TIONS &
ANSWERS

Criminal Law

QUESTIONS & ANSWERS SERIES

Company Law

Constitutional and Administrative Law

Conveyancing

Criminal Law

EC Law

English Legal System

Equity and Trusts

Family Law

Land Law

Landlord and Tenant

Law of Contract

Law of Evidence

Law of Torts

Wills, Probate and Administration

Other titles in preparation

QUESTIONS & ANSWERS

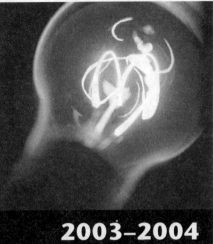

2003–2004

Criminal Law

THIRD EDITION

Geoff Douglas

LLM, Solicitor
Lecturer in Law, University of the West of England, Bristol

OXFORD
UNIVERSITY PRESS

OXFORD
UNIVERSITY PRESS

Great Clarendon Street, Oxford OX2 6DP

Oxford University Press is a department of the University of Oxford.
It furthers the University's objective of excellence in research, scholarship,
and education by publishing worldwide in

Oxford New York

Auckland Bangkok Buenos Aires Cape Town Chennai
Dar es Salaam Delhi Hong Kong Istanbul Karachi Kolkata
Kuala Lumpur Madrid Melbourne Mexico City Mumbai Nairobi
São Paulo Shanghai Taipei Tokyo Toronto

Oxford is a registered trade mark of Oxford University Press
in the UK and in certain other countries

Published in the United States
by Oxford University Press Inc., New York

First published
Blackstone Press 1999
Second edition 2001

© Geoff Douglas, 2003

British Library Cataloguing in Publication Data
Data available

Library of Congress Cataloging in Publication Data
Data available
ISBN 0–19–926081–8

1 3 5 7 9 10 8 6 4 2

Typeset by RefineCatch Limited, Bungay, Suffolk
Printed in Great Britain by
Ashford Colour Press, Gosport, Hampshire

Contents

The Q&A Series

Key features

The Q&A series provides full coverage of key subjects in a clear and logical way. This new edition contains the following features:

- Question
- Commentary
- Bullet point list
- Suggested answer
- Further reading
- Diagrams

Preface

Whilst lecturing criminal law for many years, I have had to set and mark many criminal law exams. Some answers have been exceptionally good, whilst others have been so bad as to be incapable of being awarded a pass mark. The vast majority, however, fall into that 42–58 per cent category, where the marker is often thinking, 'if only the student had used this technique or eliminated this destructive practice, I could have given him or her a few more marks, perhaps a grade higher'.

I have therefore tried to identify and apply the procedures and techniques that will hopefully enable you to achieve your maximum potential in your exam. But remember, this is the icing on the cake. Unless you have the necessary knowledge and understanding of the criminal law — a major, but interesting task in itself — exam technique means little.

I would like to thank the many students and colleagues who have directly and indirectly assisted me with this book, but in particular, Berni Bell, with whom I have had numerous discussions on the topics I have included.

Finally, I would like to thank my wife, Cynthia, son, Richard, and daughter, Nicola, for their unstinting support.

Geoff Douglas
2002

Foreword

Geoff Douglas died unexpectedly in October 2002 just two months after completing the new edition of *Q&A Criminal Law*.

Geoff was a highly respected and dedicated law teacher whose distinguished career as an academic spanned over 27 years at Bristol Polytechnic, later the University of West of England. As a specialist in Criminal Law, he was very much an adherent of the case method approach adopted by the late Professor Brian Hogan. . . . He used it as a means for his students to develop sharp analytical skills and a conceptual understanding of Criminal Law in a manner that was intellectually demanding, rigorous, fascinating and, above all, thoroughly enjoyable. His final academic work is a fitting tribute to those teaching methods that he utilised so successfully for the benefit of the many hundreds of undergraduates and CPE students whom, in his modest words, he felt 'so privileged to guide and support.'

The new edition embodies Geoff's educational philosophy of ensuring that students should be able to engage with the most up-to-date materials, focused upon the key issues of Criminal Law in a clear and logical manner that will stimulate enquiry, reflection, and further reading. As a most experienced teacher and assessor, he was well aware of the importance of examination technique and the essential need for students to present well-structured, pertinent answers based upon careful analysis and application of relevant materials. He has chosen, and devised with great care, questions that will cover all of the main areas of Criminal Law and include a considerable number of issues. His commentaries and suggested answers provide an excellent digest of Criminal Law and a fine exemplar of examination practice that should ensure that students achieve their maximum potential.

I am sure that Geoff would wish me to express thanks to the students and colleagues who assisted him, through various ways, in the writing of this new edition, as well as to Professor Ed Cape who has generously undertaken the final proof reading of the book.

Professor Alan Bensted
Dean of the Faculty of Law
University of the West of England

Table of Cases

Table of Statutes

Introduction: exam technique

Many students mistakenly believe that techniques required to succeed in examinations are totally distinct from what they have learnt throughout the year-long course. This is not the case; although certain techniques may need to be modified for exam purposes, a student will be well served by following the skills and disciplines that have been acquired during the course.

It is therefore very important to acquire good habits as early in the course as possible. When a problem or essay question is set for discussion in lectures or seminars, you should treat it as a possible exam question, but with the luxury that you are not under the pressure of the examination room. You will therefore have much longer to prepare, research and consider your answer; but when this has been done, you will obtain the maximum future benefit if you tackle it in the same way as an examination question. In this way you will acquire good habits, which may need only minor modification in the examination.

The plan

Stage 1 is to plan your answer. Identify the issues raised and make a list of all the offences you must consider, writing down the *actus reus* and *mens rea* of each offence. Then briefly note the relevant defences that may be available, and add the case names that you may be using as authority or discussing in detail. Then re-read the question and check your list to ensure that you have not missed anything. You are now in a position to put your list into logical order — in other words an organised plan — in which you can identify those issues which need to be discussed in detail and those which can be referred to briefly; which cases should be used to illustrate your points and which ones you will briefly quote as authority for a principle.

Lastly, still at the planning stage, you should consider your conclusion. More is said regarding the conclusion later, but the advantage of considering a conclusion at this stage is that it helps to crystallise your thoughts and identify any errors in your plan; and, possibly more importantly, it does give you confidence when you start to write your answer, because you know what conclusion you are working towards.

Answer the problem

Give more space to the more important points. If the problem raises various possibilities, start with the most serious or the most obvious.

What has to be proved for a conviction for the most serious offence? Do not forget to deal with both *actus reus* and *mens rea* where appropriate.

Are there any defences? Note the scope and applicability of those.

Is there doubt about liability? If so, may a lesser offence be proved? Here again, deal with the relevant considerations for liability.

The basic point is to answer the question set — apply the law to the facts given. Take the facts as stated in the problem as conclusive — you must examine the facts as proved. Sometimes the facts are deliberately vague, e.g., what exactly was D's state of mind when he killed V? If this is the case, you may have to discuss murder, manslaughter and accident. Do not be afraid in some circumstances to fail to reach a rock solid conclusion. It may be perfectly acceptable — indeed highly appropriate — to say, for instance: 'If . . . then he may be liable for murder, if . . . then he may be liable for manslaughter'. Identifying unclear areas is a skill in itself, where either the facts or the law itself are unclear.

You may have a problem which involves the potential liability of several parties. If this is the case, there is no need, for instance, to reiterate the ingredients of say, murder. There may, however, be differences which must be noted e.g., one party being under 10, one being an accomplice rather than a principal offender. It often helps to discuss the parties in order of their appearance in the problem.

Your statements of law should be backed up by reference to authorities, statute or case law. You may also refer to relevant articles and textbook theories, and draw an analogy or use hypothetical examples.

The question may say 'discuss'. This will require discussion of all the possibilities raised by the facts, all offences, all parties and any possible defences. Alternatively, you may be asked to 'advise A' or 'discuss the criminal liability of D'. Your answer clearly will have to be tailored to suit. Irrelevant material, however well researched or presented, will gain no marks but will waste time and space.

Be prepared to see both sides of the question. For instance, give proper weight to defences which may be applicable. There is no need to discuss potential defences not raised by the facts, e.g., if the problem says 'A kills Y' you need not go into the question of whether perhaps A was nine years old. If you were required to discuss infancy, the problem should involve facts to lead you to do so. The permutations otherwise would be endless! Do not forget to deal with the burden of proof, where appropriate.

Some identifiable pitfalls

A cardinal fault is irrelevance. Even if a question seems squarely on a certain area of law, it should not be a case of 'writing all you know' on such a topic. Instead, your answer should demonstrate your ability to recognise what is in issue and apply legal principles to it, backed up by authorities. Your ability in selecting the relevant areas for in-depth treatment will also be assessed; a problem question may contain minor points as well as central issues. Be selective in the way you answer, giving priority to the main points, dealing briefly with the rest.

Mistakes identified as common include illogical order, inadequate introduction and conclusion, repetition, poor or inappropriate use of authority and a conclusion which does not follow from the evidence. Not only do such mistakes cost you marks, they give the marker a negative view of the rest of your answer or entire paper. So the favourable impression you may have created earlier quickly disappears. It is therefore essential to eliminate sloppy, fundamental errors. Most markers accept that in the heat of the examination certain errors will be made, but they heavily penalise errors that reveal a lack of technique or lawyerly skill.

Examination technique

Two central pieces of advice are these:

   (a)   Answer the required number of questions.

   (b)   Keep to time.

If you answer, for instance, three questions instead of the four required, you are immediately giving yourself an absolutely total potential maximum of 75 per cent rather than 100 per cent. If one calls 50 per cent an average secure pass, your 'score' (assuming such standard of answer to three questions) would be 50 per cent of 75, i.e., 37 or 38, a *fail*. It cannot be stressed too strongly: it is vital that you attempt the required number of questions. Be careful to read through the 'rubric', the instructions on the examination paper. You may be asked to answer so many questions from part A, part B and so on. One or more questions may be compulsory. Some questions may have particular instructions built into them. Accurate interpretation of such instructions is *very important*. You should be given an indication by the relevant lecturer of what will be required, but do ask in advance if you are not sure. You ought to know when you are revising what exactly it is that you are revising for. If certain aids are allowed in the examination, you should know this — and be familiar enough with the aids to use them.

It is most important that you make the maximum use of time. Most exams are now of three hours duration, with an addtional initial 10 minutes reading time. In my experience, it is rarely the case that a student will run out of time during a criminal law exam. The usual problem for a weak student is that he or she has completed the answers, and there is still some 30 minutes left. Obviously in some cases this is because the student does not possess enough knowledge, but in the vast majority of cases, the problem is that the student has panicked and rushed into the answer without preparing a plan. At the start of an exam, there is a feeling that, as there is so much to do, the answers must be started immediately. This temptation must be resisted, for it is at the start of your exam that you are freshest and best able to plan your answers, and the order in which you tackle them. You do not want to be panicking with 45 minutes to go, and it is therefore worthwhile considering leaving one of your stronger answers to the end, to enable you confidently to cover material you are sure of, rather than dealing with troublesome topics with a tired mind.

In an ideal situation, your four and five answers will all be strong, but unfortunately experience shows that on even the best of scripts, there is often one relatively weak answer.

It is well worth using some calm time at the beginning of the examination to look through the *whole* paper. Read slowly through the questions, deciding which you will choose (or be forced) to answer. To do this at the outset saves a lot of potential 'dithering' time during the course of the examination. You may find as you initially go through the paper that certain issues or cases leap out at you as you read. It is worth making a marginal note of such matters as you go through, because it may be that you may not be able to bring them to mind later on.

Having stressed the importance of *timing*, the need to *read the questions carefully* must also be highlighted. You will be asked questions which are often quite specific in their terms. It is unlikely that you will be asked to write 'all you know about conspiracy, strict liability etc.'. Much more likely would be a question investigating a certain aspect of the topic in question. It is here that you have to be very precise and concentrated in your reading of the question so that you answer the *question posed*, not something like it and not the question you would have liked to have been asked!

If you have worked out the time allocation for each individual question, you can proceed to your first answer. It is strongly recommended that you stick strictly to your time plan, leaving one question and passing on to another when the allotted time is up. You can always return to add the finishing touches. Just leave a gap, start a new page and *press on*. Remember, when you are working out the amount of time you will allow for each question, you have to take into account thinking time, calming time and note-making time.

It is suggested that the making of an answer plan is essential. This should help to get your thoughts in order and promote the feeling of your being in control. Your answer structure will be greatly assisted by the formulation of a plan in advance. The best approach is to prepare plans for all answers before actually writing the first answer. This requires discipline and nerve, but arguably you are doing your most important thinking while your mind is at its freshest.

You will know your own strengths and weaknesses. You should, for instance, know if you are better at answering problems/writing essays; theory/practice; history/modern angle; broad/detailed questions. You have to choose as far as you can in line with your knowledge of your own abilities generally, and the selection you see before you. (Of course, on the day you may see a wonderful essay question on a topic you have fully revised and decide to answer that instead of the problem you would normally go for.)

Some things should be watched out for, guarded against. Be careful to *answer* the *question*. This may sound daft, but it cannot be emphasised enough. If the question has several parts, make sure you answer *every part*. If there is a quotation to be discussed in an essay question, you have to really pick the quote to pieces so that you discuss every facet of it. Obviously, the angle you take will depend on the wording of the question — does it say 'Evaluate', or 'Contrast' or 'Critically analyse', for instance? Beware latching on to one key word in the question and writing all you can drag up about the subject.

This is a really crucial point. All you write has to be *relevant* in order to gain you marks. Irrelevancies lose you precious time and will gain no marks. You have to aim for balance in your answer, too. Devote most time to the central issues in a problem, for instance, making brief reference only to subsidiary points.

Problem questions

If you have a long problem question involving, say, several parties to a crime and several substantive offences, and you are told at the beginning of the question that 'A and B agree to . . .', then you would not be expected to enter into a lengthy discourse about conspiracy law. The question here calls for the briefest of references to that possible offence. It would be different if the question appeared to hinge largely on the issue of conspiracy.

If a problem gives you no indication of the possible relevance of a particular defence then you would not be expected to deal with that issue, otherwise the permutations would be endless. If the problem mentions, for instance, a serious injury to a person but there is no mention of death, there is no need to develop an argument about what the situation would be if the victim died.

What this really means is that you have to interpret what it is the examiner is trying to test. What is the question essentially about? Within that question, you then have to decide what emphasis you think should be accorded to various aspects of the question.

It is very important to include in your answer clear definitions where appropriate. For instance, if you are going to discuss insanity, make sure that you state what amounts to insanity; if you are discussing provocation, say what it is. Clear definitions set the tone of your answer and put the marker in an optimistic frame of mind. The same is true of a good, clear opening paragraph — it bodes well and is worth aiming for.

It is also very important to display your understanding clearly concerning the burden of proof, particularly in relation to defences. Be careful that you do not suggest that there is a burden of proof on the defence when there is not. As you revise, you should be very alert to this point.

While on the question of displaying your knowledge, if you have read a relevant article or have been swayed by a particular writer's approach, make sure that you state this. Show the marker that you have read widely. Capitalise on your research. Get the credit.

In answering a problem question, don't feel that you have to come to a rock solid conclusion. Very often it will be impossible to do so. It is perfectly acceptable to say, for example, 'If D is found to have intended grievous bodily harm then. . . .' and so on. As long as you indicate what the issues are, what the relevant principles of liability are, that is sufficient. There is no need to predict the decision of the jury/magistrates, although you do have to indicate, where appropriate, how the jury should be directed, for instance.

Your conclusion may differ from that of another student, and may differ from that of the marker. This does not matter. So long as you can illustrate why you reach your conclusion by reference to authorities, analogy and argument, that is fine. It is quite likely that you cannot, on the facts presented, reach a definite conclusion. It may depend, for instance, on whether the jury believed that A had the necessary intention to kill or cause grievous bodily harm. If they did the verdict could be guilty of murder unless the jury considered that A had used reasonable force in self defence, in which case he would be acquitted of all charges. In situations like this, it would be wrong to conclude that A was definitely guilty or not guilty. What you must do is cover the alternatives — this demonstrates your understanding of the position. In certain questions there may be many alternative outcomes. Remember that the marks allocated for the conclusion are not simply given for arriving at the same result as the examiner (e.g., A guilty of murder) but for analysis and awareness.

Essay questions

In answering essay questions it is necessary to include the traditional introduction, followed by discussion, followed by conclusion. Neither the introduction nor the conclusion need be lengthy. The advantage of the essay question is that you can play to your strengths — so long as what you write is relevant. Beware writing all you know on a topic; it is essential to be discriminating, to tailor your answer to the way the question is worded.

In this author's experience, people sometimes tend to forget authorities when answering essay-style questions, particularly under examination conditions. You still need reference to case law, statutory definitions and general principles in an essay answer. The onus is more on you, since in a problem the facts will (or should) suggest which authorities you are being asked to discuss.

If the essay question revolves around a particular case, clearly you will need to concentrate on that decision — but the odds are that you will still need plenty of reference to other case law and statutory provisions, to place the case in its historical perspective, or to highlight the way in which the central decision will or may affect existing law.

The major task in essay writing, given that you know the subject matter, is to structure the material. You have to determine for yourself the scope and shape of your answer. It is easy to tell when marking essay answers who has followed a plan — it really shows.

Conclusion

In an exam your goal must be to obtain the highest mark possible, given your knowledge and ability. Student A may have the same attributes as student B, but student A may obtain 10–20 more marks in the exam because of good exam technique. It is therefore essential that you incorporate into your answer the style and techniques covered in this chapter. So remember to:

- read the instructions thoroughly;
- answer the correct number of questions;
- prepare your answer plan;
- answer the question set;
- deal with one issue fully before going on to the next;
- write a logical conclusion which does not conflict with the rest of your answer;
- read through your answers at the end of the exam.

The elements of a crime: *actus reus* and *mens rea*

Introduction

The traditional starting point for the study of criminal law is the constituents of a criminal offence: *actus reus* (the prohibited conduct) and *mens rea* (the mental element). Commentators and students alike want to find consistency and certainty in the application and development of the criminal law, and the chapters on this area in most criminal law textbooks try to state principles that the student should see consistently applied in later chapters covering specific offences. The main problem is that the offences have developed in a piecemeal fashion, exhibiting no underlying rationale or common approach. Thus in examining *actus reus*, the student might be covering an offence defined in modern terms, e.g., Criminal Damage Act 1971, or in obscure outdated language, e.g., Offences Against the Person Act 1861, or which has a common law definition, recently amended by statute, e.g., murder.

Similarly, when we examine our approach to *mens rea*, we can see little common ground. If the offence requires the prosecution to prove intention, this must generally be left to the jury without detailed guidance from the trial judge (*R v Moloney* [1985] 1 All ER 1025); but if recklessness is the issue, a detailed direction, spelling out to the jury what they must find, is given (*Metropolitan Police Commissioner* v *Caldwell* [1981] 1 All ER 961). If dishonesty is the *mens rea* (for Theft Act offences) the jury must consider two specific questions, but it is a question of fact for them to resolve (*R v Ghosh* [1982] 2 All ER 689). In other words, three different approaches in establishing the *mens rea* for different offences. A search for consistency is therefore a futile exercise!

A student should therefore be aware that studying the chapters on *actus reus* and *mens rea* can produce a distorted impression of the criminal law. You are dealing with concepts in isolation and you may form the impression that these general principles are consistently applied. That this is not the case can be demonstrated time and time again, but the following example aptly illustrates the problem.

In *DPP* v *Camplin* [1978] 1 All ER 1236, the House of Lords held that in considering the defence of provocation on a murder charge, the jury should take into account the characteristics of the accused's age (15) when considering whether a reasonable person would have done as the accused did. In *R* v *R (Stephen Malcolm)* (1984) 79 Cr App R 334, a 15-year-old boy was charged under s. 1(2) of the Criminal Damage Act 1971 with causing criminal damage, being reckless as to whether life would be endangered. His counsel argued that the jury in assessing recklessness — on authority of *Camplin* — had to take into account the fact that the accused was aged 15. The Court of Appeal turned down this argument deciding that the test for recklessness (following *Metropolitan Police Commissioner* v *Caldwell*) was purely objective, i.e., was this an obvious risk to the reasonable man.

How can this divergent approach be justified? The criminal law commentator would simply point out that *Camplin* was concerned with murder and provocation, and therefore had no relevance in considering recklessness for the purpose of the Criminal Damage Act 1971. Others would bemoan the fact that there appears to be no underlying rationale adopting either a subjective or an objective approach, and the offences develop independently of each other. You can understand why Sir Henry Brooke (the former head of the Law Commission) and many others wish for codification of some, if not all, of the criminal law (see [1995] Crim LR 911 — 'The Law Commission and Criminal Law Reform').

Even established concepts that have been applied for many years by the courts, may suddenly come under attack and be interpreted differently by the judiciary. Thus the House of Lords in *Attorney-General's Reference (No. 3 of 1994)* [1997] 3 All ER 936, reversed the Court of Appeal decision ([1996] 2 WLR 412), holding that the doctrine of transferred malice could not apply to convict an accused of murder when he deliberately injured a pregnant woman in circumstances where the baby was born alive but subsequently died. Lord Mustill criticised the doctrine as having no sound intellectual basis and involving a fiction, although the *Criminal Law Review* disagrees with his view ([1997] Crim LR 830).

In this chapter questions have been chosen to cover all major aspects of this area. There are some problem questions, but you would expect the essay questions in an exam to be selected from these topics. Essays are therefore included on the important aspects of *mens rea*, intention and recklessness.

A question is also included based on the Law Commission's recommendations on corporate killing (Law Com. No. 237). The Law Commission has made many suggestions on most areas of the substantive criminal law, and it is helpful to be aware of their views as they highlight the defects and anomalies in the existing law. However, when answering problem questions, the examiner will want you to cover the existing principles, stating what the law actually is rather than what it should be. You should also be aware that very few of the Law Commission's recommendations are implemented in practice. Nevertheless, the question of corporate liability is a controversial area and it appears likely that here the Law Commission's recommendations will be implemented.

Q Question 1

The practice of leaving the issue of intention to the jury without any judicial guidance as to its meaning is unworkable and likely to produce inconsistent decisions.
Discuss this statement with reference to decided cases.

Commentary

There have been so many important decisions on this important aspect of criminal law, that it is always likely to be the subject of an examination question.

Because the facts of *R* v *Moloney* [1985] 1 All ER 641 are so well known, there is a temptation simply to regurgitate them with the House of Lords' decisions. This must be resisted as there are many ingredients in the answer, which requires careful planning and organisation.

In summary, this is a question where it is quite easy to obtain a pass mark but difficult to obtain a high grade.

* *Mens rea*

* Intention — definition

* *Moloney* [1985] — 'the golden rule'

* *Woollin* [1998] — direction on intention

* Law Commission No. 218

:Q: Suggested answer

Except with strict liability offences, in order for an accused to be found guilty of a criminal offence, the prosecution must prove that the accused committed the *actus reus* of the offence with the appropriate *mens rea*. *Mens rea* generally signifies a guilty mind, although in *R* v *Kingston* [1994] 3 All ER 353, the House of Lords confirmed that the accused was guilty of an offence requiring the prosecution to prove intention, although he was morally blameless. *Mens rea* is the mental element, which varies from one offence to another; but generally, for the more serious offences, it comprises intention or recklessness, with intention being reserved for the most serious crimes.

One would therefore think that, being of such fundamental importance, intention would be specifically defined and rigidly applied, but this is not the case. There have always been difficulties with the concept of intention within the criminal law. What is it? How should it be defined? How do the prosecution prove it? How does the trial judge direct the jury? These issues have been the subject of much judicial and academic debate in recent years.

Although the word 'intention' implies purpose or even desire, there have been many diverse definitions by the judiciary, and commentators have also identified different types of intention. First, direct intent, where it was the accused's purpose or motive to bring about a result. Thus in *R v Steane* [1947] 1 All ER 813, the accused, who assisted the enemy during the war, had his conviction quashed as the court decided that he did not intend to assist the enemy; he intended to protect his family, who would have been harmed had he not cooperated. Secondly, oblique intent, where the accused does not necessarily desire the result but foresees it as highly probable. Thus in *Hyam* v *DPP* [1974] 2 All ER 41, the House of Lords upheld the conviction for murder of the accused who set fire to the victim's house, as she foresaw that death or grievous bodily harm was highly probable. Thirdly, ulterior intent, where it must be shown that in intentionally doing one act the accused has a related purpose. Thus to be guilty of burglary under s. 9(1)(a) of the Theft Act 1968, it is necessary for the prosecution to prove that the accused, when deliberately entering a building as a trespasser, did so with a specific related purpose in mind, e.g., to steal or rape. It would not be sufficient if the accused intentionally broke into the house with the sole purpose of sheltering from the weather. Other forms of intention, specific and basic, are also used to apply the defence of intoxication to certain offences (*DPP* v *Majewski* [1976] 2 All ER 142).

Although there is an overlap between intention on the one hand and motive and foresight on the other, and these latter concepts assist the jury in their deliberations on intention, it is clear that the concepts are not synonymous. Motive is the reason why a person acts, while intention is his or her mental awareness at the time of the act. Foresight can be evidence of intention, but it is not conclusive proof of it. Section 8 of the Criminal Justice Act 1967 states that a court shall not be bound in law to infer that the accused intended or foresaw a result of his actions by reason only of its being a natural and probable consequence of those actions, but 'shall decide whether he did intend or foresee that result by reference to all the evidence, drawing such inferences from the evidence as appear proper in the circumstances'.

The issue of intention was debated by the House of Lords in *R* v *Moloney* [1985] 1 All ER 641 and *R* v *Hancock and Shankland* [1986] 1 All ER 641. In the former case, Moloney shot his stepfather from point blank range and was convicted of murder after the trial judge (following *Archbold Criminal Pleading Evidence and Practice*, 40th edn, para. 17–13, p. 995) directed the jury that:

In law a man intends the consequence of his voluntary act:

(a) when he desires it to happen, whether or not he foresees that it probably will happen, or

(b) when he foresees that it will probably happen, whether he desires it or not.

The House of Lords quashed the conviction on the basis that this was a misdirection, Lord Bridge stating that:

> the golden rule should be that, when directing a jury on the mental element necessary in a crime of specific intent (i.e., intention), the judge should avoid any elaboration or paraphrase of what is meant by intent, and leave it to the jury's good sense to decide whether the accused acted with the necessary intent, unless the judge is convinced that, on the facts and having regard to the way the case has been presented to the jury in evidence and argument, some further explanation or elaboration is strictly necessary to avoid misunderstanding.

Although the decision may be criticised on the ground that their Lordships missed a golden opportunity to define intention, it is in keeping with the modern trend of leaving more and more issues to the jury, especially the meaning of words in common use. For example, *Brutus* v *Cozens* [1972] 2 All ER 1297 (insulting); *R* v *Feely* [1973] 1 All ER 341 (dishonestly).

This decision was followed by the House of Lords on this principle in *R* v *Hancock and Shankland*, where Lord Scarman also made the point that if intention required a detailed direction it was best to leave this to the discretion of the trial judge who would have had the benefit of hearing all the witnesses and gauging the ability of the jury. He added that the trial judge could not do as Lord Bridge suggested and simply direct the jury to consider two questions: first, was death or really serious injury in a murder case a natural consequence of the defendant's voluntary act?; secondly, did the defendant foresee that consequence as being a natural consequence of his act? — further instructing them that if they answer 'Yes' to both questions it is a proper inference for them to draw that the accused intended that consequence. Lord Scarman stated that the trial judge must refer to the concept of probability — the more probable the consequence, the more likely the accused foresaw it and intended it.

Despite clear House of Lords *dicta* to the contrary, the Court of Appeal in *R* v *Nedrick* [1986] 3 All ER 1 did lay down some guidelines to the effect that the jury should not infer intention unless they considered that the accused foresaw the consequence as a virtual certainty. However, this decision has attracted criticism, and the Court of Appeal in *R* v *Walker and Hayles* [1990] 90 Cr App R 226 stated 'we are not persuaded that it is only when death is a virtual certainty that the jury can infer intention to kill'.

Nevertheless, the status of *Nedrick* was confirmed by the House of Lords' discussion in *R* v *Woollin* [1998] 4 All ER 103. The House, stating that where the simple direction was not enough, the jury should be further directed that they were not entitled to find the necessary intention unless they felt sure that death or serious bodily harm was a virtual certain result of D's action (barring some unforeseen intervention) and, that D had appreciated that fact.

This decision also illustrates one of the difficulties of the present approach, i.e., when is the issue of intention so complicated as to warrant a detailed direction? In *R* v *Walker and Hayles*, the Court of Appeal decided that 'the mere fact that a jury calls for a further direction on intention does not of itself make it a rare and exceptional case requiring a foresight direction'. On the other hand, in *R v Hancock and Shankland*, the House of Lords confirmed that the trial judge was right to give a detailed direction, even though the content of the direction was wrong.

A further problem is that different juries may have different ideas as to what constitutes intention, some insisting on purpose being necessary, while others are prepared to accept that only foresight of a probable consequence is required. There is clearly the risk of inconsistent decisions and it is therefore not surprising that the Law Commission (Nos 122 and 218) have recommended that the following standard definition of intention be adopted:

> a person acts intentionally with respect to a result when
>
> (i) it is his purpose to cause it; or
>
> (ii) although it is not his purpose to cause that result, he knows that it would occur in the ordinary course of events if he were to succeed in his purpose of causing some other result.

Q Question 2

Explain and evaluate the effect on the concept of recklessness of the House of Lords' decision in *Metropolitan Police Commissioner v Caldwell* [1981] 1 All ER 961.

Commentary

Few cases have provoked such widespread discussion and hostile reaction as the House of Lords' decision in *Caldwell*. This decision — together with the one the following day in *R v Lawrence* [1981] 1 All ER 974 — changed the concept of fault and seemed to signify the end of subjective recklessness overnight. Although its influence is waning, it is nevertheless still a case of such stature as to attract an examination question.

The answer requires a thorough analysis of the case with a clear statement of its *ratio decidendi* and why Lord Diplock arrived at this conclusion. You must also analyse the way *Caldwell* was interpreted in subsequent cases, and lastly examine the application of *Caldwell*. In view of the importance of this topic, this is a very comprehensive answer.

- **Subjective recklessness**

- *Caldwell* **[1981] — House of Lords' decision**

- *Elliot* v C **[1983] — Lord Diplock's rationale**

- *Reid* **[1992] — the lacuna**

- **Limited impact — the cases**

⌖ Suggested answer

The House of Lords decided in *R v Moloney* [1985] 1 All ER 1025 that intention, being a word in common use, easily understood by the public, did not generally require a long direction from the trial judge. Recklessness, another important component of *mens rea*, had always received a clear uniform direction from the trial judge, generally following the Law Commission's recommendations:

a person is reckless if

(a) knowing that there is a risk that an event may result from his conduct or that a circumstance may exist if he takes that risk; and

(b) it is unreasonable for him to take it having regard to the degree and nature of the risk which he knows to be present.

This test had been applied in many cases and is sometimes referred to as 'the *Cunningham* test' following *R v Cunningham* [1957] 2 All ER 412. However, this settled approach was shattered by the House of Lords' decision in *Metropolitan Police Commissioner* v *Caldwell* [1981] 1 All ER 961.

The facts of this case are straightforward. The accused had a grudge against the owner of an old people's home, and while drunk he set fire to it. He was convicted under s. 1(1) of the Criminal Damage Act 1971 of recklessly damaging another's property, and of the more serious offence under s. 1(2) of the Act, destroying or damaging any property:

(a) intending to destroy or damage any property or being reckless as to whether any property would be destroyed or damaged; and

(b) intending by the destruction or damage to endanger the life of another or being reckless as to whether the life of another would be thereby endangered.

The Court of Appeal quashed his conviction under s. 1(2) of the 1971 Act. Although they certified a point of law of public importance as to whether intoxication can be a defence to this offence, the issue that most concerned the House of Lords was the applicable definition of recklessness.

The accused contended that he was not reckless since, because of his drunken state, he had not even considered that there was a risk that life might be endangered. However, Lord Diplock (giving the majority judgment) stated that recklessness encompassed both a decision 'to ignore a risk of harmful consequences resulting from one's act that one had recognised as existing, but also failing to give any thought to whether or not there is a risk in circumstances where, if any thought were given to the matter it would be obvious that there was'.

Thus, in relation to criminal damage, a person is reckless if:

(a) he or she does an act which in fact creates an obvious risk that property will be destroyed or damaged; and

(b) when he or she does the act he or she either has not given any thought to the possibility of there being any such risk, or has recognised that there was some risk involved and has nevertheless gone on to do it.

Thus the majority of their Lordships concluded that the Court of Appeal was wrong to quash the accused's conviction as he was reckless, and intoxication was not a defence to recklessly endangering life.

While the outcome for the accused is not controversial, the reasoning of Lord Diplock certainly is. Despite the fact that the minority, Lords Edmund-Davies and Wilberforce, agreed with the sources to be used to arrive at a definition (the dictionary, the Law Commission reports, the Malicious Damage Act 1861, the American model Penal Code, Professor Kenny), they interpreted them in such a way as to justify using the traditional subjective approach.

Lord Diplock reasoned that the new definition had a number of benefits, as subjective recklessness was not being abandoned, remaining part of the '*Caldwell*' definition. First, it would make it much easier for juries to decide whether or not the accused was reckless. Sometimes the accused would not give evidence or would be uncertain as to what happened, making it difficult or impossible for the jury to ascertain the accused's mental state. With the new objective test, this would not be a problem. Secondly, Lord Diplock argued that there was no difference in the culpability of person A who considered the risk and unreasonably decided to take it, and person B who could not even be bothered to first consider if there was a risk.

Although Lord Diplock insisted that the court had to ascertain a state of mind, the Court of Appeal in *R v R (Stephen Malcolm)* [1984] 79 Cr App R 334, and the Queen's Bench Division of the High Court in *Elliot v C (A Minor)* [1983] 2 All ER 1005, gave the *ratio decidendi* of the case an objective interpretation. In the latter case, a 14-year-old schoolgirl of low intelligence, who was tired and hungry, spilt some inflammable spirit and then dropped a lighted match on the wooden floor of a garden shed. She was charged under s. 1(1) of the 1971 Act. It was argued that she did not foresee the risk of fire, nor would she had she addressed her mind to the possible consequences of her action. Although Goff LJ stated that a test for recklessness which allowed the court to take into account the individual characteristics of the accused had much merit, he felt bound by the doctrine of precedent to follow *Caldwell*, and therefore the magistrates should have convicted the accused as the correct test was 'if this is an obvious risk to a reasonable man'. A similar result was reached in *R v R (Stephen Malcolm)* where the Court of Appeal rejected the appellant's argument that as the accused was aged 15, by analogy with *R v Camplin* [1978] 1 All ER 1236 the question for the jury should have been was this an obvious risk to a reasonable 15-year-old.

Thus objective recklessness was equated with negligence, and a person was at fault for failing to come up to the standard of the reasonable man. Traditionally this had been the dividing line between criminal and civil liability, *mens rea* requiring an awareness of the prohibited consequence. As a result of *Caldwell*, for offences requiring recklessness there was no difference between advertent and inadvertent conduct, both were blameworthy.

Commentators also argued that, following *Caldwell*, the accused would not be reckless if he had considered the matter and decided that there was no risk. Thus in *Chief Constable of Avon and Somerset Police* v *Shimmen* (1986) 84 Cr App R 7, the accused (a martial arts expert) while demonstrating his skills demolished a shop window. He maintained that he had recognised the risk, but had then in his opinion eliminated it, by standing a few inches further back from the window when carrying out his manoeuvre. Although the Divisional Court decided that he was reckless, they suggested that if he had given thought to but had missed the obvious and serious risk, that might not have been recklessness. Although the existence of the lacuna was recognised by the House of Lords in *R* v *Reid* [1992] 3 All ER 673, it has never resulted in the defendant's conviction being quashed.

Initially commentators also believed that despite *R* v *Lawrence* [1981] 1 All ER 974 applying *Caldwell* recklessness to the offence of causing death by reckless driving (Road Traffic Act 1988, s. 3), adding that the risk must be obvious and serious, subjective recklessness would still apply to common law as opposed to statutory offences. However, this belief ended with the House of Lords' decision in *R* v *Seymour* [1983] 2 All ER 1058, where, holding that *Caldwell* recklessness applied to manslaughter, Lord Roskill stated that the *Caldwell* definition of recklessness should be applied to all offences 'unless Parliament has otherwise ordained'.

At this time it appeared that *Caldwell* in its objective form would be universally applied, but since then there has been a retreat, with the courts refusing to apply *Caldwell* recklessness to many offences. In *W (A Minor)* v *Dolbey* (1983) 88 Cr App R 1, the Queen's Bench Division refused to apply it to s. 20 of the Offences Against the Person Act 1861 (malicious wounding), holding that 'maliciously' required foresight on the accused's behalf. This has been followed and extended by the House of Lords' decision in *R* v *Savage and Parmenter* [1991] 4 All ER 698, to other non-fatal offences against the person such as assault and battery and assault occasioning actual bodily harm (Offences Against the Person Act 1861, s. 47). A similar development took place in rape with *R* v *Satnam* (1983) 78 Cr App R 149, the Court of Appeal refusing to apply *Caldwell* on the basis that *Caldwell* was concerned with a property offence, whereas rape was an offence against the person.

In *Blakely and Sutton* v *DPP* [1991] Crim LR 763 the Queen's Bench Division held that *Caldwell* recklessness did not apply to accomplice responsibility and stated that recklessness was a word to be avoided when directing juries. Finally, in *R* v *Adomako* [1993] 4 All ER 935, the House of Lords effectively overruled *R* v *Seymour*, holding that if death arose out of a duty situation, gross negligence (not recklessness) was the test to be applied in determining whether the accused was guilty of manslaughter.

A different form of attack, an attempt to modify the *Caldwell* direction itself, also came from the House of Lords' decision in *R* v *Reid* (above), where the House was asked to overrule *Caldwell*. Their Lordships refused to do this, but said that trial judges did not have to give the *Caldwell* direction *verbatim*. As Lord Browne-Wilkinson stated: 'I cannot believe that a direction in that abstract conceptual form is very helpful to a jury'. Further, Lord Keith suggested that an accused would not be reckless 'where he acted under some excusable and understandable mistake, or where his capacity to appreciate risks was adversely affected by some condition not involving fault on his part'. Using this approach the schizophrenic tramp in *R* v *Stephenson* [1979] 2 All ER 198, would still not be convicted of criminal damage, even though he failed to recognise a risk that was obvious to the reasonable man. But note that *Elliot* v *C (A Minor)* (above) was applied in the case of *R* v *Coles* (1995) 1 Cr App R 157.

The influence of *Caldwell* has been further diminished by the replacement of s. 3 of the Road Traffic Act 1988 with s. 2 of the Road Traffic Act 1991 (dangerous driving replacing reckless driving) thereby severely limiting the effect of the other major House of Lords' decision applying objective recklessness, *R* v *Lawrence*. Thus *Caldwell* recklessness now appears to apply only to offences under the Criminal Damage Act 1971 and to certain statutory regulatory offences, e.g., under the Data Protection Act (*Data Protection Registrar* v *Amnesty International* [1995] Crim LR 633). Nevertheless, the case of *Caldwell* is still the subject of strong criticism which is likely to continue until the Law Commission's recommendations (Draft Criminal Law Bill (cl. 1)), abolishing objective recklessness and using instead the traditional subjective approach, are implemented.

Q Question 3

You are told that the Ancient Book Act 1997 has just received the Royal Assent and that s. 1 provides, 'It shall be an offence to destroy any book printed before 1800'.
Discuss the criminal liability of each party in the following situation.
Arthur owns 200 books, which he thinks are worthless. He is concerned in case any of the books were printed before 1800 and consults Ben, an expert on old books, who assures him that all the books were printed long after 1800. Arthur destroys the books and is now horrified to discover that three of them were printed in 1750.

Commentary

This is an unusual question which has caused students difficulties, with many writing about the offence of criminal damage. This is a mistake as the question requires a detailed analysis of the *mens rea* requirement of the Ancient Book Act 1997, and in particular analysis of the concept of strict liability.

In a survey by Justice referred to in an article by A. Ashworth and M. Blake, 'The Presumption of Innocence in English Criminal Law' [1996] Crim LR 306, it is estimated that in over one half of criminal offences either strict liability is imposed, or the prosecution have the benefit of a presumption. It is obviously an important topic, and popular with examiners!

A good answer will require a detailed consideration of the possibility of this offence being one of strict liability and the effect of this. You should also consider the position if the courts decide that intention or recklessness is the appropriate mental state.

- **Strict liability** — *Sweet* v *Parsley* [1969]

- **Presumption of** *mens rea* — *B* v *DPP* [2000]

- **The exceptions**

- **Recklessness**

- **Mistake** — *Morgan* [1975]

- **Aiding and abetting** — *Callow* v *Tillstone* [1900]

:Q: **Suggested answer**

As s. 1 of the Ancient Book Act 1997 is silent as to the *mens rea* requirement of the offence, there is a possibility that it will be deemed an offence of strict liability. That is an offence where it is not necessary for the prosecution to prove intention, recklessness or negligence in relation to any one or more of the elements of the *actus reus*. Thus in *Pharmaceutical Society of Great Britain* v *Storkwain* [1986] 2 All ER 635, the House of Lords upheld the conviction of a pharmacist who had given drugs to a patient with a forged doctor's prescription, although the court found the pharmacist blameless. This decision demonstrates the inherent unfairness of strict liability, but is justified on the basis that the misuse of drugs is a grave social evil and therefore should be prevented at all costs.

The first case of statutory strict liability was *R* v *Woodrow* (1846) 15 M & W 404, where the accused was found guilty of being in possession of adulterated tobacco, even though he did not know that it was adulterated. Many early decisions revealed an inconsistent approach as the courts were trying to interpret old statutes in ascertaining the will of Parliament. However, Lord Reid in the House of Lords' decision in *Sweet* v *Parsley* [1969] 1 All ER 347 laid down the following guidelines:

(a) Wherever a section is silent as to *mens rea* there is a presumption that, in order to give effect to the will of Parliament, words importing *mens rea* must be read into the provision.

(b) It is a universal principle that if a penal provision is reasonably capable of two interpretations, that interpretation which is most favourable to the accused must be adopted.

(c)   The fact that other sections of the Act expressly require *mens rea* is not in itself sufficient to justify a decision that a section which is silent as to *mens rea* creates an absolute offence. It is necessary to go outside the Act and examine all relevant circumstances in order to establish that this must have been the intention of Parliament. So in *Cundy* v *Le Coq* (1884) 13 QB 207, a publican was found guilty of selling intoxicating liquor to a drunken person under s. 13 of the Licensing Act 1872, even though the publican did not know and had no reason to know that the customer was drunk; whereas in *Sherras* v *De Rutzen* [1895] 1 QB 918, a publican was not guilty under s. 16(2) of the Licensing Act 1872 of serving alcohol to a police constable while on duty when the accused did not know or have reason to know that the police constable was on duty. The former case was held to be an offence of strict liability, whereas in the latter, in order to obtain a conviction, the prosecution had to prove *mens rea* on behalf of the publican, which they were unable to do.

Despite the fact that there is a presumption in favour of *mens rea* when a statute is silent, the courts have been prepared to rebut this presumption on many occasions. The leading case on this point is *Gammon* v *Attorney-General for Hong Kong* [1985] AC 1, where Lord Scarman set out the applicable principles. If the offence is truly criminal in character the presumption is particularly strong, but it can be displaced where the statute is concerned with an issue of social concern. Thus, in *Gammon*, as the accused's activities involved public safety, the Privy Council were prepared to hold that the legislature intended the offence to be one of strict liability.

On analysis these principles appear inconsistent. It could be argued that all crimes by definition are grave social evils, yet if the offence is truly criminal in character, strict liability does not apply. In practice, the courts have adopted a flexible approach, but it is recognised that certain spheres of activity are always likely to attract the conclusion that this is an offence of strict liability. Thus inflation (*R* v *St Margaret's Trust Ltd* [1958] 2 All ER 289), pollution (*Alphacell Ltd* v *Woodward* [1972] 2 All ER 475), and dangerous drugs (*Pharmaceutical Society of Great Britain* v *Storkwain*, above) are traditional areas where strict liability has been imposed. However, it does seem in recent years that the category of grave social concern is expanding to encompass new social activity to include acting as a director whilst disqualified (*R* v *Brockley* [1994] Crim LR 671) and unauthorised possession of a dangerous dog (*R* v *Bezzina* [1994] 1 WLR 1057).

However, the House of Lords have again emphasised the need for the prosecution to prove *mens rea* in *B (A minor)* v *DPP* [2000] 1 All ER 833, where Lord Hutton stated (at p. 855), 'the test is not whether it is a reasonable implication that the statute rules out *mens rea* as a constituent part of the crime — the test is whether it is a necessary implication'. Further in *R* v *Lambert* [2001] 3 All ER 577, the House held that although s. 28 of the Misuse of Drugs Act 1971 required the defence to prove a defence, this only meant introduce evidence of, rather than establish a defence on the balance of probabilities.

In view of these developments, it is submitted that it would be most unlikely for s. 1 of the Ancient Book Act 1997 to be an offence of strict liability, and therefore Arthur will only be guilty if the prosecution can establish that he had the necessary *mens rea*.

If the court decides that the prosecution must prove intention, it is submitted that Arthur cannot be guilty. As he has obtained the opinion of Ben, an expert, he clearly did not desire or even foresee the consequence. Arthur has made a mistake, and even if an accused makes an unreasonable mistake, in accordance with the House of Lords' decision in *DPP* v *Morgan* [1975] 1 All ER 8, he is entitled to be judged on the facts as he believed them to be.

If the court decides that the offence could be committed recklessly, it would still be very difficult for the prosecution to establish the appropriate *mens rea*. For subjective recklessness, the prosecution must show that the accused foresaw the consequence and took an unjustified risk (*R* v *Cunningham* [1957] 2 All ER 412); and even if the court were to apply the objective recklessness test, as expounded in *Metropolitan Police Commissioner* v *Caldwell* [1981] 1 All ER 961, the prosecution would have to show that the accused gave no thought to the possibility of an obvious risk. As Arthur sought the opinion of an expert it is difficult to see how it could be argued that the risk was obvious, or his conduct unjustified.

It is therefore submitted that Arthur could be guilty of the offence only if the court decides that s. 1 of the Ancient Book Act 1997 creates an offence of strict liability. This would be a very harsh outcome bearing in mind that the real culprit in the circumstances is Ben, the expert. It is also ironic that Ben could not be guilty of aiding and abetting a strict liability offence as a result of the decision in *Callow* v *Tillstone* (1900) 19 Cox CC 576. In this case the defendant, a vet, was convicted of abetting the exposure for sale of unsound meat, an offence of strict liability. At the request of a butcher he examined the carcass of a heifer and negligently gave the butcher a certificate confirming that the meat was sound. Despite the fact that the butcher was convicted of the offence, the defendant's conviction for abetting was quashed, the court holding that *mens rea* was required for an accessory and that negligence was not sufficient. It is submitted that this is a further argument for holding that the Ancient Book Act 1997 does not create a crime of strict liability.

Q Question 4

Gloria, Wood's eccentric aunt, aged 57, was invited to stay with Wood and his girlfriend Mary at their property on the coast. It was agreed that Gloria would stay for three weeks and would occupy 'the lodge' in the garden of the Wood's house some 30 yards away. Gloria also agreed to pay £40 to cover the electricity she would use in the lodge.

Everything went well for two weeks with all three sharing meals at the house. However, a change of mood then came over Gloria who decided that she no longer wanted to have meals with Wood and Mary, and who spent more and more time by herself at the lodge.

After 20 days of the holiday Gloria, whose physical condition had visibly deteriorated, announced that she refused to leave the lodge and was going to stay there the rest of the winter. This so enraged Wood and Mary that the next day they told her to leave immediately, which she did.

Six hours later, at 11 pm, Gloria rang their bell pleading to be let in as she was cold and hungry and had nowhere else to go. Wood and Mary refused, and during that night Gloria was taken to hospital suffering from hypothermia.

While in hospital, Gloria fell unconscious and was placed on a life support machine. After five days she was correctly diagnosed by Dr Spock as being in a persistent vegetative state with no hope of recovery. He accordingly disconnected the machine.

Discuss the criminal responsibility (if any) of Wood and Mary.

Commentary

This problem concerns one of the more difficult areas of criminal law, criminal responsibility for omission to act. The Law Commission No. 143 proposed very detailed conditions concerning this topic, but these provisions were jettisoned in the revised Code (Law Com. No. 177) on the basis that the courts would be able to develop the correct principles. As Professor Glanville Williams pointed out, 'the law is in a state, if not of disarray, then of mystery'.

The question is based on the major case of *R v Stone and Dobinson* [1977] 2 All ER 341. A detailed knowledge of, and an ability to analyse this case is therefore essential in order to tackle the problem successfully.

As often is the case, a problem covering omission will also involve a consideration of causation.

Note: You are not required to consider the responsibility of Dr Spock.

- Involuntary manslaughter

  - Constructive

  - Gross negligence — *Adomako* [1994]

- Omission — general rule

- Duty of care

- Causation

☀ Suggested answer

Wood and Mary could be charged with involuntary manslaughter, unlawful homicide without malice aforethought. It is submitted that they could not be convicted of murder as from the facts there is no evidence that they intended either to kill or to cause grievous bodily harm, and they therefore lack the *mens rea* of murder (*R* v *Moloney* [1985] 1 All ER 1025).

They would not be charged on the basis of constructive manslaughter as the prosecution must establish an intention to do an act which is unlawful and dangerous (*R* v *Church* [1965] 2 All ER 72). In this problem, the accused have omitted to act, and in *R* v *Lowe* [1973] 1 All ER 805 the Court of Appeal indicated that an omission could not constitute the unlawful act for constructive manslaughter.

The basis of manslaughter that would be argued is gross negligence, which was analysed by the House of Lords in *R* v *Adomako* [1994] 4 All ER 935, where their Lordships held that an accused would be guilty of manslaughter if the following four conditions were satisfied:

(a) the accused owed a duty of care to the victim;

(b) that duty was broken;

(c) the conduct of the accused was grossly negligent;

(d) that conduct caused the victim's death.

The first issue to consider is the difficult one of whether Wood and Mary owed Gloria a duty of care.

Traditionally, the criminal law has always drawn a clear distinction between acts and omissions, being loath to punish the latter. Other European countries — such as Greece, France and Germany — do not exhibit the same reluctance, and there is dispute as to whether the English approach is correct. See in particular the different views of Professors A. Ashworth (1989) 105 LQR 424 and G. Williams (1991) 107 LQR 109. However, apart from the numerous statutes that impose a duty to act, e.g., s. 170 of the Road Traffic Act 1988, it appears that the common law will impose a duty to act only in very limited circumstances. Clearly a duty to act for the purposes of criminal responsibility can arise under a contract of employment, e.g., *R* v *Pittwood* (1902) 19 TLR 37, where a railway gate operator was guilty of manslaughter when a person was killed crossing a railway line as a result of the accused leaving the gate open when a train was coming. Similarly, if the accused creates a dangerous situation he will owe a duty to try to minimise the danger. So, in *R* v *Miller* [1983] 1 All ER 978, the House of Lords upheld the accused's conviction for criminal damage where he had inadvertently started a fire and then, when he realised what he had done, simply left the building without making any attempt to prevent the fire spreading or to call the fire brigade.

In *R* v *Gibbins and Proctor* (1918) 13 Cr App R 134, the Court of Appeal held that parents owed a duty of care to their infant children living in the same household; but the most relevant authority to this problem is the controversial case of *R* v *Stone and Dobinson* [1977] 2 All ER 341. Stone, a 67-year-old man of low intelligence, partially deaf and almost blind, lived in a house with his mistress Dobinson, who was ineffectual and inadequate, and Stone's subnormal son. Stone's sister Fanny came to live with them and contributed to the rent. Fanny suffered from anorexia nervosa, and was in other ways regarded as eccentric. In due course she refused to leave her room and her condition deteriorated. Stone and Dobinson made minimal efforts to check on her condition, and she was eventually found dead in bed by Dobinson in a scene of appalling filth.

The accused were found guilty of manslaughter and appealed on two grounds to the Court of Appeal, the first being that they had simply omitted to act and, as they did not owe Fanny a duty of care, there was no *actus reus*. This argument was rejected by the Court of Appeal, Lord Lane CJ stating: 'Whether Fanny was a lodger or not she was a blood relative of Stone; she was occupying a room in his house, and Dobinson had undertaken the duty of looking after her'.

Thus the court must decide if a duty of care was owed. In *R* v *Khan* [1998] Crim LR 830, the Court of Appeal stated that it was for the judge to rule whether, on the facts, a duty was capable of arising and for the jury to decide whether it did arise. However, in *R* v *Gurphal Singh* [1999] Crim LR 582, the Court of Appeal approved the practice of the trial judge deciding, as a matter of law, that a duty was owed.

Their second contention was that they lacked the necessary *mens rea* required for manslaughter as they did not foresee the risk of death or grievous bodily harm. Again the Court of Appeal rejected this argument, holding that the accused had acted in reckless disregard of danger to the health and welfare of an infirm person. Lord Lane CJ said: 'Mere inadvertence is not enough. The defendant must be proved to have been indifferent to an obvious risk of injury to health or actually to have foreseen the risk but to have determined nevertheless to run it'.

However, Wood and Mary could point out that their situation is not identical to that of Stone and Dobinson. Gloria is not Wood's sister but only his aunt, and Mary does not appear to have undertaken to look after Gloria in the same way as Dobinson did Fanny. Further, they can argue that Gloria was not actually living in the same house, as she was staying in the lodge at the end of the garden. To impose the same duty on them as was imposed on Stone and Dobinson, where a different type of arrangement existed, would be very harsh, especially when it is generally agreed that *Stone and Dobinson* is a very difficult decision without a clear *ratio decidendi*.

Further, the House of Lords' decision in *R* v *Adomako* has altered the test in cases where a duty situation exists. Gross negligence and not recklessness is used, and the jury will have to consider whether the extent to which the accuseds' conduct departed from the proper standard of care incumbent upon them, involving as it must have done a risk of death to the victim, was such that it should be judged criminal. It is therefore much more difficult for the prosecution to prove that there was a risk of death as opposed to a risk of injury to health and welfare.

The final issue to be resolved is causation. Whether an omission, as opposed to an act, can actually cause a consequence is a moot point. However, the law clearly accepts that it can and there was no appeal on this point in *Stone and Dobinson*.

It is not necessary for the prosecution to prove that the accuseds' conduct was the sole or main cause, merely that it contributed significantly to the victim's death (*R v Cheshire* [1991] 3 All ER 670). The accused could argue that the doctor's turning off the life support system constituted a *novus actus interveniens*, breaking the chain of causation; but this argument was rejected by the House of Lords in *R v Malcherek*; *R v Steel* [1981] 2 All ER 422, where Lord Lane CJ stated that 'the fact that the victim has died, despite or because of medical treatment for the initial injury given by careful and skilled medical practitioners, will not exonerate the original assailant from responsibility for the death'.

It is therefore clear that Wood and Mary could not succeed with the argument that they did not cause Gloria's death. However, it is submitted that they would not be guilty of manslaughter, on the basis that either they did not owe Gloria a duty of care or, if they did, that they were not grossly negligent with regard to the risk of death.

Q Question 5

Critically analyse with reference to decided cases, the reasons why the development and application of the criminal law is often unpredictable and inconsistent.

Commentary

Warning: do not attempt this type of question in an exam unless you are very competent and confident.

Occasionally an exam will contain a question which requires you to take a wider view of the criminal law. This is such a question. You cannot simply home in on a specific area and cover it in detail. You must try to think of instances throughout the syllabus that can be used in your arguments to answer the question. Avoid the common mistake of interpreting the question to read 'Choose one area of the criminal law where there are difficulties and write all about them'!

This question has been included as it enables you to think more widely about the role of the criminal law within the legal system and society as a whole. Not an easy task, but this author feels that the struggle is worth the effort. It is to be hoped that you agree.

- **Constant change** — *R v R* [1991]

- **Lack of code** — *Caldwell* [1981], *Morgan* [1975]

- **Logic v Policy**

- **Role of House of Lords — *Clegg* [1995]**

ːଦ୍ː Suggested answer

The development of many areas of law follows a consistent and logical course. The basic foundations, their concepts and application are accepted by the vast majority, and only fine tuning or adjustments of these principles are required to meet new situations. Unfortunately this cannot be said about criminal law, where the debate about fundamental concepts — such as whether recklessness should be interpreted subjectively or objectively and whether a mistake should have to be on reasonable grounds — and controversial issues — such as whether duress should be a defence to a charge of murder and whether a battered woman should have the defence of provocation — is still ongoing.

One of the problems is that the criminal law is subject to constant change. It has to adapt to cover new phenomena, such as stalking, and to reflect society's changing social and moral standards. As the House of Lords stated in *R v R* [1991] 2 All ER 257, abolishing the husband's marital rape exemption, the common law is capable of evolving in the light of social, economic and cultural developments, and the status of women has changed out of all recognition from the time (*Hale's Pleas of the Crown 1736*) when the husband's marital rape exemption was initially recognised. Similarly, society once believed that it was a crime to take your own life, and if you failed you were guilty of attempted suicide and should be punished. However, attitudes softened and it was recognised that such a person needed help, not a criminal trial; the law was consequently amended by the Suicide Act 1961. A new Government is also likely to produce changes in certain aspects of the criminal law, e.g., public order offences.

There is no doubt that the development and application of the criminal law would be more consistent and predictable if we had an overall uniform approach. The problem is illustrated by two House of Lords' decisions: *Metropolitan Police Commissioner* v *Caldwell* [1981] 1 All ER 961, where an objective approach to recklessness was used, and *DPP* v *Morgan* [1975] 2 All ER 347, where a subjective approach to mistake was applied. Commentators may argue that two different areas of the criminal law were being considered (criminal damage and rape), but as the Law Commission have recognised (Law Com. No. 143) in suggesting codification, 'the criminal law could then exhibit a uniform approach to all crimes and defences'.

This perhaps, above all other factors, is the source of the problem — the lack of a code. All other major European countries (France, Germany, Spain) have a detailed criminal code, with a uniform approach providing a starting point for interpreting the law. Our criminal law has developed in a piecemeal fashion, with one offence's development showing little consistency with another's. So often it is difficult to say what our law actually is, even before we start to debate how it should be applied, e.g., *R* v *Savage and Parmenter* [1991] 4 All ER 698, interpreting (after over 130 years of use) the provisions of the Offences Against the Person Act 1861. A code could be expressed in clear language with definitions of fundamental concepts such as intention and recklessness, as suggested by the Law Commission's Draft Criminal Code; although, as the former chairman of the Law Commission Justice Henry Brooke stated ([1995] Crim LR 911): 'Nobody in their right mind would want to put the existing criminal law into a codified form'.

Often our criminal law follows a logical approach in its application; but as it does not exist in a vacuum and is not simply the application of academic principles, policy considerations sometimes prevail. As Lord Salmon stated in *DPP* v *Majewski* [1976] 2 All ER 142, regarding the defence of intoxication, 'the answer is that in strict logic the view [intoxication is no defence to crimes of basic intent] cannot be justified. But this is the view that has been adopted by the common law which is founded on common sense and experience rather than strict logic'. Policy considerations are also behind s. 1(3) of the Criminal Attempts Act 1981, whereby in the offence of attempt, the facts are to be as the accused believes them to be. Thus an accused objectively viewed may not be doing a criminal act but he or she can still be guilty of attempt, as in *R* v *Shivpuri* [1986] 2 All ER 334.

There is often no means of predicting which approach will prevail. In *Jaggard* v *Dickinson* [1980] 3 All ER 716, the accused, who had been informed by her friend X that she could break into X's house to shelter, while drunk mistakenly broke into V's house. She was charged with criminal damage under s. 1(1) of the Criminal Damage Act 1971, but argued that she had a lawful excuse under s. 5(2) of the Act as she honestly believed that she had the owner's consent. Although the prosecution contended that this was a crime of basic intent and therefore drunkenness was no defence (citing the House of Lords' decisions of *Metropolitan Police Commissioner* v *Caldwell* and *DPP* v *Majewski* in support), the Court of Appeal quashed her conviction, giving priority to the statutory provision of s. 5(2) of the 1971 Act.

One important aspect of the criminal law process in recent years which has caused uncertainty is the role of the House of Lords in changing the criminal law. Clearly judges are there to say what the law is, not what it should be; but Lord Simon in *DPP for Northern Ireland* v *Lynch* [1975] 1 All ER 913 said: 'I am all for recognising that judges do make law. And I am all for judges exercising their responsibilities boldly at the proper time and place . . . where matters of social policy are not involved which the collective wisdom of Parliament is better suited to resolve'. Thus in *R* v *R*, the House of Lords changed the law of rape, by abolishing the husband's defence of marital rape immunity without waiting for Parliament to implement the Law Commission's recommendations. However, their Lordships took the opposite view in *R* v *Clegg* [1995] 1 All ER 334, where they refused to follow the Law Commission's suggestion that a person who was entitled to use force in self-defence but who used unreasonable force, thereby killing the victim, would be guilty of manslaughter, not murder. Lord Lloyd stated:

> I am not adverse to judges developing law, or indeed making new law, when they can see their way clearly, even where questions of social policy are involved. [A good recent example is *R v R*.] But in the present case I am in no doubt that your Lordships should abstain from law making. The reduction of what would otherwise be murder to manslaughter in a particular class of case seems to me essentially a matter for decision by the legislature.

It is difficult to appreciate the essential difference in issues in these two cases, despite Lord Lowery's justifications in *R v Clegg* that '*R v R* dealt with a specific act and not with a general principle governing criminal liability'. Clearly there is a difference in opinion amongst the Law Lords as to the correct application of these principles. This is well illustrated by the House of Lords' decision in *R v Gotts* [1992] 1 All ER 832. The majority decision not to allow duress as a defence to attempted murder was on the basis that duress was no defence to murder. The minority view to the contrary revealed a different analysis. They argued that duress is a general defence throughout the criminal law with the exceptions of the offences of murder and treason. It is for Parliament, and not the courts, to limit the ambit of a defence; and as attempted murder is a different offence to murder, duress must therefore be available.

It is submitted that these are the main reasons why the development and application of the criminal law is often uncertain and unpredictable. There are other factors, such as whether an issue is a question of law for the judge or fact for the jury, e.g., the meaning of 'administer' (*R v Gillard* (1988) 87 Cr App R 189); the difficulty in ascertaining the *ratio decidendi* of many cases, e.g., *R v Brown* [1993] 2 All ER 75 (consent); and the possible effect of the decisions of the European Court of Human Rights. But it is the lack of a code and uniform principles which are the main factors causing the inherent uncertainty.

Q Question 6

Arthur and Bert are the directors of Malo Ltd, a British ferry company. The directors know that their workforce is under enormous pressure during the tourist season, and that safety requirements are not always closely followed. They know that on several occasions their ferries have sometimes started their journeys with the bow doors slightly open, in breach of recognised procedure. However, as there have been no disasters or loss of life on its ferries, the company has not employed additional workers or improved its safety precautions.

Sid is the assistant bosun who is responsible for ensuring that all bow doors are properly shut, and Dave is the captain, responsible for all aspects of passenger safety. On one journey, Sid opened the bow doors, went to his cabin and fell asleep. As a result the bow doors remained open at the start of the voyage, in breach of safety requirements, and 10 passengers were killed when the sea flooded the lower deck. It later transpired that Dave had not bothered to make his customary check of the bow doors, as he had been too busy dealing with his other duties.

Discuss the criminal liability of Malo Ltd, Arthur and Bert for manslaughter.

Commentary

The outcomes of many recent disasters — such as Hillsborough, the *Marchioness*, Clapham Railway junction, the Kings Cross fire and the Zeebrugge ferry disaster — have focused attention on the question of corporate criminal responsibility. The results of these cases were considered by the vast majority of the public and commentators to be very unsatisfactory. Manslaughter charges were brought only after intense public pressure in one case alone, the Zeebrugge disaster, and those charges were dismissed. In the vast majority of the disaster cases the corporate body escaped with a fine. It is therefore not surprising that the Law Commission has turned its attention to this area (Law Com. No. 237) and that it can form the basis of an examination question.

Apart from covering the basis of corporate responsibility and the important case of *R v P&O European Ferries (Dover) Ltd* (1991) 93 Cr App R 72 (the Zeebrugge disaster), it is also necessary to state the existing bases of involuntary manslaughter and briefly consider causation.

If you were instructed to cover the criminal responsibility of the employees, you would need to analyse the issues of omission and causation in full. Detailed coverage of omission can be found in other suggested answers in this and the following chapter.

- Corporate liability — *Tesco Supermarkets v Nattrass* [1972]

- Involuntary manslaughter

- *R v P&O European Ferries (Dover) Ltd* [1991]

- *R v OLL Ltd* [1994]

- Causation

:Ö: Suggested answer

A corporation can be liable to the same extent as an individual for criminal acts carried out by certain employees: first, by holding that a corporation is vicariously liable for the acts of its employees where a natural person would similarly be liable, for example when a statute imposes criminal liability; secondly, by way of the judicially developed principle of identification.

The fact that a company could be guilty of an offence requiring *mens rea* was recognised in *R v ICR Haulage Ltd* [1944] 1 All ER 691, where a company was convicted of a common law conspiracy to defraud, the court holding that the intent of the managing director represented the intent of the company. Denning LJ stated:

> a company may in many ways be likened to a human body. It has a nerve centre which controls what it does. The directors and managers represent the directing mind and will of the company and control what it does. The state of mind of these managers is the state of mind of the company and is treated by the law as such.

This principle was applied by the House of Lords in *Tesco Supermarkets* v *Nattrass* [1972] AC 153, where their Lordships held that the company may be criminally liable for the acts of only 'the board of directors and perhaps other superior officers of a company who carry out the functions of management and speak and act as the company'.

In *R* v *P&O European Ferries (Dover) Ltd* (1991) 93 Cr App R 72, Turner J recognised the need to look at the company's articles of association to ascertain the company's controlling mind; and although the courts have held that the company may not be identified with a branch manager of a supermarket (*Tesco* v *Nattrass*) or a depot engineer (*Magna Plant Ltd* v *Mitchell* [1996] Crim LR 396), it is quite clear that it will be identified with the company's directors. Indeed, the decisions by the Privy Council in *Meridian Global Funds Management Asia Ltd* v *Securities Commission* [1995] 2 AC 500 and the House of Lords in *Re Supply of Ready Mix Concrete, Re* [1995] 1 AC 456, indicate that the courts are now more prepared to widen the identification principle to other employees within the company such as the company's financial investment manager.

It is therefore submitted that Arthur and Bert as directors would be identified as the company, but not Sid as assistant bosun of a ship. The position of Dave as ship's captain is less clear-cut, but the prosecution would argue that he should be included as control of the ship has been delegated to him. Nevertheless, the defence would counter with the submission that his position can be equated to that of the supermarket manager in *Tesco* v *Nattrass*, where the House of Lords held he could not be so identified.

Thus in order for Malo Ltd to be found guilty of manslaughter, the prosecution must prove that the directors Arthur or Bert (or possibly the captain Dave) had committed involuntary manslaughter. This can be defined as unlawful homicide without malice aforethought and has two bases: first, constructive manslaughter, where the accused intended to do an act which was unlawful and dangerous (*DPP* v *Newbury and Jones* [1976] 2 All ER 365); secondly, where the accused has been reckless or grossly negligent (*R* v *Adomako* [1994] 3 All ER 79).

Quite clearly, this is not an example of constructive manslaughter as it is perfectly lawful to operate a ferry service; and even if the company was acting negligently so as to be committing a minor offence, this would still not be sufficient for constructive manslaughter. As Lord Aitkin said in *Andrews* v *DPP* [1937] 2 All ER 552: 'There is an obvious difference in the law of manslaughter between doing an unlawful act and doing a lawful act with a degree of carelessness which the legislature makes criminal'. Although this *dictum* has been heavily criticised, this House of Lords' decision is still good law and would apply here.

However, the prosecution would be able to present a strong case on the gross negligence basis. Following *R v Adomako*, the prosecution must prove that: (i) a duty of care was owed; (ii) there was a breach of that duty; (iii) the breach was grossly negligent and caused the victim's death. It is submitted that the first two conditions could be easily satisfied, and it is then a question for the jury to decide if the breach was grossly negligent. As Lord Mackay stated in *R v Adomako*:

> This will depend on the seriousness of the breach of duty committed by the defendant in all the circumstances in which the defendant was placed when it occurred. The jury will have to consider whether the extent to which the defendant's conduct departed from the proper standard of care incumbent upon him, involving as it must have done a risk of death to the [victim] was such that it should be judged criminal.

The company would of course be judged on the standard of the reasonable prudent ferry operator, not that of the reasonable man.

The leading case on this topic is *R v P&O European Ferries (Dover) Ltd* (1991) 93 Cr App R 72. The roll-on roll-off ferry, *The Herald of Free Enterprise*, capsized just outside Zeebrugge harbour in March 1987, after leaving the harbour with its bow doors open, resulting in the death of many passengers. The assistant bosun whose job it was to ensure that the doors were shut was asleep in his cabin. The captain had no means of confirming from the bridge whether or not the doors had been shut. They, together with the directors and the company, were tried for manslaughter. Evidence was given that the system had worked without mishap for seven years in which there were upward of over 60,000 sailings. Further, although it would have been easy to reduce or eliminate the risk of the ship ever sailing with its doors open — by a system of positive reporting or the installation of bridge indicator lights — neither the Department of Transport nor Lloyds insurers required these measures, and P&O's system was no different to that of the other ferry operators. As a result, Turner J ruled that on an application of the objective recklessness test (as stated by Lord Diplock in *Metropolitan Police Commissioner v Caldwell* [1981] 1 All ER 961 and *Lawrence v Metropolitan Police Commissioner* [1981] 2 All ER 1253) the reasonable man could not conclude that there was an obvious and serious risk of death or serious harm from operating a ferry in this manner, and directed the jury to acquit all defendants.

Despite this decision it is not certain that the jury would rule in Malo Ltd's favour on this point, for the following reasons: first, as a result of Zeebruggee and other disasters, public opinion has hardened, and the dangers of defective systems are well known; secondly, in *R v OLL Ltd, Kite and Stoddart* (the Lyme Bay canoeing disaster — (1994), unreported), a company and its managing director were convicted of manslaughter at Winchester Crown Court after the jury had found that they were grossly negligent in allowing schoolchildren to go canoeing on the sea without proper super-vision thereby causing their death; and thirdly, in a duty situation, the applicable test is, after *Adomako*, gross negligence and not recklessness.

There is also the possibility that the court might accept the aggregation principle, whereby the negligence of a number of company operatives could be added together to hold that the company was grossly negligent. Despite Devlin J in *Armstrong* v *Strain* [1952] 1 All ER 139 stating 'You cannot add an innocent state of mind to an innocent state of mind and get as a result a dishonest state of mind', commentators argue strongly that there is a place for this doctrine in a crime of gross negligence such as manslaughter.

The final condition for the prosecution to establish is causation. Malo Ltd and the directors would argue that the deaths were caused by the negligence of Sid and Dave, and therefore that the defendants should be exonerated. However, the prosecution need only establish that the defendants' conduct significantly contributed to the deaths. It is not necessary to prove that it was the main cause or even a substantial cause (*R* v *Cheshire* [1991] 3 All ER 670). Further, the court will rarely accept in crim-inal cases the *novus actus interveniens* argument (see, for example, *R* v *Pagett* (1983) 76 Cr App R 141), and it is therefore submitted that it is quite probable that Malo Ltd, Arthur and Bert will be found guilty of manslaughter.

▣ Question 7

How would your answer to Quesiton 6 differ if the recommendations of the Law Commission on involuntary and corporate manslaughter (Law Com. No. 237) were implemented?

Commentary

In their 1980 Report, the Criminal Law Revision Committee recognised that 'so serious an offence as manslaughter should not be a lottery'; and more recently the Law Commission have pointed out that on the only occasion on which a case of corporate manslaughter has been brought to trial, the obscurities of the law of corporate responsibility were com-pounded by the obscurities of the law of manslaughter.

This comment was made before the successful prosecution of OLL Ltd for manslaughter in the 1994 Lyme Bay canoeing disaster case (*R* v *OLL Ltd, Kite and Stoddart*), before which there had been three unsuccessful prosecutions for manslaughter of a company in the history of English law.

The answer to the previous question demonstrates the uncertainty in the application of the law in this area, and many commentators have argued for a completely different approach, not based on principles applied in ascertaining individual responsibility. As Celia Wells points out ('Corporations: Culture, Risk and Criminal Responsibility' [1993] Crim LR

551): 'Corporations are different from human beings; their activities are not merely on a grander scale — their whole existence, functions and formations mark them apart. The contours of their culpability should reflect these differences'.

It is not unusual for a question (or part question) on the Law Commission's recommendations on a particular topic to be included in an examination paper if they have been covered in the course and concern a current controversial issue. They are even more likely to be included if the Government has indicated that the recommendations may be implemented.

- **Law Commission's recommendations**
- **Reckless killing**
- **Killing by gross carelessness**
- *R v P&O Ferries Ltd* **[1991]**
- **Corporate killing**

:Q: Suggested answer

The Law Commission has recommended that the existing offence of involuntary manslaughter should be abolished and replaced by new offences of reckless killing and killing by gross carelessness. Generally when recommending changes, the Law Commission will try to utilise some of the existing established principles, but here the Commission decided that there were so many inconsistencies in constructive manslaughter and uncertainties with gross negligence or reckless manslaughter, that the best approach would be to scrap the existing bases and start again.

Reckless killing would occur when: (i) a person by his or her conduct causes the death of another; (ii) he or she is aware that his or her conduct will cause death or serious injury; and (iii) it is unreasonable for him or her to take that risk, having regard to the circumstances as he or she believes them to be.

Killing by gross carelessness would take place if the following conditions were satisfied:

(a) a person by his or her conduct causes the death of another;

(b) a risk that his or her conduct will cause death or serious injury would be obvious to a reasonable person in his or her position;

(c) he or she is capable of appreciating that risk at the material time; and

(d) either —

(i) his or her conduct falls far below what can reasonably be expected of him or her in the circumstances, or

(ii) he or she intends by his or her conduct to cause some injury or is aware of,

THE ELEMENTS OF A CRIME: *ACTUS REUS* AND *MENS REA* **33**

and unreasonably takes, the risk that it may do so, and the conduct causing (or intending to cause) the injury constitutes an offence.

Applying these tests to the facts of the question, it would still be extremely difficult for the prosecution to establish reckless killing. Although condition (ii) requires only an awareness of the risk of causing death or grievous bodily harm, and this would be much easier to prove than intention or even perhaps subjective recklessness, the prosecution must still establish in condition (iii) that it was unreasonable to take the risk. It would certainly not be unreasonable to operate roll-on roll-off ferries simply because there is a risk of death or serious injury, but if the directors know that the company's system and safety procedures are defective, the prosecution may be able to satisfy this condition.

It is, however, more likely that the company could be convicted of killing by gross carelessness. Certainly there would be no difficulty in establishing the first three conditions, and the prosecution would have a good chance of proving condition (d)(i) (that the company's conduct falls far below what can reasonably be expected of it in the circumstances). If the error is due solely to an individual employee's momentary lapse (for example, a train driver's failure to spot a red signal light) the company will not be guilty: if, on the other hand, the accident could have been prevented by using readily available safety measures or by changing the general practices and procedures, the company could be found guilty.

Commentators argued that the company should have been found guilty of manslaughter in *R v P&O European Ferries Ltd* (1991) 93 Cr App R 72, as the corporate management were negligent in allowing pressure to build on the crew to improve turnaround times and for failure to enforce corporate instructions on bow doors. Collective management's response to several requests for bow-door indicator lights was poor and no attempt was made to assess the effectiveness of existing monitoring procedures. The Sheen Enquiry concluded that management response displayed 'an absence of any proper sense of responsibility'.

As the directors of Malo Ltd knew the crew were under intense pressure at turnaround times, it is therefore extremely likely that a jury would find the conditions for killing by gross negligence satisfied, and the company would be found guilty. Similarly, on the tests proposed by the Law Commission, it is submitted that the directors would also be found guilty of this offence.

If the company could not be convicted of reckless killing, it does appear that it would be guilty under the Law Commission's proposed completely new offence of corporate killing. A corporation would be guilty of corporate killing if:

(a) management failure by the corporation is the cause or one of the causes of a person's death; and

(b) that failure constitutes conduct falling far below what can reasonably be expected of the corporation in the circumstances.

The provisions also state that there is a management failure by the company if the way in which the activities are managed or organised fails to ensure the health and safety of persons employed in or affected by those activities. Thus once there is evidence that employees have perceived a risk, even a small one, of serious consequences, it will be appropriate to look critically at the company's system for transmitting that knowledge to the appropriate level of management and for acting on the knowledge received. The court will therefore be able to analyse the company's organisation, attitude and concern for safety in general in considering whether or not there has been a management failure.

The new offence will also not face so many difficulties on the issue of causation, as the proposals provide that management failure may be regarded as a cause of the victim's death notwithstanding that the immediate cause is the act or omission of an individual. Thus Malo Ltd would still be found guilty even though the court might rule that the employees Sid and Dave were the immediate cause of death.

Thus a company and its directors could be guilty of the offences of reckless killing and killing by gross negligence; but only the company could be found guilty of corporate killing, a proposed offence which would recognise that criminal responsibility should fall on organisations who fail to impose a safe system of work, thereby making their operations a risk to public safety.

Further reading

Ashworth, A., 'Interpreting Criminal Statutes' [1991] LQR 419.

Ashworth, A. and Blake, M., 'The Presumption of Innocence in English Criminal Law' [1996] Crim LR 306.

Field, S. and Lynn, M., 'Capacity, Recklessness and the House of Lords' [1993] Crim LR 127.

Norrie, A., 'Oblique Intent and Legal Politics' [1989] Crim LR 793.

Smith, J.C., 'R v Woollin' [1998] Crim LR 890.

Sullivan, B., 'Corporate Killing — Some Government Proposals' [2001] Crim LR 31.

Unlawful homicide

Introduction

One of the themes of this book, and of the substantive criminal law itself, is the constant pressure for change and consequent uncertainty. This is aptly illustrated by the offences of murder and manslaughter, which have been before the House of Lords in recent years and have also been the subject of Law Commission reports (in particular involuntary manslaughter: No. 237 1996).

It is odd that, despite the fact of having the Homicide Act 1957 and the Law Reform (Year and a Day Rule) Act 1996, we still have a common law definition for murder containing the misleading term for *mens rea*, 'malice aforethought'. This of course does not require premeditated evil but, after *R v Moloney* [1985] 1 All ER 1025, simply an intention to kill or cause grievous bodily harm. That this is the *mens rea* for murder has now been settled for over 10 years (this may not seem a long period, but the criminal law is constantly changing), although the debate as to whether it should be the *mens rea* has been fuelled by Lord Mustill's *obiter dicta* in *Attorney-General's Reference (No. 3 of 1994)* [1997] 3 All ER 936. He was critical of the conspicuous anomaly that intention to cause grievous bodily harm is sufficient *mens rea* for murder. This anomaly has also been recognised by the Law Commission, whose Draft Code (cl. 54) provides that an intention to cause serious personal harm *being aware that death may occur* should be required. However, this suggestion, together with those abolishing the mandatory life sentence for murder, is likely to go unheeded on the basis that such changes would send the wrong message to society, in as much as the public would think that the crime of murder was no longer regarded as such a serious offence.

The need for legislation in this area was also recognised by the Law Lords in *Airedale NHS Trust v Bland* [1993] 1 All ER 821, concerning the criminal responsibility of doctors regarding euthanasia. This was another example of the problems caused by the absence of a criminal code, highlighting the fact that sometimes we do not actually know what the law is until it is formulated in a House of Lords' decision. It is certainly most unsatisfactory that their Lordships had to resort to the distinction between acts and omissions, in deciding that disconnecting the naso-gastric tube was an omission (to give further treatment), in order to hold that a doctor in these circumstances would not be committing murder or manslaughter.

The Law Commission has also recognised the urgent need to reform the law on involuntary manslaughter, to the extent that in their 1996 Report (Law Com. No. 237) they proposed the abolition of the common law offence and its replacement by two separate offences based on subjective recklessness and gross carelessness. It is an unusual step when the Law Commission decide to scrap all of the applicable principles, but in 1980 the Criminal Law Revision Committee stated that 'so serious an offence as manslaughter should not be a lottery'. Nevertheless, all the anomalies and inconsistencies must still be applied in trying to answer questions on this troublesome area. The author has accordingly included in this chapter typical problem questions concerning all the important aspects of these topics, as well as a full question on the partial defence of provocation, always an examination favourite.

Q Question 1

Mary, intending to give her neighbours Jill and Stan a fright, lit a fire in their letterbox not knowing whether anybody was in the house. In fact, Jill and Stan had gone out for the evening, but their aged parents, Meg and Hugh, who were staying at their home, were overcome by fumes. Owing to an administrative error, two ambulances arrived to take the victims to hospital; and the ambulance in which Hugh was transported was driven so negligently that it was involved in an accident and by the time it arrived at hospital Hugh had died.

Meg arrived at hospital and was informed that a blood transfusion would save her life. However, owing to religious beliefs, she refused and died two days later.

Discuss the criminal liability of Mary.

Commentary

All criminal law exams will contain a question on murder, and this question is typical. Whenever you cover murder you must always consider involuntary manslaughter as most questions will leave the issue of malice aforethought in doubt. In this answer the constructive basis of involuntary manslaughter is dealt with in detail.

The other major area that must be covered in detail is causation. Again this is a topic which you will often find included in questions based on unlawful homicide, and in this answer the cases concerning medical treatment as a *novus actus interveniens* must be analysed.

Although there are difficulties surrounding these topics a well-prepared student would be confident of obtaining a high mark on a question of this nature.

- Murder — malice aforethought

- Transferred malice

- Constructive manslaughter

- Causation

- Criminal Damage Act 1971

:Q: Suggested answer

The most serious offences which Mary may be charged with are murder and manslaughter. Murder is the unlawful killing of a human being within the Queen's peace with malice aforethought. After the Law Reform (Year and a Day Rule) Act 1996, it is not necessary that the death takes place within a year and a day of the unlawful act or omission. The mental state for murder, malice aforethought, is satisfied by the prosecution establishing that the accused intended to kill or cause grievous bodily harm. This was stated in *R* v *Moloney* [1985] 1 All ER 1025 and confirmed by the House of Lords in *R* v *Hancock and Shankland* [1986] 1 All ER 641. This is a question of fact for the jury, and in *Moloney* the House of Lords stated that unless intention was a very complicated issue because of the facts of the case the trial judge should avoid any elaboration or paraphrasing of what is meant by intention, but simply leave it to the jury's good sense as intention is a word in common use and easily understood by the public.

If the issue is complex the trial judge might follow the guidelines laid down by the House of Lords in *R* v *Woollin* [1998] 4 All ER 103, where it was stated that if the simple direction was not enough, the jury should be further directed that they were not entitled to find the necessary intention unless they felt sure that death or serious bodily harm was a virtually certain result of D's actions (barring some unforeseen intervention) and that D had appreciated that fact.

However, Lord Scarman in *R* v *Hancock and Shankland* did emphasise that there is no magic formula that the trial judge must follow, although he should point out to the jury that the more probable the consequence the more likely the accused foresaw it and intended it. Nevertheless, foresight of consequence is not conclusive proof of intention, although it is evidence from which the jury may infer intention.

Mary may argue that she intended only to frighten the occupants of the house and not to cause death or grievous bodily harm. She may also argue that she did not intend to harm Hugh and Meg, but this argument will fail because of the doctrine of transferred malice, i.e., if Mary has the *mens rea* for a particular offence against a particular victim but she actually commits that crime against a different victim, the *mens rea* will be transferred to the actual victim and Mary will be guilty of that offence. Thus in *R* v *Mitchell* [1983] 2 All ER 427, the accused was found guilty of manslaughter when he deliberately hit a 72-year-old man who fell against an 89-year-old woman, knocking her over and causing her to break a femur. This required an operation and she died as a result of complications arising from it. The Court of Appeal rejected the accused's argument that the doctrine could only apply if the actual victim and the intended victim were identical; and more recently in *Attorney-General's Reference (No. 3 of 1994)* [1996] 1 Cr App R 351, the court held that the doctrine could apply to convict an accused of murder who stabbed a pregnant woman with the result that the baby was born alive but later died as a result of injuries inflicted by the accused (although this decision was reversed by the House of Lords: [1997] 3 All ER 936).

As intention is a question of fact for the jury, it is not possible to be certain that they would conclude that Mary had malice aforethought. They may accept that her action was directed at simply damaging the house or simply frightening the occupants. If this was the case, Mary could still be convicted of involuntary manslaughter which is unlawful homicide without malice aforethought. There has always been uncertainty as to what the appropriate *mens rea* for this offence should be, and indeed actually is. As Lord Aitkin stated in *Andrews* v *DPP* [1937] 2 All ER 552 at pp. 554–5, 'of all crimes manslaughter appears to afford most difficulties of definition, for it concerns homicide in so many and so varying conditions'.

There are two broad categories of involuntary manslaughter. First, manslaughter by an unlawful and dangerous act, where the prosecution must prove that the accused intended to do an act which was unlawful and dangerous. Secondly, manslaughter by gross negligence or recklessness as to the risk of death (*R* v *Adomako* [1994] 3 All ER 79).

The constructive basis (as the first category is often known) is the one on which the prosecution would concentrate as it is easily established. It is not necessary for the prosecution to prove that Mary knew the act was unlawful or dangerous, simply that she intended to do that act, i.e., set fire to the house. Whether the act is unlawful is clearly a question for the judge and jury. It is clear that Mary has committed the *actus reus* of criminal damage, and although the jury must be satisfied that Mary had the necessary *mens rea* for this offence (*R* v *Jennings* [1990] Crim LR 588), she clearly intended to start the fire.

Mary may argue that she did not realise that this was dangerous, but this contention will not succeed as the House of Lords in *DPP* v *Newbury and Jones* [1976] 2 All ER 365 confirmed that this is a question of fact for the jury and the prosecution do not have to prove that the accused recognised the risk of danger. Further, the appropriate direction to the jury is that the accused's act is dangerous if 'all sober and reasonable people would inevitably recognise [that it] must subject the other person to, at least, the risk of some harm resulting therefrom, albeit not serious harm' (*per* Edmund Davies J in *R* v *Church* [1965] 2 All ER 72 at p. 70). It is quite clear that if you set fire to a residential property not knowing whether the house is occupied there is a risk of physical harm, and therefore the prosecution would easily satisfy this condition.

In *R* v *Dalby* [1982] 1 All ER 916, the Court of Appeal appeared to introduce a third condition into constructive manslaughter, i.e., the act must be directed at the victim and likely to cause immediate injury. This was quickly amended by *R* v *Mitchell* to an act directed at another (not necessarily the victim). However, in *R* v *Goodfellow* (1986) 83 Cr App R 23, where the accused, intending to be rehoused by the council, set fire to his house, thereby causing the death of some of his family, the aimed-at doctrine was rejected and the accused was convicted of constructive and reckless manslaughter. Thus it appears that as long as there is no intervening act, this condition is satisfied.

Mary would therefore be guilty of murder or manslaughter unless the court was satisfied that she did not cause the victims' deaths. However, the prosecution do not have to prove that Mary's actions were the main cause or even a substantial cause of the victims' deaths, merely that they made a significant contribution to the consequence (*R* v *Cheshire* [1991] 3 All ER 670). Mary would argue in respect of Meg's death that her decision to refuse a blood transfusion was unreasonable and constituted a *novus actus interveniens* which broke the chain of causation. This point was resolved in *R* v *Blaue* [1975] 1 WLR 1411 where, on similar facts, the court applied the 'egg-shell skull' principle that you take your victim as you find him. Thus an accused will not be exonerated merely because the consequences of the accused's act are exacerbated by the susceptibilities of the victim. As Lawton LJ stated in *R* v *Blaue*: 'It has been the policy of the law that those who use violence on other people must take their victims as they find them. This in our judgement means the whole man, not just the physical man'. In *Blaue* the court refused to say that the victim's decision was unreasonable, but even if it was, on the authority of *R* v *Holland* (1841) 2 Mood and R 351, it would still not exonerate Mary. In this case the accused severely cut the victim's hand with an iron sword. The victim refused to have his fingers amputated although he was given medical advice that failure to do so would result in lockjaw and his death. Unfortunately, the diagnosis proved correct and the victim died. Nevertheless the accused was convicted of murder.

The position regarding Hugh's death is more complicated. Mary would argue the authority of *R* v *Jordan* (1956) 40 Cr App R 152, which decided that if the medical treatment received was the sole cause of death and was also grossly negligent, the chain of causation will be broken. However, later cases have isolated *R* v *Jordan*, demonstrating that it is very difficult to succeed with this argument. Thus in *R* v *Smith* [1959] 2 All ER 193, the accused stabbed the victim in a barrack room brawl. The victim was dropped twice while being taken to the medical orderly who failed to diagnose the full extent of his wounds. Not surprisingly the victim died, but the accused's conviction for murder was upheld as the court held that as the original wound was still an operating cause of death the chain of causation was not broken. Similarly in *R* v *Cheshire* (above), on facts similar to *R* v *Jordan*, the Court of Appeal upheld the accused's conviction for murder, Beldam LJ stating 'it will only be in the most extraordinary and unusual case that such treatment can be said to be so independent of the acts of the accused that it could be regarded in law as the cause of the victim's death to the exclusion of the accused's act'.

So even if the evidence was able to show that the injuries sustained by Hugh in the ambulance accident were the sole cause of death, the court might still conclude that this was not 'so independent of the acts of the accused' and therefore not sufficient to break the chain of causation.

In the unlikely event of Mary's arguments on causation succeeding, she would still be guilty of offences under the Criminal Damage Act 1971. In particular, arson under s. 1(3) and intentionally or recklessly endangering life under s. 1(2). On the other hand, it is unlikely that she would be convicted of attempted murder, as the prosecution must prove that Mary intended to kill — an intention to cause grievous bodily harm is not sufficient (*R* v *Jones* [1990] 1 WLR 1057).

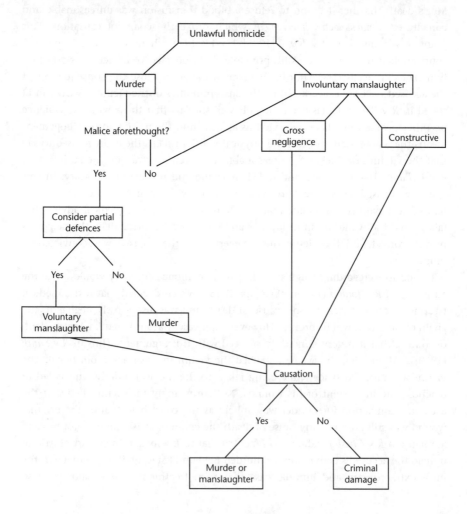

Q Question 2

Discuss Don's criminal liability for murder and manslaughter in the following circumstances.

On a very cold winter's night Don, accompanied by Mrs X, is driving along a lonely country road. Don's attention is distracted by his talking with Mrs X and he knocks down Tim, a pedestrian. Don is worried that Mrs X's husband may somehow learn of their relationship and therefore drives on although he can clearly see that Tim is injured and unconscious. Tim's body is not discovered until the following morning, by which time he has died from exposure to the exceptional cold. If he had received proper medical treatment the previous night, he would not have died.

Commentary

Although this question, like the previous one, involves murder and manslaughter, and there are some basic elements which must be covered, there are different elements of these offences which must be emphasised here.

The key to writing a good answer to this question is to recognise that in effect there are two incidents to analyse. First, Don inadvertently knocking over Tim; and, secondly, Don's decision to leave him exposed to the elements. This enables you to analyse in full the different mental states involved in relation to the offences.

In most answers you have to make decisions about how much material to include on specific elements. In this answer, as a conviction for murder is most unlikely, very little is said about malice aforethought; whereas in the answer to the previous question, as this issue was in some doubt, there was extensive coverage of the issue of intention. On the other hand, manslaughter is analysed in great detail here, with emphasis on applying the law to the facts of this problem.

You are not required to consider the criminal responsibility of Mrs X, or offences other than murder or manslaughter, although clearly Don would be guilty of offences under the Road Traffic Act 1991.

- Murder — malice aforethought

- Manslaughter

- Constructive manslaughter

- Gross negligence manslaughter

- Duty of care

- Causation

ːQ̇ː Suggested answer

The most serious offences with which Don may be charged are murder and manslaughter. Murder is defined as the unlawful killing of a human being within the Queen's peace with malice aforethought. Before the Law Reform (Year and a Day Rule) Act 1996, it was necessary to show that death followed the unlawful act or omission within a year and a day, but this is no longer the case. In *Hyam* v *DPP* [1974] 2 All ER 41, the House of Lords stated that malice aforethought included an intention on the accused's behalf knowingly to expose the victim to the risk of death. However, this decision was 'clarified' in *R* v *Moloney* [1985] 1 All ER 1025, where the House of Lords stated that only an intention to kill or cause grievous bodily harm would be sufficient to constitute malice aforethought.

Their Lordships in *Moloney* also held that as intention is a word in common use, easily understood by the public, it should be left to the jury by the trial judge without any elaborate definition or direction. It is submitted that as Don was simply inadvertent when initially knocking Tim over, there is no question of malice aforethought and accordingly this issue should not be left to the jury.

Manslaughter is divided into two categories: voluntary and involuntary. Voluntary manslaughter occurs when the accused causes the victim's death with malice aforethought but has one of the three partial defences under the Homicide Act 1957, i.e., provocation, diminished responsibility, or death arising as a result of a suicide pact. On the facts of this question there is no evidence of these elements and voluntary manslaughter would not be considered by the court.

Involuntary manslaughter is unlawful homicide without malice aforethought. The prosecution must prove that the accused caused the victim's death and either intended to do an act which was unlawful and dangerous (constructive manslaughter), or was grossly negligent or reckless as to the risk of death (*R* v *Adomako* [1994] 3 All ER 79).

It is very easy for the prosecution to establish the *mens rea* for constructive manslaughter as it is not necessary to prove that the accused realised his or her act was either unlawful or dangerous. Whether the act was unlawful is a question for the judge and jury (*R* v *Jennings* [1990] Crim LR 588) and whether it was dangerous is a question of fact for the jury. It is not necessary for the prosecution to prove that Don recognised the danger (*DPP* v *Newbury and Jones* [1976] 2 All ER 362); it is simply for the jury to decide whether the act of the accused was such as 'all sober and reasonable people would inevitably recognise must subject the other person to at least the risk of some harm resulting therefrom albeit not serious harm' (Edmund Davies J in *R* v *Church* [1965] 2 All ER 72 at p. 70).

At first sight it would therefore appear that Don would be guilty of manslaughter under the constructive basis. However, the criminal law is not always based on pure logic and often policy considerations are important in shaping the applicable principles. Thus in *Andrews* v *DPP* [1937] 2 All ER 552, in a case concerning causing death by dangerous driving, Lord Aitkin expressly distinguished between intrinsically unlawful acts and acts that become unlawful because they are performed negligently: 'There is an obvious difference in the law of manslaughter between doing an unlawful act and doing a lawful act with a degree of carelessness which the legislature makes criminal'. Although this *dictum* has been heavily criticised it is still good law, and therefore Don's act of driving carelessly will not be treated as an unlawful act for the purposes of constructive manslaughter. We must therefore consider the second basis of involuntary manslaughter.

The terms 'recklessness' and 'gross negligence' have for many years been used to describe the second basis of involuntary manslaughter. These terms have often been used interchangeably, and in *R* v *Seymour* [1983] 2 AC 493 the House of Lords applied an objective recklessness test as to a risk of death or physical injury. However, this decision was in effect overruled by the House of Lords in *R* v *Adomako* where their Lordships decided that in cases of death resulting from a duty of care situation, gross negligence was the appropriate test.

Thus, in order to find the accused guilty of gross negligence manslaughter, the prosecution must prove the following conditions:

(a)   the accused owed a duty of care to the victim;

(b)   the accused acted in breach of that duty;

(c)   the accused's conduct was grossly negligent; and

(d)   that conduct caused the victim's death.

Whether or not conduct is grossly negligent is a question of fact for the jury and will depend upon the seriousness of the breach in all the circumstances in which the accused was placed when it occurred. 'The jury will have to consider whether the extent to which the accused's conduct departed from the proper standard of care incumbent upon him involving as it must have done a risk of death to the victim was such that it should be judged criminal' (*per* Lord Mackay in *R* v *Adomako*).

If Don had been only momentarily distracted while driving and the incident took place on a lonely country road where there was little possibility of other traffic or pedestrians, it is unlikely that the jury would find him grossly negligent as to the risk of death. However, as Don realised that he had knocked Tim over and then deliberately left him, his responsibility must now be analysed in respect of this fact.

Again, it is most unlikely that the jury would consider that he possessed malice aforethought. Even if Don were to admit that he foresaw that by leaving Tim there was a risk of death or grievous bodily harm, the House of Lords stated in *R* v *Moloney* that foresight is not the same as intention, and therefore Don lacks the necessary malice aforethought required for murder. However, he is now much more likely to have the necessary *mens rea* for manslaughter. It is possible that this would be constructive manslaughter, although there is doubt as to whether an omission can constitute an unlawful and dangerous act for this purpose. The uncertainty stems from the Court of Appeal decision in *R v Lowe* [1973] 1 All ER 805; and in *R v Shepperd* [1980] 3 All ER 899, the House of Lords distinguished between omissions and commission stating:

> If I strike a child in a manner likely to cause harm it is right that if that child dies I may be charged with manslaughter. If, however, I omit to do something with the result that it suffers injury to its health which results in its death, we think that a charge of manslaughter should not be an inevitable consequence even if the omission is deliberate.

Turning to the gross negligence basis, it is clear that Don as a motorist would owe a duty of care to Tim, a pedestrian he has just knocked over; but although he was in breach of a duty in the manner in which he drove, would Don be in breach of his duty in failing to assist Tim? Don would no doubt argue that this is simply an omission to act, and the law does not generally punish omissions. It is submitted that Don's argument would fail, as in *R v Miller* [1983] 1 All ER 978 the House of Lords stated that a duty owed by someone who had created a danger was broken when that person deliberately failed to take steps to minimise that danger. Lord Diplock said:

> I see no rational ground for excluding from conduct capable of giving rise to criminal liability conduct which consists of failing to take measures that lie within one's power to counteract a danger that one has oneself created, if at the time of such conduct one's state of mind is such as constitutes a necessary ingredient of the offence.

This principle would apply to impose a duty on Don to summon medical assistance.

Considering the third element of the test, was Don grossly negligent with regard to the risk of death? It is now much more likely the jury will conclude that he was. The victim was unconscious; it was a lonely country road, and there was therefore little possibility of a passer-by coming to his assistance; and it was an extremely cold night which meant that Tim's condition would rapidly deteriorate.

Don might argue that the factor of the weather means that the fourth condition cannot be fulfilled, namely that Don did not cause the victim's death. However, the prosecution has to establish only that Don's conduct was a significantly contributing cause (*R v Cheshire* [1991] 3 All ER 670). The courts are also traditionally reluctant to accept the argument that a *novus actus interveniens* has broken the chain of causation and it cannot be envisaged that the extreme cold weather could be deemed the sole cause of death thereby exonerating Don.

It is therefore submitted that the prosecution should now be able to establish all the ingredients of gross negligence and that Don would be found guilty of involuntary manslaughter.

Q Question 3

Prescilla is pregnant and Richard (as he well knows) is responsible for her condition. They become very depressed about the future and decide to commit suicide, by attaching themselves together by way of an electric cable which Richard connects to the mains. Richard then pulls the switch, but although a strong current passes through them and they are both badly burnt they are not killed. They are both taken to hospital and treated for first degree burns. Prescilla gives birth to a premature baby who, as a result of injuries caused by the electrocution, suffers severe respiratory problems. She is placed on a ventilator; but after five days, because she is now in a persistent vegetative state with no hope of recovery, Dr Spock decides to turn the machine off and the baby dies.

Discuss the criminal responsibility of the parties.

Commentary

This question involves a number of interesting issues concerning unlawful homicide and the doctrine of transferred malice. It also requires detailed analysis of two recent controversial cases: *Attorney-General's Reference (No. 3 of 1994)* [1997] 3 All ER 936 and *Airedale NHS Trust* v *Bland* [1993] 1 All ER 821.

The student must also consider the question of suicide, and how the provisions of the Suicide Act 1961 and the Homicide Act 1957 affect the position. Consideration of the offence of abstracting electricity without the owner's consent under s. 13 of the Theft Act 1968 is not required!

• **Murder**

• **s. 2 Suicide Act 1961**

• **Transferred malice**

• **Causation**

• *Airedale NHS Trust* v *Bland* **[1993]**

☼ Suggested answer

Richard could be charged with a number of offences arising out of this incident. Regarding Prescilla, he could be charged with attempted murder, unlawful wounding under s. 18 of the Offences Against the Person Act 1861, and aiding and abetting suicide under s. 2 of the Suicide Act 1961. Regarding the baby who is born alive, he could (following *Attorney-General's Reference (No. 3 of 1994)* [1997] 3 All ER 936) be guilty of murder.

To be found guilty of attempted murder the accused must have done more than a merely preparatory act (Criminal Attempts Act 1981, s. 1) with an intention to kill (*R v Whybrow* (1951) 35 Cr App R 141); an intention to cause grievous bodily harm is not sufficient (*R v Jones* [1990] 3 All ER 886). It is submitted that the jury would conclude that turning on the electricity after wiring up Prescilla is more than merely preparatory, and as Richard and Prescilla intended to die the prosecution could easily establish *mens rea*. However, in view of the alternative offences and the provisions of the Suicide Act 1961, the Crown Prosecution Service might decide that attempted murder is not the most appropriate charge. Incidentally, although the existence of a suicide pact (within the meaning of s. 4(3) of the Homicide Act 1957) is a defence, reducing murder to manslaughter, it is not available on a charge of attempted murder.

Instead Richard could be charged under s. 2 of the Suicide Act 1961, i.e., 'a person who aids, abets, counsels or procures the suicide of another shall be liable on conviction on indictment to imprisonment for a term not exceeding 14 years'. *R v McShane* [1977] Crim LR 737 demonstrates that Richard can be convicted of attempting to commit the offence, and it is submitted that as the facts clearly show that he has sufficient *mens rea* he will be found guilty of this offence.

Similarly there appears to be little doubt that a conviction under s. 18 of the Offences Against the Person Act 1861 would also follow. The severe burns would constitute either a wound or grievous bodily harm and Richard clearly has the intention to bring about this consequence (*R v Belfon* [1976] 3 All ER 46). It is most unlikely that Prescilla's consent would be a defence.

Richard could also be charged with murder of the baby. Murder is the unlawful killing of a human being within the Queen's peace, with malice aforethought. After the Law Reform (Year and a Day Rule) Act 1996, it is not necessary that the death takes place within a year and a day of the unlawful act or omission. If a foetus is injured in the womb and is not born alive, the appropriate charge is abortion or child destruction. However, in this problem, the baby had an existence independent of the mother, and Richard could be charged with murder. He will argue that he lacked malice aforethought as he did not intend to kill or cause grievous bodily harm to the baby (*R v Moloney* [1985] 1 All ER 1025). Nevertheless, the prosecution can contend that the doctrine of transferred malice applies. Thus, where an accused has the *mens rea* for one particular crime but the actual victim is different from the intended victim, the accused will be guilty of the manslaughter of the actual victim. This long-established principle has been applied in many cases, e.g., in *R v Mitchell* [1983] QB 741, the accused was found guilty of the manslaughter of V when he deliberately hit X causing him to fall onto V thereby breaking her femur, an injury from which she eventually died.

However, the House of Lords held in *Attorney-General's Reference (No. 3 of 1994)* [1997] 3 All ER 936, that the doctrine could not apply to convict an accused of murder, who stabbed a pregnant woman with the result that the baby was born alive but later died as a result of the injuries inflicted by the accused. The House reversed the decision of the Court of Appeal reasoning that they could not extend the doctrine to what they regarded as a double transfer of intent — from the mother to the foetus, and from the foetus to the child. Lord Mustill stated that the doctrine 'is useful enough to yield rough justice in particular cases, and it can sensibly be retained notwithstanding its lack of any sound intellectual basis. But it is another matter to build a new rule upon it'.

Surprisingly, in view of their rejection of the Court of Appeal's reasoning, the House held that the accused could be guilty of the manslaughter of the baby. Thus Richard could be convicted of the manslaughter of the baby, on the basis that he intended to do an act which was unlawful and dangerous.

Richard may also argue that he did not cause the baby's death, as the chain of causation was broken by Dr Spock turning off the life support machine. However, the prosecution only have to show that Richard's act significantly contributed to the baby's death (*R v Cheshire* [1991] 3 All ER 670). In *R v Steel and Malcherek* [1981] 2 All ER 422, Lord Lane CJ said (at pp. 696–7) that 'the fact that the victim has died despite or because of medical treatment for the initial injury given by careful and skilled medical practitioners will not exonerate the original assailant from the responsibility for the death'. It is therefore submitted that the prosecution would be able to establish causation by Richard.

Dr Spock may also face charges of murder or manslaughter in respect of the baby's death, and his responsibility may depend on the application of the House of Lords' decision in *Airedale NHS Trust v Bland* [1993] 1 All ER 821. Although only a civil case, the House of Lords did consider at great length the criminal responsibility of a doctor who decided to disconnect the naso-gastric tube which was feeding the victim who was in a persistent vegetative state. Their Lordships concluded that in the unlikely event of a prosecution for murder, there might be difficulties for the prosecution in establishing malice aforethought. However, the reason why they have believed there would be no conviction for murder or manslaughter was based on the traditional approach in dealing with omissions to act.

Their Lordships' reasoning was that disconnecting the naso-gastric tube would be viewed as discontinuing treatment and would therefore constitute an omission to act. Omissions are not punishable unless there is a duty to act, with breach of that duty causing the prohibited consequence. Clearly in a doctor/patient relationship the doctor owes a duty to act in the patient's best interests (*R v Adomako* [1993] 4 All ER 935), but it is not always in the patient's best interests to be kept alive in any circumstances. Thus if a doctor decides on bona fide grounds in accordance with accepted medical practice that it is in the patient's best interest to discontinue treatment and allow the patient to die with dignity, the doctor will not be acting in breach of his duty and cannot therefore be criminally responsible. Of course if he does a positive act which accelerates death this reasoning cannot apply and he could be found guilty of murder or manslaughter or attempted murder, as in the case of *R* v *Cox* [1992] *The Times*, 18 November, where a doctor, at the request of an incurably ill patient and with the consent of her relatives, gave her a drug with no analgesic qualities to relieve pain, but thereby hastening her death.

Although it is more likely that Prescilla will be the main prosecution witness in Richard's trial, she could also face charges of aiding and abetting an attempted suicide under the Suicide Act 1961. The prosecution could also contend that she should be convicted of manslaughter on the gross negligence basis. Clearly her conduct has significantly contributed to the baby's death and she was grossly negligent with regard to the risk of the baby's death when taking part in the suicide attempt. The key issue would be, for the purposes of criminal law, does a pregnant woman owe a duty of care to her unborn child? It is submitted that she does and Prescilla would therefore be found guilty if charged with manslaughter.

Q Question 4

The conditions that must be satisfied for the defence of provocation to succeed are unfair to the accused.

Discuss this statement with reference to decided cases.

Commentary

The recent decisions — including *R* v *Ahluwalia* [1992] 4 All ER 894 and *R* v *Thornton (No. 2)* [1996] 2 All ER 1023 — concerning battered women who kill their husbands have brought to public attention the defence of provocation. Many people were surprised that this defence was not available in the circumstances of the cases; and because there have been other important decisions such as in *R* v *Morhall* [1995] 3 All ER 659, *R* v *Smith* [2000] 3 WLR 654 and *Luc Thiet Thuan* v *R* [1997] 2 All ER 1033, the controversial defence is a suitable topic for an essay question.

The answer must obviously include reference to the important cases, but you must avoid the pitfall of simply giving the facts and decisions of a list of cases. The ingredients of the defence must be covered in full and the cases used to illustrate how these principles are applied.

Lastly, with regard to the conclusion for an essay question of this nature, there is a tendency simply to agree with the examiner's implied or expressed opinion. This is a mistake. Your conclusion should logically reflect the points you have made in your answer. Certainly, with this issue, an opinion either way can be justified, although in this answer the author has chosen to disagree with the given statement.

- s. 3 Homicide Act 1957

- Subjective test

- Objective test — *Camplin* [1978]

- *Smith* [2000]

- Cumulative provocation

- Burden of proof and the judge's duty

:Q: Suggested answer

Since provocation was recognised as a partial defence to murder, reducing the conviction to manslaughter, there have always been difficulties in deciding the precise limits of the defence. It is therefore not surprising that the modern controversial issue of whether a battered woman who kills her partner who has caused her suffering over a long period of time should have the defence of provocation, has highlighted the uncertainties surrounding the defence.

Provocation is a common law defence now defined in s. 3 of the Homicide Act 1957, which states:

> Where on a charge of murder there is evidence on which the jury can find that the person charged was provoked (whether by things done or by things said or by both together) to lose his self-control, the question whether the provocation was enough to make a reasonable man do as he did shall be left to be determined by the jury; and in determining that question the jury shall take into account everything both done and said according to the effect which, in their opinion, it would have on a reasonable man.

The defence therefore involves the consideration of three elements, the first being: 'Was the accused provoked thereby losing self-control?' In the vast majority of cases this subjective condition is easily satisfied. If there is any evidence of provocation the trial judge must leave the issue to the jury. Thus in *R v Doughty* (1986) 83 Cr App R 319, the Court of Appeal quashed the murder conviction of the accused who killed a 17-day-old baby because she was crying, because the trial judge had wrongly refused to put the issue of provocation to the jury. However, there have been many cases where the Court of Appeal has confirmed the trial judge's decision that as there was no loss of self-control provocation was not available as a defence. For example, in *R v Cocker* [1989] Crim LR 740, the defendant's wife suffered from an incurable disease and repeatedly begged him to kill her. She had grown increasingly irritable, and after a particularly harrowing sleepless night again told him to kill her. He did so, but the trial judge refused to put the issue of provocation to the jury, the accused being convicted of murder. This decision was upheld by the Court of Appeal on the basis that the accused had not lost his self-control but had killed in cold blood.

Similarly, if a long time has elapsed between the act of provocation and the retaliation, the defence will fail as the law insists that there must be 'a sudden and temporary loss of self-control, rendering the accused so subject to passion as to make him or her for the moment not master of his (or her) mind' (*per* Devlin J in *R* v *Duffy* [1949] 1 All ER 932). So in *R* v *Ibrams* (1981) 74 Cr App R 154, a delay of five days in the accused's response ruled out the defence. An insistence on this condition being satisfied has led to the failure of the defence in several cases involving battered women, including *R* v *Thornton* [1992] 1 All ER 306, *R* v *Thornton (No. 2)* [1996] 2 All ER 1023 and *R* v *Ahluwalia* [1992] 4 All ER 894; and although in the latter case the court accepted that the subjective element would not, as a matter of law, be negatived simply because of delayed reaction, the Court of Appeal has approved the principle that 'circumstances which induce a desire for revenge are inconsistent with provocation since the conscious formulation of a desire for revenge means that a person has had time to think, to reflect and that would negative a sudden temporary loss of self-control, which is of the essence of provocation' (*per* Devlin J in *R* v *Duffy*). This is the reason why some commentators believe this condition to be unfair, as an immediate aggressive response is perceived as being a typically male reaction, whereas a woman will often take time to contemplate appropriate action.

Greater flexibility exists with the second condition, which until *DPP* v *Camplin* [1978] 2 All ER 168 was a purely objective test: 'Would a reasonable man have lost his self-control?' In *Camplin*, a 15-year-old had been sexually assaulted and taunted by the victim, who died when the accused hit him over the head with a chipati pan. The House of Lords decided that the jury should have been directed to consider if a reasonable 15-year-old boy (not a reasonable man) would have done as he did. Lord Diplock said:

> the reasonable man referred to is a person having the power of self-control to be expected of an ordinary person of the sex and age of the accused but in other respects sharing such of the accused's characteristics as they think would affect the gravity of the provocation to him, and whether such a person would in like circumstances be provoked to lose his self-control but would also react to the provocation as the accused did.

According to *R* v *Newell* (1980) 71 Cr App R 331, not only did the characteristic have to be something permanent, separating the accused from the ordinary man, but to be relevant the provocation had to be related to that characteristic. In recent cases this principle has not been vigorously applied and many differing characteristics have been taken into account. Thus in assessing the objective condition juries have been asked to put themselves into the position of a person with a mental age of nine (*R* v *Raven* [1982] Crim LR 51); a glue sniffer (*R* v *Morhall* [1995] 3 All ER 659); an immature attention seeker (*R* v *Humphreys* [1995] 4 All ER 1008); an eccentric with obsessional personality traits (*R* v *Dryden* [1995] 4 All ER 987); and a woman suffering from battered woman syndrome and severe depression (*R* v *Ahluwalia*, above).

This trend has been extended by the House of Lords' decision in *R* v *Smith* [2000] 3 WLR 654, where the House held that a jury could take into account mental characteristics of the defendant reducing his or her power of self-control. This controversial majority decision gives the jury a wide discretion as to what characteristics of the defendant are to be taken into account, as Lord Hoffmann for the majority stated that juries may be told that they 'may think that there was some characteristic of the accused, whether temporary or permanent which society could reasonably have expected of him and which it would be unjust not to take into account'. The majority also stated that jealousy, obsession, exceptional pugnacity and excitability should be ignored, but no model direction is offered. This approach was criticised by Lord Hobhouse who stated that 'it is not acceptable to leave the jury without definite guidance as to the objective criterion to be applied', and it does appear that the objective element of the defence has been reduced to next to nothing, if in fact it still exists at all.

In view of these recent decisions which have severely softened the harshness of the traditional 'reasonable man approach', it cannot be seriously argued that this condition is unfair to the accused, although it may be unfair to the jury trying to put themselves in the position of an accused with these characteristics.

The linked third condition — 'Would a reasonable man have done as the accused did?' — is a question of fact for the jury. In *Mancini* v *DPP* [1941] 3 All ER 272, the House of Lords stated that the mode of retribution must bear a reasonable relationship to the provocation if the offence is to be reduced to manslaughter; and although Lord Diplock stated in *R* v *Camplin* that this is not to be treated as a rule of law, nevertheless it is a factor which will influence the jury. Thus in *R* v *Clarke* [1991] Crim LR 383, the jury ruled out the defence of provocation where the accused had head-butted and strangled the victim and then put live wires into her mouth thereby electrocuting her, presumably on the basis that whereas the accused had (and a reasonable man might have) lost self-control, a reasonable man would never have taken this extreme action.

Many of the collateral rules relating to the defence are favourable to the accused. First, the principle of cumulative provocation is recognised. Thus even if the accused reacts violently to a relatively trivial act, the defence of provocation can succeed on the 'final straw basis'. So in *R* v *Davies* (1975) 60 Cr App R 253, the trial judge informed the jury that they could take account of 'the whole course of conduct of the parties right through that turbulent year of 1972'; and more recently, in *R* v *Humphreys* (above) the Court of Appeal, in quashing a murder conviction, stated that there should have been a careful analysis by the trial judge of the different strands of provocative behaviour by the victim over the period of their relationship.

Secondly, the provocation can be directed at a third party and be sufficient for the accused to have a defence. Thus in *R* v *Pearson* [1992] Crim LR 193, where two brothers killed their tyrannical father, the Court of Appeal quashed the conviction of William as the trial judge had failed to direct the jury that in considering William's defence they should take into account the victim's actions against his brother

Malcolm. Similarly, if the provocation has come from a third party this will not rule out the accused's defence. Thus in *R v Twine* [1967] Crim LR 710, the defence succeeded when the accused was provoked by his girlfriend's conduct with the victim, and as a result killed him. Even the doctrine of transferred malice can be used. So in *R v Gross* (1913) 23 Cox CC 455, the defence succeeded when the defendant, who was provoked by her husband, fired at him intending to kill him but missed and killed the victim.

Thirdly, even if the accused is the aggressor, this will not automatically deprive him or her of the defence. The Privy Council in *Edwards v R* [1973] 1 All ER 152, did state that if the provocation was self-induced it could not succeed. So, if a blackmailer was attacked by his victim and responded by killing him, he could not succeed with the defence unless the victim's response had been extreme and totally unpredicted. However, this was not followed in the more recent case of *R v Johnson* [1989] Crim LR 738, where the Court of Appeal held that the accused was not precluded from the defence even though the attack was the inevitable result of his conduct.

Fourthly, in keeping with the general principles applicable to mistake, where the accused is provoked partly as a result of a mistake of fact, he or she is entitled to be judged on the facts as he or she believed them to be. Thus in *R v Letenock* (1917) 12 Cr App R 221, the Court of Criminal Appeal substituted a manslaughter verdict as there was evidence which suggested that the accused, who was drunk, believed that he was going to be attacked. This decision indicates that even if the accused's mistake is unreasonable, this principle will apply.

Lastly, unlike the other partial defence of diminished responsibility, where the accused has the burden of proof, here, once the accused has raised some evidence of provocation, the burden of disproving it remains on the prosecution. In fact in a line of cases culminating in *R v Cambridge* [1994] 2 All ER 760, the Court of Appeal confirmed that even if the accused did not raise provocation, if the evidence suggested the existence of the defence, the trial judge was obliged to direct the jury on it. However, in *R v Acott* [1977] 1 All ER 706, the House of Lords confirmed that there must be some evidence of provocation, Lord Steyn stating that 'if there is such evidence the judge must leave the issue to the jury. If there is no such evidence, but merely the speculative possibility that there has been an act of provocation, it is wrong for the judge to direct the jury to consider provocation'.

Given these conditions and the fact that words alone can constitute provocation, it is submitted that the conditions that must be satisfied for the defence to succeed are not unfair to the accused in the vast majority of cases. It is only in the situation when the defence has been denied to battered women who kill their partners that the defence has arguably been unfairly denied, and the injustice of a murder conviction in these circumstances should perhaps be mitigated, not by changing the defence of provocation, but by extending the principles of self-defence, or by abolishing the mandatory life sentence for murder.

Q Question 5

Craig, who was very short-sighted, argued with Melanie, who unknown to Craig was eight months pregnant. Melanie pointed her finger at Craig which so annoyed him that he kicked Melanie in the stomach intending to hurt her badly. Melanie was taken to hospital with severe internal bleeding, and also as a result of the kick she gave birth prematurely, to Siamese twins. The twins had been injured by the kick and a team of medical experts concluded that the only way Zoey, the stronger twin would survive was to operate to separate them, although this would inevitably result in the weaker twin, Abigail's death. The operation was carried out by Doctor Spock, and two days later Abigail died.

Discuss the criminal liability of Craig and Doctor Spock.

Commentary

This question involves detailed knowledge of a number of offences against the person, but as important is an ability to explain and apply two very controversial decisions: *Re A (Children) (Conjoined Twins: Surgical Separation)* [2000] 4 All ER 961, and *Attorney-General's Reference (No. 3 of 1994)* [1997] 3 All ER 936. Unless you know these cases very well, you should not attempt this question as it is very easy to cover irrelevant issues. For example, if you stated that the doctrine of transferred malice was applicable to the question of whether Craig was guilty of murder (the view of the Court of Appeal in *Attorney-General's Reference*) you would then discuss the partial defence of provocation in detail. However, this would be wrong because the House of Lords in *Attorney-General's Reference* (reversing the Court of Appeal's decision) held that the doctrine of transferred malice would not apply in these circumstances, and therefore Craig could only be guilty of involuntary manslaughter, thus making a discussion on provocation irrelevant.

Avoiding this pitfall is essential, but there is still plenty to cover in order to attain a good mark.

- Aggravated assault

  - *Savage and Parmenter* [1991]

- Consider murder

  - *Attorney-General's Reference (No. 3 of 1994)* [1997]

- Transferred malice

- Involuntary manslaughter

- Causation

Doctor Spock

• Unlawful homicide

 − *Airedale NHS Trust* v *Bland* [1993]

• Necessity

 − *Dudley and Stephens* [1881–5]

 − *Re A (Children) (Conjoined Twins)* [2000]

:Q: Suggested answer

Craig could be charged with a number of offences against the person, the most serious being the murder of Abigail. There is also the possibility that Doctor Spock could be guilty of murder or manslaughter despite the decision in *Airedale NHS Trust* v *Bland* [1993] 1 All ER 821, and *Re A* [2000] 4 All ER 961.

It is quite clear that Craig would be guilty of an offence under the Offences Against the Person Act 1861 (OAPA 1861). The most serious offence is s. 18, wounding or causing grievous bodily harm with intent. Although internal bleeding is not a wound (*C (A Minor)* v *Eisenhower* [1984] QB 331), it could amount to grievous bodily harm (*R* v *Smith* [1960] 3 All ER 161). However, in order to obtain a conviction under s. 18, the prosecution must prove that Craig intended to cause grievous bodily harm. As Craig appears to have only kicked Melanie once, and probably did not know that she was pregnant, the *mens rea* may be difficult to establish (unless he does admit that he intended to hurt her badly). The prosecution may instead choose to charge Craig under s. 20. Although the *actus reus* is also wounding or causing grievous bodily harm, the *mens rea* is maliciously, and this has been interpreted as the accused foresaw that some physical harm might result (*R* v *Savage and Parmenter* [1991] 4 All ER 698). Clearly, as Craig deliberately kicked Melanie, he will have the *mens rea* for this offence.

In the unlikely occurrence that the jury decide that Melanie's injuries do not constitute grievous bodily harm, but only actual bodily harm, Craig would be convicted under s. 47 OAPA 1861 (assault occasioning actual bodily harm). For this offence the prosecution need only prove that Craig had the *mens rea* for common assault (*R* v *Savage and Parmenter* [1991] 4 All ER 698).

As Abigail has died as a result of Craig's acts, it is possible that the CPS would consider prosecuting him for murder, i.e., the unlawful killing of a human being within the Queen's peace with malice aforethought. Abigail has an existence separate from her mother and would therefore be regarded as a human being, and the prosecution would be able to show that Craig had malice aforethought if they could prove that he intended to kill or cause grievous bodily harm (*R* v *Moloney* [1985] 1 All ER 1025). However, even though he may have intended to cause Melanie grievous bodily harm, this would not satisfy the *mens rea* requirement in respect of Abigail's death in view of the House of Lords' decision in *Attorney-General's Reference (No. 3 of 1994)* [1997] 3 All ER 936. In this case, on similar facts the House decided that it would not be possible to use the doctrine of transferred malice to find an accused guilty of the murder of a baby in such circumstances because a foetus was not a live person protected by the law of murder, and that there was no *mens rea* towards the foetus. Accordingly, when A acts without intent to injure the foetus, the intent to injure the mother cannot be transferred from the mother to the foetus. Lord Mustill stated that the doctrine 'is useful enough to yield rough justice, in particular cases, and it can sensibly be retained notwithstanding its lack of any sound intellectual basis. But it is another matter to build a new rule upon it'.

This controversial decision means that Craig could not be guilty of murder because he lacks malice aforethought with regard to Abigail. However, he could be guilty of involuntary manslaughter as although the House of Lords decided that the doctrine of transferred malice could not apply to murder in these circumstances, they did conclude that an accused would be guilty on the basis of constructive manslaughter. This offence is easily established as the prosecution need only prove that Craig intended to do an act which was unlawful and dangerous. It is not necessary to prove that Craig knew the act was unlawful or dangerous (*R v Newbury and Jones* [1976] 2 All ER 365). The first question is for the judge and the jury to resolve (*R v Jennings* [1990] Crim LR 588), and the second is for the jury to resolve whether all reasonable and sober people would realise the risk of some physical harm (*R v Church* [1965] 2 All ER 72). As Lord Mustill in *Attorney-General's Reference* pointed out, 'in this case the act which had to be shown to be an unlawful and dangerous act was the stabbing of the child's mother. There can be no doubt that all sober and reasonable people would regard that act, within the appropriate meaning of this term, as dangerous. It is plain that it was unlawful as it was done with the intention of causing her injury. As the defendant intended to commit that act, all the ingredients necessary for *mens rea* in regard to the crime of manslaughter were established, irrespective of who was the ultimate victim of it'. Thus, as Craig deliberately kicked someone, which would at least constitute common assault, he would be guilty of manslaughter unless the jury decided that he did not cause Abigail's death.

Although Craig would argue that death was the result of the operation performed by Doctor Spock, the prosecution only have to prove that Craig's act was a significant contribution to the consequence (*R v Cheshire* [1991] 3 All ER 670). Craig would maintain that the operation constituted an intervening act breaking the chain of causation and exonerating him. However, in *R v Steel and Malcherek* [1981] 2 All ER 422, Lord Lane CJ stated (at pp. 696–7) that 'the fact that the victim has died despite or because of medical treatment for the initial injury given by careful and skilled practitioners, will not exonerate the original assailant from the responsibility for the death'. Clearly the victim would not have been in this position but for Craig's action and if the treatment given was in accordance with medical practice it would not break the chain of causation. It is therefore submitted that Craig would be guilty of manslaughter.

Simply because the court may decide that the chain of causation was not broken, it does not automatically follow that Doctor Spock could not be guilty of murder or manslaughter. It is possible to have two people held responsible for the victim's death if their independent actions have significantly contributed to this consequence. The case of Doctor Spock can be distinguished from the House of Lords' decision in *Airedale NHS Trust* v *Bland* [1993] 1 All ER 821, because in that case the House of Lords held that disconnecting the naso-gastric tube, which was keeping the victim alive, was not an act, but an omission to give further treatment. As it was done in the patient's best interest, there was no breach of duty and therefore no criminal liability. However, Doctor Spock has done a positive act, and therefore this reasoning cannot be employed.

Judges and commentators alike have had difficulty in concluding whether a doctor in such circumstances either lacks malice aforethought, has not caused the victim's death, or has a specific defence of lawful treatment (see *R* v *David Moor* [2000] Crim LR 31), and in *Bland*, Lord Goff stated (at p. 898), 'Moreover, where the Doctor's treatment of his patient is lawful, the patient's death will be regarded in law as exclusively caused by the injury or disease to which the condition is attributable'. Although the principles are not as yet clearly formulated, further guidance has been given by the Court of Appeal in *Re A* [2000] 4 All ER 961, where in identical circumstances the court decided that the doctor would have the defence of necessity. It was previously thought that in the light of the decision in *R* v *Dudley and Stephens* [1881–5] All ER Rep 61, that necessity would never be recognised as a defence to murder. However, in distinguishing this case, Brooke LJ decided that the operation would be lawful even though it would inevitably bring about the death of the weaker twin as the three necessary requirements of necessity would be fulfilled; namely:

(a) the act was needed to avoid inevitable and irreparable evil;

(b) no more should be done that was reasonably necessary for the purpose to be achieved; and

(c) the evil inflicted was not disproportionate to the evil avoided.

It is therefore submitted that Doctor Spock could not be guilty of murder, and could only be guilty of manslaughter if he were grossly negligent in either arriving at the decision to operate, or in carrying out the operation (*R* v *Adomako* [1994] 3 All ER 79).

Q Question 6

Discuss Clive's criminal responsibility for murder and manslaughter only in the following circumstances:

Clive is a drug dealer. He gave a packet of prohibited drugs to Dennis, an experi-

enced drug user. Dennis took the drugs to his house, injected himself and died of a drug overdose. Clive then injected Malcolm, at Malcolm's request, with a prohibited drug. Later that same day Malcolm died from the effects of the drug as he had a weak heart. Finally Clive gave Emma, at her request, a syringe filled with prohibited drugs and encouraged her to inject herself. Emma, who had not taken drugs before, did this and then began to cough and shake uncontrollably. However, Clive simply left her and she died shortly after.

Commentary

Three recent Court of Appeal decisions, *R* v *Khan* [1998] Crim LR 830, *R* v *Kennedy* [1999] Crim LR 65 and *R* v *Dias* [2002] Crim LR 490, have highlighted one of the recurring problems that periodically confronts the criminal law, i.e., the public's perception of the appropriate response of the law. All three cases involve the supply of drugs causing the death of a young victim who may have been experimenting with the drug for the first time. Obviously there are offences under the Misuse of Drugs Act 1971 which are designed to cover the illegal supply of drugs, but when a victim dies this leads the public to demand a more serious offence such as murder or manslaughter.

The many miscarriage of justice cases, especially those involving terrorism, where there is much public hysteria, demonstrate that the criminal justice system is then at its most vulnerable with established procedures and safeguards often being disregarded. A similar situation applies to the substantive criminal law, and although in *Khan*, *Kennedy* and *Dias* the accused were convicted of manslaughter, this could only be achieved by stretching the boundaries of some of the established principles concerning omissions and causation. It is then left to the appellate courts and commentators to assess the situation after the dust has settled.

Apart from the three recent decisions, there are also two other important manslaughter cases involving the supply of drugs: *R* v *Cato* [1976] 1 All ER 260, and *R* v *Dalby* [1982] 1 All ER 916. A good answer will therefore contain an analysis of all four cases within the context of involuntary manslaughter. In addition, the concepts of omission and causation must be applied in order to arrive at conclusions for the three incidents.

- Consider murder

- Involuntary manslaughter

  - constructive

  - *Khan* [1998]

  - *Kennedy* [1999]

  - *Dias* [2002]

  - *Cato* [1976]

- *Dalby* [1982]

- gross negligence

- *Adomako* [1995]

• **Causation**

- intervening act

- egg-shell skull principle

:Ọ: Suggested answer

Clive might be charged with murder — the unlawful killing of a human being within the Queen's peace with malice aforethought. In *R* v *Moloney* [1985] 1 All ER 1025, the House of Lords confirmed that malice aforethought is an intention to kill or cause grievous bodily harm. Although this is a question of fact for the jury, and Clive may have foreseen the risk of death or grievous bodily harm, it is submitted that the prosecution would find it very difficult to establish beyond reasonable doubt that Clive had the necessary intention. It is therefore much more likely that Clive will be charged with manslaughter.

Involuntary manslaughter is unlawful homicide without malice aforethought, and can either be on the basis of constructive or gross negligence. Constructive manslaughter occurs when A has caused V's death and intended to do an act which was unlawful and dangerous. Its ingredients can be very easily established by the prosecution, as they do not have to prove that A knew the act was either unlawful or dangerous. It is a question for the judge and jury as to whether A's act was a criminal offence, although the jury do have to be satisfied that A had the necessary *mens rea* for that offence (*R* v *Jennings* [1990] Crim LR 588). Similarly, the test for dangerous is an objective one: 'the unlawful act must be such as all sober and reasonable people would inevitably recognise must subject the other person to at least the risk of some harm resulting therefrom, albeit not serious harm' (Edmund-Davies J in *R* v *Church* [1965] 2 All ER 72).

In *R* v *Dalby* [1982] 1 All ER 916, the Court of Appeal held that on similar facts to Dennis, there was an unlawful and dangerous act. However, the court in quashing the conviction for manslaughter decided that the unlawful act of the supply of the dangerous drug by A to the deceased did not constitute the *actus reus* of manslaughter. This was on the basis that the unlawful act of supplying drugs was not an act directed against the person of V, and did not cause any direct injury to him. This controversial decision appeared to add a new ingredient to constructive manslaughter, the act had to be directed at the victim. However, in *R* v *Goodfellow* [1986] 83 Cr App R 23, the Court of Appeal rejected this submission and the House of Lords in *Attorney-General's Reference (No. 3 of 1994)* [1997] 3 All ER 916, made it clear that it is not a requirement of constructive manslaughter that A's unlawful act be directed at the victim.

Nevertheless, Clive could still argue that because Dennis voluntarily took the drug, and he was an experienced drug user, Clive did not cause his death. Although the prosecution has only to prove, in order to satisfy the causation element, that Clive's acts were a significant contribution to V's death (*R* v *Cheshire* [1991] 3 All ER 670), there is a powerful argument that a voluntary act by the victim operates as an intervening act. This view is stated by Professor Glanville Williams, *Textbook on Criminal Law* (2nd edition), p. 39: 'what a person does (if he had reached adult years, is of sound mind and is not acting under mistake, intimidation or similar pressure) is his own responsibility and is not regarded as having been caused by other people. An intervening act of this kind, therefore breaks the causal connection that would otherwise have been perceived between previous acts and the forbidden consequence'.

However, this principle was not applied by the Court of Appeal in *R* v *Kennedy* [1999] Crim LR 65, where *Dalby* was also distinguished to uphold A's conviction for manslaughter. In this case A's conduct in supplying the drug and encouraging V to inject himself was deemed an unlawful act (under s. 23, Offences Against the Person Act 1861) and preparing the mixture and handing it to V for immediate injection was capable of amounting to a significant cause of death. It would therefore appear that Clive could be guilty of the manslaughter of Dennis, but the outcome is not certain in view of the most recent Court of Appeal decision in *R* v *Dias*. In this case *Kennedy* was distinguished and the Court of Appeal held, in quashing the accused's conviction for manslaughter, that the chain of causation was broken by the victim's act of self-injection.

The prosecution would also use constructive manslaughter regarding Clive's responsibility for Malcolm's death. The circumstances are very similar to the Court of Appeal's decision in *R* v *Cato* [1976] 1 All ER 260. In this case there was some dispute as to what constituted the unlawful act, but even though Malcolm consented to Clive injecting him, this could still constitute aggravated assault under the Offences Against the Person Act 1861. This is because consent is not a defence to the deliberate infliction of actual bodily harm or more serious harm, unless it is in the course of a lawful activity (*R* v *Brown* [1993] 2 WLR 556). Clearly the injecting of drugs in these circumstances would not amount to a lawful activity and therefore is an unlawful act.

Clive, however, may argue that as he did not know that Malcolm had a weak heart, his act was not dangerous. This point arose in *R* v *Watson* [1989] 2 All ER 865, where the Court of Appeal decided that for the purpose of ascertaining whether there was an obvious risk of some physical harm, the reasonable man had to be put in the same circumstances as the accused. He did not have the benefit of hindsight. So Watson's conviction was quashed, as he did not realise that the occupier of the house in which he was committing a burglary had a weak heart. However, it is submitted that there is a risk that someone without a weak heart could suffer some physical harm by being injected with prohibited drugs, and therefore Clive's act would be both unlawful and dangerous.

Similarly, Clive's argument that it was Malcolm's weak heart that was the main cause of death would also fail. *R v Cheshire* [1991] 3 All ER 670, states that the prosecution, to satisfy the causation test, only needs to prove that A's act was a significant contribution to V's death, and *R v Blaue* [1975] 1 WLR 1411 demonstrates the principle that you take your victim as you find him (the egg-shell skull principle). Thus, the fact that Malcolm is exceptionally vulnerable because he has a weak heart does not mean that Clive did not cause his death.

Despite the decision in *Kennedy*, the more appropriate basis of manslaughter with regard to Emma's death might be gross negligence. This situation is very similar to *R v Khan* [1998] Crim LR 830, where the Court of Appeal quashed A's conviction because of a misdirection by the trial judge who failed to give a direction in accordance with the House of Lords' decision in *R v Adomako* [1995] 1 AC 171.

In order to prove gross negligence manslaughter, the prosecution would have to establish the following four conditions:

(a) Clive owed Emma a duty of care;

(b) Clive was in breach of that duty;

(c) Clive's conduct was grossly negligent, i.e., having regard to the risk of death, Clive's conduct fell so far beneath the required standard, and was so bad as to amount to criminal negligence;

(d) Clive's conduct caused Emma's death.

It is submitted that the prosecution would easily establish conditions (b), (c) and (d) but there are difficulties in deciding whether a duty of care was owed. This is because the general rule in criminal law is that a duty to help others is not owed by members of the public. In *Adomako*, A was an anaesthetist involved in an operation, so it was held that because of his office, he owed a duty to his patient. A similar conclusion was reached in *R v Litchfield* [1998] Crim LR 507, where the Court of Appeal upheld the conviction of a ship's captain who caused the death of three crew members by the grossly negligent navigation of his schooner. However, in *Khan*, the court stated that to extend a duty to summon medical assistance to a drug dealer who supplies heroin to a person who subsequently dies, would enlarge the class of persons to whom on previous authorities, such a duty does arise.

Nevertheless, it is submitted that the court could use the principle from *R v Miller* [1983] 1 All ER 978, to impose a duty. In this case the House of Lords decided that if A created a dangerous situation then, if he realised this, he was under a legal duty to take steps to minimise the danger. So, *Miller*, who inadvertently set fire to property, was guilty of criminal damage when, realising what he had done, failed to call the fire brigade. The same principle should be applied to Clive. He has created the dangerous situation, and it would be easy for him to summon medical attention to minimise the danger he has caused Emma.

In conclusion, it therefore appears that on application of decided cases, Clive could be convicted of the manslaughter of all three victims. There is some doubt concerning the application of some of these principles, and it is clear that the two conflicting decisions of *Kennedy* and *Dias* would have to be resolved before the outcome concerning Dennis's death could be decided.

Further reading

Doran, S., 'Alternative Defences — the Invisible Burden on the Trial Judge' [1991] Crim LR 878.

Gardner, T. and Macklem, T., 'Compassion Without Respect? Nine Fallacies in R v Smith' [2001] Crim LR 623.

'Legislating the Criminal Code: Involuntary Manslaughter', Law Com. No. 237 (1996).

Norrie, A., 'After Woollin' [1999] Crim LR 532.

Non-fatal offences against the person

Introduction

Apart from motoring and theft-related offences, criminal assaults, batteries and woundings are the staple diet of the criminal courts, with more than 100,000 prosecutions a year. Because of the historical increase in crime there has been an increase in the number of Crown Court judges, recorders and assistant recorders, many of whom have been recruited from outside the ranks of specialist criminal practitioners. It is therefore imperative that the offences are clear, fair and easily applied. However, as the Law Commission has pointed out (Law Com. No. 177):

> the existing interface between common law and statutory provisions undoubtedly contributes to make the law obscure and difficult to understand for everyone concerned. This may lead to inefficiency, the cost and length of trials may be increased, because the law has to be extracted and clarified and there is greater scope for appeals on misdirections on points of law.

Sir Henry Brooke, the former head of the Law Commission, in announcing the Law Commission's proposals for reform of offences against the person (Law Com. No. 122) stated that it was intolerable that the courts were still wrestling with the intricacies and inconsistencies of the Offences Against the Person Act 1861, which is full of antique and obscure language and which has been the subject of many recent appeals that displayed serious disagreement as to the basic content of the law. Even after the recent House of Lords' decisions in *R v Savage and Parmenter* [1991] 4 All ER 698, *R v Brown* [1993] 2 All ER 75 and *R v Burstow* and *R v Ireland* [1997] 4 All ER 225, many aspects of the law are unsatisfactory and its application erratic (for example, see *R v Wilson* [1996] 3 WLR 125 where the Court of Appeal in quashing a conviction decided that the trial judge was wrong to apply *Brown* on the facts of the case).

The Law Commission's work on this topic has taken over 20 years and has massive support amongst judges, magistrates, the police and solicitors and barristers. If implemented the recommendations would save the waste of enormous amounts of valuable court, lawyers', and citizens' time and money simply on attempts to find out what the law is, and in correcting errors where the administration of justice has gone wrong when obscure law has been wrongly applied. The report was published in 1994, but as yet no Draft Bill has been placed before Parliament, so it appears that the problems will remain.

The questions included in this chapter cover all the typical offences against the person you would expect to find on a standard criminal law syllabus. The Public Order Act 1986 has not been included, and the only sections of the Offences Against the Person Act 1861 to appear are ss. 18, 20 and 47, the ones that have caused all the difficulties! There have been important recent decisions on the modern phenomenon of 'stalking', and although the legislature rushed through the Protection from Harassment Act 1997, it is quite probable that the more serious incidents will be prosecuted under the 1861 Act. This again demonstrates the need for a code as the present development of principles depends on the accidents of litigation and piecemeal legislation. The common law method of resolving uncertainty by retrospective declaration of the law is objectionable in principle as it may lead to the conviction of a defendant on the basis of criminal liability not known to exist in that form before he acted (e.g., *R* v *R* [1991] 4 All ER 481).

Arguably, this is one of the most difficult areas of the criminal law as far as students are concerned. Not only do you have the unsatisfactory 1861 Act to apply, but also a host of important recent cases and other changes in the law. Thus the offence of rape has been redefined by s. 142 of the Criminal Justice and Public Order Act 1994; s. 89 of the Police Act 1996 has replaced s. 51 of the Police Act 1964; and there have been (since the House of Lords' decision in *Brown*) two Law Commission reports (Law Commission Consultation Proposal No. 134 and No. 139 — some 290 pages long) on the topic of consent as a defence.

Q Question 1

The majority decision of the House of Lords in *R* v *Brown* [1993] 2 All ER 75 concerning consent as a defence to the deliberate infliction of physical harm, does not follow the legitimate aims and functions of the criminal law.

Discuss.

Commentary

This is a challenging question on a difficult issue. Consent as a defence in criminal law has always caused problems, and since *Brown* there have been two very detailed Law Commission reports on the subject. It is always likely, therefore, to be the subject of an exam question.

There is also the added complication of reference to the legitimate aims and functions of the criminal law. As our system does not have a code, there is no statute that sets out the law's aims and functions, so it is necessary to consider case law, Law Commission reports, and the views of commentators to ascertain these. In this answer, you must attempt to cover this issue, as the question is not simply an invitation to write all you know about *Brown*.

There are various versions of aims and functions for criminal law (as well as criminal justice and sentencing), but the author has chosen those set out in the American Law Institute Penal Code which are as good as any. Obviously you cannot relate all of them to the decision in *Brown*, but it provides a basis and point of reference.

You must then deal fully with the *ratio decidendi* of the case, with a detailed analysis of Lord Templeman's judgment on behalf of the majority. A discussion as to whether this does represent the legitimate aims and functions must then follow.

Obviously opinions on this issue will greatly differ, as of course they did in the House of Lords with Lords Mustill and Slynn dissenting. Your conclusion could therefore be totally different from this author's; but provided it is logically developed from your earlier analysis, it would not mean that your answer would necessarily obtain a lower mark. Indeed, it might result in a higher one!

- **Aims of the criminal law**

- **House of Lords' decision in *Brown* [1993]**

- **Lord Templeman's rationale**

- **Law and morals**

- **Role of the House of Lords**

- **Public interest**

⠅Ⓠ⠅ Suggested answer

There will never be complete agreement as to the correct aims and functions of the criminal law and, in the absence of a criminal code setting out a rationale containing fundamental principles, this issue will remain a topic of debate. However, the aims and functions of English criminal law, it is submitted, are similar to those stated in the American Law Institute Model Penal Code, i.e.:

(a) To forbid and prevent conduct that unjustifiably and inexcusably inflicts or threatens substantial harm to individual or public interests.

(b) To subject to public control persons whose conduct indicates that they are disposed to commit crime.

(c) To safeguard conduct that is without fault from condemnation as criminal.

(d) To give fair warning of the nature of the conduct declared to be an offence.

(e) To differentiate on reasonable grounds between serious and minor offences.

In addition to protecting the public from harmful activity, we also expect the criminal law to respect certain individual liberties such as freedom from coercion, deception or fear, the right to protest, demonstrate etc. Individual freedom of choice is also a liberty that we place high on our list of priorities, and it is this conflict between individual freedoms and collective interests which was one of the major issues in *R* v *Brown* [1993] 2 All ER 75.

In *Brown*, a group of middle-aged men willingly participated in sado-masochistic activities which involved the deliberate infliction of wounds. Videos were made of their activities and circulated to members of the group, but not to outsiders. The men were charged with various offences including assault occasioning actual bodily harm (Offences Against the Person Act 1861, s. 47) and malicious wounding (Offences Against the Person Act 1861, s. 20) and pleaded guilty when the trial judge ruled against their defence of consent. The Court of Appeal upheld their conviction but certified the following point of law of general public importance: 'Where A wounds or assaults B occasioning him actual bodily harm in the course of a sado masochistic encounter, does the prosecution have to prove lack of consent on the part of B before they can establish A's guilt under section 20 or section 47 Offences Against the Person Act 1861'. The House of Lords answered this question in the negative and dismissed the appeal. Lord Templeman, who gave the majority judgment, decided the issue using a mixture of precedent and public policy. He stated that consent is not a general defence where actual bodily harm or wounding has been caused. There are exceptions to this rule, and even violence intentionally inflicted will not be a criminal offence if it occurs in the course of a lawful activity, such as contact sports, surgical operations, rough horseplay or tattooing. The question for the House therefore was, can such sado-masochistic behaviour as occurred in *Brown* be a lawful activity?

Lord Templeman concluded that this could be answered only by considerations of policy and public interest. The criminal law must provide sufficient safeguards against exploitation and corruption of others, particularly those who are young, weak in body or mind, inexperienced or in a state of special physical, official or economic dependence. He referred to three reasons leading to the conclusion that such conduct was not in the public interest:

(a) It glorified the cult of violence ('pleasure derived from the infliction of pain is an evil thing').

(b) It increased the risk of AIDS and the spread of other sexually transmitted diseases.

(c) It could lead to the corruption of youth.

Lord Templeman concluded: 'I am not prepared to invent a defence of consent for sado-masochistic encounters which breed and glorify cruelty and result in offences under section 47 and section 20 of the Act of 1861'.

The minority (Lords Mustill and Slynn) interpreted the relevant cases (*R* v *Coney* (1882) 8 QBD 534; *R* v *Donovan* [1934] 2 KB 498; and *Attorney-General's Reference (No. 6 of 1980)* [1981] QB 715) and the public interest requirements differently. Lord Mustill decided that the decks were clear for the House to tackle completely anew the question whether the public interest required s. 47 to be interpreted as penalising the conduct in question. He concluded that:

> the state should interfere with the rights of the individual to live his or her life as he or she may choose no more than is necessary to ensure a proper balance between the special interests of the individual and the general interests of the individuals who together comprise the populace at large.

In relating the majority decision to aims and functions, many questions arise. First, in ascertaining public interest, how far should the Law Lords take into account society's morals? This involves reference to the Hart–Delvin debate (see Lord Devlin, *The Enforcement of Morals*) as to whether conduct should be criminalised simply because it is a moral wrong, and whether the criminal law should simply reflect society's moral standards or try to improve them. This is virtually impossible to answer briefly, but it is submitted that as it cannot be deemed morally right to encourage deliberate injury through sado-masochistic activity, the majority decision does not conflict with this objective. If the majority had not declared it unlawful, their decision could have been interpreted as condoning or even encouraging such activities.

Secondly, was the House of Lords' decision in *Brown* creating new law, or was it giving effect to the will of Parliament expressed in the 1861 Act? Again, this is difficult to answer, but the application of the defence of consent is probably correct as there has been traditionally a reluctance to extend its boundaries, partially because of the difficulties in deciding whether consent was freely given by a victim capable of understanding the nature of the act (see *Burrell* v *Harmer* [1967] Crim LR 169 — consent to tattooing given by boys aged 12 and 13 held invalid). It is submitted that their Lordships were not abolishing an existing defence (as they did when they removed the husband's marital rape immunity in *R* v *R* [1991] 4 All ER 481) but were simply declaring the boundaries of an existing offence.

Thirdly, was this a situation where respect for individual freedom should have been outweighed by the need to protect society from such conduct? The participants were middle-aged men who were in control of the activities, but the Law Lords considered that because of the risk of future, younger, inexperienced participators, the accuseds' individual liberty had to be sacrificed. This aspect of the decision was heavily criticised (e.g., N. Bamforth, 'Sado Masochism and Consent' [1994] Crim LR 661) and was considered by the Court of Appeal in *R* v *Wilson* [1996] 3 WLR 125. In this case, a husband, who at his wife's request had branded his initials on her buttocks with a hot knife, had his conviction under s. 47 of the 1861 Act quashed. The court took the view that *Brown* was not authority that consent is no defence to a charge under s. 47 in all circumstances where actual bodily harm is inflicted. Russell LJ stated:

> we are firmly of the opinion that it is not in the public interest that activities such as the appellant's in this appeal should amount to criminal behaviour. Consensual activity between

husband and wife, in the privacy of the matrimonial home, is not, in our judgement, normally a proper matter for criminal investigation, let alone criminal prosecution.

In *Wilson*, therefore, individual liberty was the deciding factor; whereas in *Brown*, the deciding factor was protection of the public. Both decisions were based to some extent on the concept of public policy, which has been described as an 'unruly horse'. Both cases demonstrate the difficulties of applying the criminal law and in deciding whether a judgment is right or wrong.

Q Question 2

Jack and Brian argue fiercely. Brian deliberately throws a pint of beer over Jack and then forcibly pushes Jack, causing him to gash his head and fall to the floor. Jack, feeling a little dazed, picks up a bottle and throws it at Brian. The bottle hits Brian causing him minor bruising, but then ricochets into PC 49, a police officer who is on duty, causing him to fall and suffer concussion.

Discuss the criminal responsibility of Jack and Brian.

Commentary

This is a typical question on assault and aggravated assault, an area of law which would be very straightforward if the Law Commission's recommendations (No. 122) had been implemented. As they have not, we still have to grapple with the notorious Offences Against the Person Act 1861, a statute riddled with inconsistencies and anomalies.

A good answer must reveal an understanding of the elements of, and differences between, s. 18, s. 20 and s. 47 of the 1861 Act, and an ability to apply them to the facts of the problem. This will be the heart of the answer, although you must also cover common assault under s. 39 of the Criminal Justice Act 1988 and assault on a police officer in the execution of his duty (Police Act 1996, s. 89). The defences of automatism and self-defence should also be considered briefly before being rejected (for obvious reasons).

No doubt the Crown Prosecution Service would consider charges under the Public Order Act 1986 in an incident of this nature, but as this topic is more likely to be found on a public law (or constitutional law) syllabus, it has been excluded from this answer.

- Common assault — s. 39 Criminal Justice Act 1988

- s. 18 Offences Against the Person Act 1861

- s. 20 Offences Against the Person Act 1861

- s. 47 Offences Against the Person Act 1861

- *Savage* v *Parmenter* [1991]

- s. 89 Police Act 1996

- Defences

☼ Suggested answer

When Brian throws a pint of beer over Jack he will have committed a common assault under s. 39 of the Criminal Justice Act 1988. This summary offence comprises both technical assault and battery. Quite clearly Brian's act would constitute a battery, i.e., 'an act by which the defendant intentionally or recklessly inflicts unlawful personal violence upon the victim' (*Fagan* v *Metropolitan Police Commissioner* [1968] 3 All ER 442). A battery can be the direct application or (as in this case) indirect application of personal violence. Thus in *R* v *Martin* (1881) 8 QBD 54, where the accused placed an iron bar across the exit of a theatre and then turned out the lights, he was guilty of inflicting grievous bodily harm (under s. 20 of the Offences Against the Person Act 1861) as the escaping audience were injured when they ran into the bar.

It is also possible that Brian also committed a technical assault on Jack, i.e., 'any act by which the defendant intentionally or recklessly causes the victim to apprehend immediate and unlawful personal violence' (*Fagan*). This would of course depend upon whether Jack apprehended the impending force of the beer!

However, the more serious consequence which Brian has caused by pushing Jack is the gash to Jack's head, and as a result he will face charges under the Offences Against the Person Act 1861. It is unlikely that this injury would constitute grievous bodily harm (words which should be given their ordinary and natural meaning, according to the House of Lords' decision in *R* v *Smith* [1960] 3 All ER 161) but it could amount to a 'wound', which requires only that the continuity of the whole skin be broken (not simply an internal rupturing of blood vessels: *C (A Minor)* v *Eisenhower* [1984] QB 331). If this is the case, Brian could be charged under s. 18 of the 1861 Act: 'Whosoever shall unlawfully and maliciously by any means whatsoever wound or cause any grievous bodily harm to any person with intent to do some grievous bodily harm . . . shall be guilty of [an offence]'. Nevertheless, the prosecution must prove an intention to cause grievous bodily harm, and it is submitted that, on the facts, this would be very difficult to establish (even though it is a question of fact for the jury in accordance with *R* v *Moloney* [1985] 1 All ER 1025).

It is more likely that Brian would be charged under s. 20 of the 1861 Act: 'Whosoever shall unlawfully and maliciously wound or inflict any grievous bodily harm upon any other person . . . shall be guilty of [an offence]'. Whereas in *R* v *Mowatt* [1967] 3 All ER 47, the House of Lords stated that the word 'maliciously' adds nothing to the *mens rea* requirement of s. 18, it is the only word used to define the *mens rea* of s. 20, and its meaning has been the subject of intense debate. The key decision on this point is the House of Lords' decision in *R v Savage and Parmenter* [1991] 4 All ER 698, where the facts were similar to this problem. Their Lordships decided that in order to establish the *mens rea* for s. 20, all the prosecution had to prove was that the accused actually foresaw that some harm might result. This is an easy test to satisfy, as it is not necessary for the prosecution to prove that the accused foresaw the risk of grievous bodily harm or a wound (the prohibited consequences under s. 20), simply that some harm might result. However, this test is subjective, the House of Lords having rejected the argument that *Caldwell* recklessness was applicable.

It is therefore submitted that as a forcible push involves the risk of some physical harm, the prosecution, if the gash was held by the judge to constitute a wound, would be able to establish the ingredients of s. 20 of the 1861 Act.

On the other hand, if the court concluded that the gash was not a wound, Brian could be found guilty under s. 47 of the Act (assault occasioning actual bodily harm). The consequence, actual bodily harm, can include psychiatric harm (*R v Mike Chan-Fook* [1994] 2 All ER 552) and minor, but not merely superficial, cuts of a sort probably requiring medical treatment. As the maximum period of imprisonment (five years) is the same for a conviction under s. 20 or s. 47, the prosecution would probably be satisfied with a conviction under s. 47. *R v Savage and Parmenter* [1991] 4 All ER 698 confirms that a s. 47 conviction is a permissible alternative verdict on a count alleging unlawful wounding contrary to s. 20, and also clarified the *mens rea* requirement for s. 47, which is satisfied by the prosecution proving that the accused had the *mens rea* for common assault. It is not necessary for the accused to have intended or foreseen the risk of actual bodily harm. Thus, as long as Brian caused the consequence with the *mens rea* of common assault, Brian will be guilty under s. 47.

Jack will also face charges under the 1861 Act. Brian's injuries would seem to constitute actual bodily harm, but the concussion suffered by PC 49 could amount to grievous bodily harm. This is a question of fact for the jury and would obviously depend on the medical evidence. If it was deemed grievous bodily harm it is likely that Jack could be found guilty under s. 18 of the Offences Against the Person Act 1861, as throwing a beer bottle at someone is evidence of intention to cause grievous bodily harm. The fact that Jack did not intend to harm PC 49 will not assist him as the doctrine of transferred malice will apply. This doctrine can also be used if Jack was charged under s. 89 of the Police Act 1996 (replacing s. 51 of the Police Act 1964) with assaulting a police officer in the execution of his duty. Thus in *McBride* v *Turnock* [1964] Crim LR 173, the accused struck at X, a private citizen, but accidentally hit V, a police officer acting in the execution of his duty. Although the accused had no intention of assaulting V, the doctrine of transferred malice applied and he was found guilty of this offence.

If Jack could bring evidence to show that as a result of gashing his head he was not in control of his faculties, he could raise the defence of automatism. However, for this defence to succeed there needs to be a total destruction of voluntary control, reduced or imperfect awareness is not sufficient (*Attorney-General's Reference (No. 2 of 1992)* (1993) 99 Cr App R 429). So the fact that Jack was able to pick up and throw the bottle would probably ensure that this defence failed.

Jack might also raise self-defence, on the basis that he had been attacked and believed that the attack was still continuing. Although the burden of proof is on the prosecution to prove that Jack was not acting in self-defence, and Jack's belief that he had to resort to violence to protect himself need not be based on reasonable grounds (*R v Williams* [1987] 3 All ER 411), it will still be very difficult for this defence to succeed, as the indiscriminate throwing of a beer bottle may not be held to be reasonable and proportionate to the push.

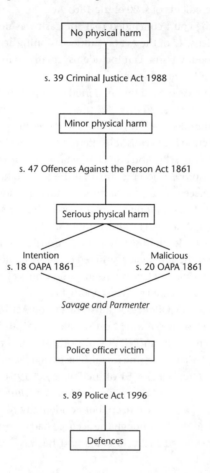

Q Question 3

While on patrol, PC 49 received a police message that a burglary was taking place. He saw a man climb through the window of a house and, believing him to be a burglar, entered the house. He identified himself to Stan, the occupant, who then started attacking PC 49. After a struggle PC 49 arrested Stan who said 'I thought you were a burglar'.

After leaving the house PC 49 saw two men with carrier bags. Thinking they might be burglars, he asked them to explain their presence. One of them, Dan, turned away and ignored PC 49's questions. PC 49 tapped him on the shoulder to attract his attention but Dan pushed him away. Undeterred, PC 49 asked the other, Trevor, what had happened, but Trevor replied 'I'm not saying anything'. PC 49 then grabbed Trevor's arm, telling him he would 'be detained until all the questions are answered'. Trevor then struck PC 49 in the face and ran away.

Discuss the criminal liability of Stan, Dan and Trevor.

Commentary

This question is based on the offences contained in s. 89 of the Police Act 1996 (formerly s. 51 of the Police Act 1964), i.e., wilful obstruction and assault on a police officer in the execution of his duty. There are many detailed provisions as to the specific procedures that police officers must follow in carrying out their duties contained in the Police and Criminal Evidence Act (PACE) 1984, but detailed knowledge of these provisions is rarely required for questions in substantive criminal law examinations.

A good answer will deal with the many important cases on this topic, with a full analysis of their application to the facts of the problem.

- s. 89(1) Police Act 1996 — assault

- Execution of duty

- *Mens rea* — mistake

- s. 89(2) Police Act 1996 — obstruction

- s. 39 Criminal Justice Act 1988 — common assault

:Q: Suggested answer

Stan, Dan and Trevor could all be charged under s. 89(1) of the Police Act 1996: 'Any person who assaults a constable in the execution of his duty, or a person assisting a constable in the execution of his duty, shall be guilty of an offence'. This offence was formerly contained in s. 51 of the Police Act 1964, and there have been many cases on the issue of whether a police officer was acting in the execution of his duty.

Despite provisions in PACE 1984, the courts have always resisted the temptation to specify comprehensively the meaning of 'in the execution of his duty'. In the leading case of *R* v *Waterfield* [1964] 1 QB 164, the Court of Criminal Appeal stated: 'In the judgement of this court it would be difficult and in the present case it is unnecessary to reduce within specific limits the general terms in which the duties of police constables have been expressed'. Thus if the police officer's conduct falls within the general scope of the duty to prevent crime and to bring offenders to justice then it would seem to be within the protection of the statute if it is lawful.

Clearly PC 49 is investigating crime, and it is submitted that he would have a right to enter Stan's property without a warrant as he has reasonable grounds to suspect that a crime is taking place.

It is stated that Stan attacks PC 49, and *prima facie* the offence would seem to have taken place. However, it is unclear whether Stan has actually assaulted PC 49. The old case of *R* v *Forbes and Webb* (1865) 10 Cox CC 362 stated that it was no defence that the accused was reasonably unaware that the victim was a police constable; but in *Blackburn* v *Bowering* [1994] 3 All ER 380, the accused's conviction for a similar offence (assaulting an officer of the court in the execution of his duty under s. 14(1)(b) of the County Courts Act 1984) was quashed as, if the accused was not guilty of assault, he could not be guilty of aggravated assault. Thus in *R* v *Williams* [1987] 3 All ER 411, the Court of Appeal, in quashing the accused's conviction for aggravated assault, where the accused had hit the victim mistakenly believing he was committing a criminal offence, decided that the accused had not committed an assault. He had to be judged on the mistaken facts as he believed them to be, and on that basis he did not intend to use unlawful force which is required for assault.

Although there has traditionally been reluctance to allow mistake to succeed as a defence to the charge of assault on a police officer in the execution of his duty, and *R* v *Fennell* [1970] 3 All ER 225 states that the accused would be guilty if he knew that the victim was a police constable even if he made an honest and reasonable mistake that the constable was acting outside his duty, it is submitted that Stan has a defence if he is unaware that PC 49 is a police officer and believes that he is a burglar.

Dan's action of pushing PC 49 away clearly amounts to an assault, but he could argue that PC 49 is not acting in the execution of his duty. In theory PC 49 is committing a battery by tapping Dan on the shoulder, and if this is the case, he clearly cannot be acting in the execution of his duty. However, in *Donnelly* v *Jackman* [1970] 1 All ER 987, the court recognised that we are deemed to consent to usual social contact, such as being slapped on the back when we have done something well or being tapped on the shoulder to gain our attention. Thus it is not every trivial interference with a citizen's liberty that amounts to a course of conduct sufficient to take the officer out of the course of his duties, and in this case it was held that the police officer on identical facts was acting in the execution of his duty. Dan would therefore appear to be guilty of assaulting PC 49 in the execution of his duty.

Although Trevor can be charged with the same offence, the position is more complicated. In *Rice* v *Connolly* [1966] 2 QB 414, it was held that an accused who refused to answer a police officer's questions when there was no legal duty to do so, was not guilty of wilful obstruction of a police officer in the execution of his duty under s. 51(3) of the Police Act 1964 (now s. 89(2) of the Police Act 1996). However, this does not mean that PC 49 is acting outside the execution of his duty in asking questions, and if he reasonably suspects that Trevor has committed an offence and Trevor, when asked, refuses to give his name, PC 49 will be entitled to exercise his power of arrest (PACE 1984, s. 25). On the facts, it does not appear that PC 49 has followed this procedure, and it is clear from *Kenlin* v *Gardner* [1967] 2 QB 510 that an officer has no power to detain for further questioning. The Court of Appeal in *Collins* v *Wilcock* [1983] 3 All ER 374 recognised that only in exceptional circumstances could a police officer be acting in the course of his duty if he is committing a tort or crime, and it is submitted that grabbing hold of Trevor's arm to detain him further would ensure that PC 49 is acting outside his duty. It therefore follows that Trevor cannot be guilty under s. 89. Further, *Kenlin* v *Gardner* and *Ludlow* v *Burgess* [1971] Crim LR 238 confirm that the use of reasonable force to escape from unlawful detention will not amount to an assault.

Thus although Trevor could still be charged with assault under s. 39 of the Criminal Justice Act 1988, he could raise this argument by way of defence. Whether Trevor's actions amount to reasonable force is a question for the jury to resolve, taking into account all the surrounding circumstances including the possibility of escaping by other means (*Bentley* v *Brudzinski* [1982] Crim LR 825). However, it is submitted that punching a police officer in the face in these circumstances is unlikely to be viewed as reasonable, and Trevor could therefore be found guilty of assault.

Q Question 4

There is no clear and coherent articulation of fundamental principles which might govern decisions in new situations nor is there any clear identification of the public policy considerations which resulted in each decision. Allen, M., *Textbook on Criminal Law*, 5th edn, London: Blackstone Press, 1999, p. 312.

Explain and discuss with regard to the issue of consent as a defence to offences against the person.

Commentary

The issue of consent is arguably one of the most difficult in the criminal law because it does involve the conflict between two fundamental issues: the freedom of the individual and the need to protect society. It is this tension which causes the radically differing opinions in this area, as recently illustrated by the majority and minority judgments in *R* v *Brown* [1993] 2 All ER 75.

Fortunately, this question is limited to consent in relation to offences against the persons as there are equal difficulties concerning consent and theft (as graphically illustrated by the House of Lords' decision in *DPP* v *Gomez* [1993] 1 All ER 1). However, there are still many principles and cases to cover in a logical and organised manner. Further there are two recent Law Commission Reports (Law Commission Consultation Papers 134 (1994) and 139 (1995)) that could be considered.

This is therefore an answer which requires a lot of careful planning and because of the diverse material the content of answers to this question will often be different in many respects. The following answer tries to relate the key issues to the question posed.

- **Consent — vitiating factors**

    - **capacity**

    - **mistake/fraud**

    - **duress/intimidation**

- **Consent and unlawful homicide**

- **Consent and aggravated assault**

:Q̇: **Suggested answer**

Consent is an issue that has always caused problems in the criminal law whether it has been treated as part of the constituents of an offence or as a defence to a criminal charge. The two main problems are (a) to which offences can (and should) consent be a defence, and (b) which conditions must be satisfied for a consent to be deemed valid. It is convenient to deal with this second issue, as the principles are clearer. The Law Commission Consultation Paper 134 has recognised the importance of having clear and consistent principles concerning the validity of consent by the victim, stating 'It is the victim's informed choice which negatives the criminal nature of the injury'. Thus a victim's consent may be held invalid if there is the presence of any one or more of the following factors:

1. *Youth.* The victim may be too young to fully understand the nature of the act. Thus in *Burrell* v *Harmer* [1967] Crim LR 169, D was convicted of assault occasioning actual bodily harm arising from tattooing two boys aged 12 and 13 which resulted in their arms becoming inflamed and painful.

2. *Immaturity, stupidity.* Not only is it the law's duty to pay special regard to protecting the young, it must also recognise the special position of the vulner-

able. Thus if the victim is suffering from some mental illness or is unusually credulous, stupid or immature, the court will hold consent to be invalid (*R v Howard* [1965] 3 All ER 684).

3. *Intimidation.* What constitutes sufficient intimidation or duress to render the consent invalid is still undecided, but the Law Commission (No. 134) stated that consent should be disregarded where induced by threats not involving violence. The underlying theory is that, whatever the nature of the threat, the victim's autonomy in relation to his own body has been interfered with without jurisdiction, and consent is therefore invalid. Thus in *R v Day* (1841) 9 C & P 722, D was charged with an assault on a nine-year-old girl. The girl had not resisted his conduct and it was argued that since she submitted, she must have consented and he therefore could not be guilty. However, he was convicted after the jury were directed that if she had submitted out of fear there would have been no true consent on her part.

4. *Fraud or mistake.* If consent has been obtained only after the nature of the act has been misrepresented or, in rape cases, the victim has been deceived about the identity of the man (*R v Elbekkay* [1995] Crim LR 163), the court will declare the consent to be invalid. This was illustrated in *R v Williams* [1923] 1 KB 340, where D obtained consent after telling the victim that he was performing a surgical operation to improve her singing voice. However, to render the consent invalid it must be a mistake concerning the fundamental nature of the act and not mere detail. Thus in *R v Linekar* [1995] 3 All ER 69 the Court of Appeal quashed the conviction for rape of D who had been found guilty because he had obtained the victim's consent by deceiving her into believing that he would pay for having sexual intercourse with her. Similarly in *R v Richardson* [1998] 3 WLR 1298 the Court of Appeal quashed the conviction for assault of a dentist who gave treatment to patients without first telling them that he was suspended from practice. However, this decision is very hard to reconcile with the Court of Appeal's decision in *R v Tabassum* [2000] 2 Cr App R 328, where the accused was convicted on three charges of indecent assault. He had represented himself as a breast cancer specialist, although he was not medically qualified. As a result of this representation, three women allowed him to examine them. His conviction was upheld as although the women had consented to the nature of his act, they had not consented to its quality as they thought that he was medically qualified. This appears to be a new distinction, but could be justified on the basis that if the accused misrepresents his qualifications thereby obtaining the victim's consent which would otherwise have not been given, this in effect amounts to a mistake as to identity, which vitiates consent.

Although there are questions of fine degree, on these issues the rules are fairly consistently applied and arguably in this respect the quote is incorrect. However, the situation is different when we turn to the first issue and in particular to what offences should consent be a defence.

It is quite clear that consent is no defence to murder. Thus in *Airedale NHS Trust* v *Bland* [1993] 1 All ER 821 the House of Lords had to resort to the principle that the discontinuance of treatment to the victim in a persistent vegetative state was an omission which did not constitute a breach of duty to enable them to conclude that the doctor disconnecting the naso-gastric tube would not be guilty of murder.

Manslaughter based on the unlawful and dangerous act basis (i.e., constructive manslaughter) is a more complex issue. As it is recognised that consent can negative a common assault, the Court of Appeal in *R* v *Lamb* [1967] 2 All ER 1282 quashed the conviction of manslaughter of a defendant who accidentally fired a gun killing the victim who had consented to the gun being pointed at him. However, in *R* v *Cato* [1976] 1 WLR 110 the Court of Appeal upheld the conviction of manslaughter of a defendant who had with the victim's consent injected him with a dangerous drug, thereby causing his death. The court held that you cannot consent to the deliberate infliction of grievous bodily harm in such circumstances.

These cases illustrate the general rule that consent is a defence to common assault but not to actual bodily harm (s. 47, Offences Against the Person Act 1861 (OAPA 1861)) or grievous bodily harm (s. 18 and s. 20, OAPA 1861). However, this is a general principle and the extent and basis of the exceptions to it has received detailed analysis by the House of Lords in *R* v *Brown* [1993] 2 All ER 75. The key question here was whether wounds inflicted in the course of consensual sado-masochistic activities between adult men constituted an offence under s. 20 of the OAPA 1861 (malicious wounding). The minority held that as consent had been obtained the defendants had not committed a crime of violence as required for s. 20. However, the majority saw the issue in a different light. They considered that consent could not be a defence to deliberate wounding unless it was given in the course of a lawful activity, for example properly conducted contact sports (*Attorney-General's Reference (No. 6 of 1980)* [1981] QB 715), surgical operation or even rough horseplay (*R* v *Jones* [1986] 83 Cr App R 375). In Lord Templeman's judgment, the question was whether the defence of consent could be extended to apply to this situation. He decided that it could not as this would not be in the public interest because it could lead to the corruption of youth, the spread of sexually transmitted diseases and it encourages the cult of violence. The decision has been heavily criticised on a number of bases, but it was upheld by the European Court of Human Rights *Laskey* v *UK* (1997) 24 EHRR 39.

However, in *R* v *Wilson* [1996] 3 WLR 125, where a husband at his wife's consent branded her buttocks with a red-hot poker, the Court of Appeal distinguished *Brown* in quashing his conviction under s. 47 of the OAPA 1861, holding that her consent was a defence. The court's rationale appearing to be that it is not in the public interest for the criminal law to invade the matrimonial home and look too closely at such consensual conduct.

Deciding any major issue on the basis of what is in the public interest is always going to lead to uncertainty if only on the basis of how do we know what public opinion is on such matters and who is to decide what that opinion is? This is no doubt the reason why many would support the view taken by Allen.

Q Question 5

Arthur is a troublesome pest who continually annoys people. For two years he had been pestering Monica. He had never previously threatened to hurt her, but has constantly followed and watched her come and go from her house. However, on one occasion she saw him standing outside her living room window and he said 'I'm going to get you Monica'. Monica was frightened and phoned the police before Arthur moved away.

Arthur had also been telephoning Violet at least twice a week for over twelve months. When she picked up the phone he would simply remain silent, until she put the phone down. This caused Violet great distress and she had to seek psychiatric help for anxiety and headaches.

However, the person who has most suffered from Arthur's actions has been Wendy. She has suffered a complete nervous breakdown as a result of his conduct involving constant telephoning, sending hate mail and persistently following her.

Discuss the criminal responsibility of Arthur.

Commentary

The criminal law has to adapt to cope with new social ills and many recent cases have demonstrated the extent of the problem of stalking.

There is inevitably a time before a decision is made as to whether the existing offences encompass such conduct or whether new legislation is required. Unfortunately the existing provisions of the notorious Offences Against the Person Act 1861 (OAPA 1861) have to be considered in relation to this conduct and the reported stalking cases again highlight the difficulties in applying this troublesome Act.

The question requires an analysis of the offences of assault and battery and the aggravated assaults as well as the recent important Court of Appeal and House of Lords decisions.

I have also very briefly mentioned the Protection from Harassment Act 1997, Parliament's response to stalking, and the Telecommunications Act 1984 and the Malicious Communications Act 1988, although these Acts may not be included in a typical criminal law syllabus.

For further reading see *Stalking: The Criminal Law Response*, Celia Wells [1997] Crim LR 463.

- **Words alone — assault**
- *Constanza* [1997]

- s. 47 Offences Against the Person Act 1861 — *Ireland* [1997]
- s. 20 Offences Against the Person Act 1861 — *Burstow* [1997]
- s. 4 Protection from Harassment Act 1997

☿ Suggested answer

The most serious offences that Arthur will be charged with are under the OAPA 1861. In particular s. 18 wounding or causing grievous bodily harm, s. 20 malicious wounding and s. 47 assault occasioning actual bodily harm. However, in the first incident with Monica it must first be considered if an assault has taken place.

An assault is any act by which the defendant intentionally or recklessly causes the victim to apprehend immediate and unlawful personal violence whereas a battery is any act by which the defendant intentionally or recklessly inflicts unlawful personal violence upon the victim. The House of Lords in *R v Savage and Parmenter* [1991] 4 All ER 698 confirmed that intention or subjective recklessness is sufficient *mens rea*, Lord Ackner stating (at p. 711): 'It is common ground that the mental element of assault is an intention to cause the victim to apprehend immediate and unlawful violence or recklessness whether such apprehension be caused.' Common assault, a term covering both assault and battery, should be charged under s. 39 of the Criminal Justice Act 1988.

The prosecution would face two problems regarding the *actus reus* of assault in this case. First, the fact that there was no threatening gesture from Arthur raises the question whether words alone can constitute an assault. For many years it was thought that they could not, the *dicta* of Holroyd J in *R v Meade and Belt* (1823) 1 LEW CC 184, 'No words or singing are equivalent to an assault' being accepted. However, in *R v Wilson* [1955] 1 All ER 744, Lord Goddard stated that the words 'get out the knives' in themselves would constitute an assault even if they were not accompanied by a threatening gesture. Similarly in the recent case of *R v Constanza* [1997] Crim LR 576, the Court of Appeal in upholding the accused's conviction under s. 47 of the OAPA 1861 for assault occasioning actual bodily harm rejected the appellant's submission that an assault could not be committed by words alone without a physical action.

The second problem is that the victim must apprehend immediate violence and Arthur could argue that as he was outside Monica's house he was in no position to immediately carry out the threat. However, this condition has been liberally interpreted and in *Smith v Superintendent of Woking Police Station* [1983] 76 Cr App R 234, the accused was convicted of assault by looking through the window of the victim's bedsitting room with intent to frighten her. More recently in *R v Ireland* [1997] 4 All ER 225 the House of Lords upheld the accused's conviction under s. 47 of the OAPA 1861 where the accused had phoned the victim and remained silent. The court held that the accused had put himself in immediate contact with the victim and when she lifted the telephone she was placed in immediate fear and suffered psychological harm. This decision was applied in *R* v *Constanza* [1997] Crim LR 576, where the court held that the Crown must prove that the victim feared violence 'at some time not excluding the immediate future' and rejected the defence submission that a person cannot have a fear of immediate violence unless they can see the potential perpetrator.

It is therefore submitted that in view of these recent developments expanding the concept of assault and the fact that the appropriate *mens rea* of intention or subjective recklessness can be easily established, that Arthur will be guilty of assaulting Monica.

The House of Lords' decision in *R* v *Ireland* establishes that silence can amount to an assault and Arthur would therefore face a charge under s. 47 of the OAPA 1861 in respect of Violet. The main difficulty for the prosecution would be in establishing that Violet suffered actual bodily harm. It is hard to envisage that the draftsmen of this offence considered that this phrase covered any harm other than physical injury, but it is now recognised that the distinctions between physical and mental injury may often be manifested by physical symptoms. In *R* v *Mike Chan-Fook* [1994] 2 All ER 552 the Court of Appeal held that psychiatric injury was actual bodily harm provided that the prosecution could bring sufficient expert psychiatric evidence to establish it. Further, it does not cover mere emotion, fear or hysteria. Thus whether Arthur's conduct has occasioned actual bodily harm would very much depend on expert evidence.

It is submitted that again the prosecution would have little difficulty in establishing Arthur's *mens rea*. This is because the House of Lords in *R* v *Savage and Parmenter* [1991] 4 All ER 698, confirmed that the *mens rea* for s. 47 of the OAPA 1861 was the same as for common assault. It is therefore not necessary for the prosecution to prove that the accused intended to cause or foresaw the risk of causing actual bodily harm.

In *R* v *Burstow* [1997] 4 All ER 225 the House of Lords held that grievous bodily harm can include psychiatric injury and therefore in respect of Wendy, Arthur could be convicted under s. 18 or s. 20 of the OAPA 1861. Both these offences involve the consequence of the victim suffering a wound or grievous bodily harm but whereas s. 18 uses the word 'cause', s. 20 uses 'inflict'. The effect of the difference between these two words have troubled the judiciary and commentators for many years but in *R* v *Burstow* Lord Bingham referred to the House of Lords' decision in *R* v *Mandair* [1994] 99 Cr App R 250 where Lord Mackay stated 'In my opinion, as I have said, the word cause is wider or at least not narrower than the word inflict' to justify the conclusion that there is not any radical divergence between the meaning of the two words and that an accused could be guilty under s. 20 even though the psychiatric injury was not the result of physical violence.

The major difference between s. 18 and s. 20 is the *mens rea*. Section 18 requires an intention to do grievous bodily harm or an intent to resist or prevent the lawful apprehension or detainer or any person. *R* v *Bryson* [1985] Crim LR 669 decided that intention has the same meaning as in the law of murder and therefore in accordance with *R* v *Moloney* [1985] 1 All ER 1025 the trial judge should not give a complex direction on the meaning of intent as it is a word in common use easily understood by the jury. As this case involves psychiatric harm the judge might take the view that this complicates the issue and that a direction is required.

In *R* v *Ireland* and *Burstow* where the facts were very similar to this problem the persons accused were convicted under s. 20 of the OAPA 1861. It is often difficult for the prosecution to establish the necessary intent required for a s. 18 conviction, but s. 20 only requires proof of maliciousness. Although the prohibited consequence of s. 20 is wounding or grievous bodily harm the House of Lords in *R* v *Mowatt* [1967] 3 All ER 47 stated that this meant the accused foresaw the risk of some physical harm, not necessarily grievous bodily harm. This decision was followed by the House of Lords in *R* v *Savage and Parmenter* [1991] 4 All ER 698 where it was confirmed that the test was subjective, *Caldwell* recklessness having no application to this offence.

It is therefore submitted that Arthur would be convicted under s. 20 of the OAPA 1861 in respect of his activities towards Wendy. No doubt he could also face charges under s. 4 of the Protection from Harassment Act 1997 where to satisfy the *mens rea* the prosecution has only to prove that a reasonable person would realise that the effect of the accused's conduct would be a fear of violence or sense of harassment. He has also clearly committed offences under s. 43 of the Telecommunications Act 1984 and s. 1 of the Malicious Communication Act 1988, but his conduct and its consequences are so serious as to warrant convictions under the OAPA 1861.

Q Question 6

Dave, in the course of a conversation with his friends Bill and Steve, repeatedly says that all women really mean yes when they say no to sexual intercourse. Steve invites his friends home where his wife Linda is asleep. Dave goes into the bedroom and starts to have sexual intercourse with Linda who is still asleep. On waking, Linda believing that Dave is her husband initially continues but then on realising Dave's true identity tells him to stop. However, Dave disregards her protests and continues.

Steve suggests to Bill that he has sexual intercourse with Linda, stating that her struggling is really a sign of enjoyment. Bill then forces Linda to have sexual intercourse with him. Afterwards Steve forces Linda to have sexual intercourse.

A week ago Linda had filed a petition for divorce.

Discuss the criminal liability of Steve, Dave, and Bill.

Commentary

Rape is a criminal offence which has undergone a number of important changes in recent years. Not only has there been a new definition imposed by s. 142 of the Criminal Justice and Public Order Act 1994 and a House of Lords decision (*R* v *R* [1991] 4 All ER 481) abolishing the husband's marital role immunity, but also a number of very important Court of Appeal decisions (e.g., *R v Elbekkay* [1995] Crim LR 163; *R v Larter and Castleton* [1995] Crim LR 75).

This question requires detailed knowledge and application of these new developments as well as consideration of the general issues of mistake and recklessness. This inevitably requires mention of *DPP v Morgan* [1975] 1 All ER 8 and the direction on recklessness that should be given to a jury in accordance with *R v Satnam* (1983) 78 Cr App R 149.

Finally, do not be put off by reference in the question to the fact that Linda has recently petitioned for divorce. This is a red herring!

- **Rape — definition**

- *R v R* **[1991]**

- **Consent — case law**

- *Mens rea* **—** *Satnam* **[1983]**

- **Mistake —** *Morgan* **[1975]**

:Ọ: Suggested answer

All three men would be charged with the offence of rape and Steve could also be charged with the inchoate offence of incitement.

Under s. 1(2) of the Sexual Offences Act 1956 as substituted by s. 142 of the Criminal Justice and Public Order Act 1994. A man commits rape if—

(a) he has sexual intercourse with a person (whether vaginal or anal) who at the time of the intercourse does not consent to it, and

(b) at the time he knows that the person does not consent to the intercourse or is reckless as to whether that person consents to it.

Before the House of Lords' decision in *R v R* [1991] 4 All ER 481, a husband could only be guilty of raping his wife in very limited circumstances for example if she had obtained a decree nisi or a judicial separation order (see *R v Roberts* (1986) 84 Cr App R 117). This was because of the fiction (dating back to Hale's Pleas of the Crown 1736) that a woman by marrying and thereby becoming the property of her husband had irrevocably given her consent to sexual intercourse with him. Fortunately the House of Lords (in effect implementing the recommendations of the Law Commission No. 116) recognised that the status of married women in modern society had changed out of all recognition from the bygone age when the fiction was applied. They therefore decided not to create another exception to the husband's immunity, but rather to abolish it completely so that a husband could be guilty of raping his wife in the same way as any man could be guilty of raping any woman. The fact that Linda has petitioned for divorce is therefore irrelevant, apart from adding further support to the prosecution evidence that Linda did not consent and that Steve was aware of this. Thus providing the prosecution can establish the *mens rea* of rape which on the facts it appears that they can, Steve will be guilty.

Even before the House of Lords' decision a husband could be guilty of aiding and abetting the rape of his wife (*R* v *Cogan and Leak* [1976] QB 217) and it is possible that Steve's presence together with his actions in encouraging his friends would amount to aiding and abetting (see *R* v *Clarkson* [1971] 3 All ER 344).

Even if Bill is acquitted of rape, this is no bar to Steve being convicted of aiding and abetting (*R* v *Millward* [1994] Crim LR 527).

However, the prosecution might instead charge Steve with the inchoate offence of incitement to rape, as he has clearly encouraged Bill to commit the offence and Steve has the necessary *mens rea* of contemplating the offence knowing that Bill could have the necessary *mens rea* for it.

The position of Dave is far more complex, especially concerning the issue of consent. Initially when he has sexual intercourse Linda does not protest because she is asleep. In the recent case of *R* v *Larter and Castleton* [1995] Crim LR 75 the appellants appealed against their conviction of rape of a 14-year-old girl who gave evidence to the effect that she remained asleep during the act and remembered nothing of what had happened. The appellants argued that the judge should have given an express direction as in *R* v *Howard* (1956) 50 Cr App R 56 that the prosecution had to prove either that the complainant physically resisted or if she did not, that her understanding and knowledge were such that she was not in a position to decide whether to consent or resist. However, in rejecting their appeal the court stated that the essential element in the definition of rape is the absence of consent. The position was governed by *R* v *Olugboja* [1982] QB 320 and that the jury should be told that 'consent' is to be given its ordinary meaning and if necessary that there is a difference between consent and submission in as much that it did not follow that a mere submission involved consent.

Nevertheless, Dave could argue that the initial lack of consent could be cured by Linda's apparent willingness on awakening to continue. However, the criminal law has long recognised that an apparently free consent can nevertheless be invalidated because of a number of factors. For example, in *R* v *Fletcher* [1859] Bell CC 63 the court held that as the complainant was only aged 13 and of weak intellect, her consent was invalid. The law has also emphasised that a mistake as to the identity of the man will also invalidate consent. This was recently confirmed by the Court of Appeal's decision in *R* v *Elbekkay* [1995] Crim LR 163. The complainant (V) lived with her boyfriend X, and one evening they went out drinking with A. They came back drunk and V went to bed alone. During the night V was awakened by another person in the bed. She thought it was her boyfriend X and agreed to sexual intercourse. However, she then realised that it was A, punched him and made him stop. On appeal A contended that

V had consented and that he could not therefore be guilty of rape. However, the Court of Appeal again referring to *R v Olugboja* [1982] QB 320 confirmed that the question for the jury was simply 'at the time of the sexual intercourse did the woman consent'. Clearly consent to have sexual intercourse with X was not consent to have intercourse with A whose conviction was upheld.

In *Elbekkay* the accused could not argue that he honestly believed that V was consenting because he was drunk at the time and the Court of Appeal held in *R v Fotheringham* (1989) 88 Cr App R 206 (following *R v O'Grady* [1987] QB 95) that drunkenness ruled out the possible defence of honest mistake as to the victim's consent. As drunkenness is no defence to rape (*R v Woods* (1982) 74 Cr App R 312) this contention was doomed to failure. However, as Dave was not drunk he might raise this argument and before we consider it in detail in the context of *mens rea*, we must first deal with the remaining issue concerning consent which is 'can consent be effectively withdrawn when it was originally given?'

For many years the only authority on this point was the Privy Council's decision in *Kaitamaki v R* [1985] AC 147 where it was held that if the victim had informed A that she was no longer consenting and A did not stop the act of intercourse, then he would be guilty of rape. This was viewed by many as a very harsh decision, but it has been recently followed and applied by the Court of Appeal in *R v Cooper and Schaub* [1994] Crim LR 531. It is therefore clear that the prosecution can establish the *actus reus* of rape in their case against Dave.

Both Dave and Bill would argue that they lacked the *mens rea* for rape as they believed that Linda was consenting. This has proved a troublesome area for trial judges in recent years with the House of Lords supplying a subjective approach to intention and mistake in *DPP v Morgan* [1975] 1 All ER 8 but an objective approach to recklessness in *R v Caldwell* [1981] 1 All ER 961. The Court of Appeal have attempted to reconcile these difficulties in their decision in *R v Satnam* [1983] 78 Cr App R 149, where they stated:

> the judge should in dealing with the state of mind of D first of all direct the jury that before they could convict of rape the Crown had to prove that either D knew that the woman did not want to have sexual intercourse or was reckless as to whether she wanted to or not. If they were sure he knew that she did not want to they should find him guilty of rape knowing there to be no consent. If they were not sure about that then they would find him not guilty of such rape and should go on to consider reckless rape. If they thought he might genuinely have believed that she might want to even though he was mistaken in this belief they would find him not guilty. If they were sure he had no genuine belief that she wanted to they would find him guilty. If they came to the conclusion that he could not care less whether she wanted to or not, but pressed on regardless, then he would have been reckless and could not have believed that she wanted to and they would find him guilty of reckless rape.

Therefore in order to succeed, Dave and Bill would have to give evidence to the effect that they honestly believed that Linda was consenting and in accordance with *Morgan* provided their belief was honestly held it would not matter that such belief was also unreasonable in the circumstances. However, the more unreasonable the belief the less likely it will be that the jury would conclude that it was honestly held. Dave and Bill will therefore face difficulties on this point. Dave's belief seems to be based mainly on his prejudices whereas Bill, although he can argue that he believed Steve's statement about his wife's consent, faces the obvious problem that she clearly made it known to him that she was not consenting. It is therefore submitted that they would both probably be found guilty of rape.

Q Question 7

Betty, aged 15, was persuaded by her boyfriend, Eric, aged 18, to have sexual intercourse. She informed her doctor, Dr Spock, who gave her some contraceptives so that she did not become pregnant. While Betty and Eric were in the act of sexual intercourse, Betty's mother Doris entered the room, and without their being aware of it, silently watched what they were doing.

Discuss the criminal liability of the parties.

Commentary

This question involves two major topics: unlawful sexual intercourse (Sexual Offences Act 1956), and aiding and abetting. There are a number of points to mention, including the exam favourite: 'Can mere presence at the scene of the crime amount to aiding and abetting?' But there is not that much material to cover, and the answer is shorter than many in this book. It is a question from an exam paper requiring five (instead of the usual four) answers. Nevertheless, organisation and planning are, as always, essential.

- s. 6 Sexual Offences Act 1956

- Aiding and abetting — *Tyrrell* [1894]

- s. 8 Accessories and Abettors Act 1861

- Omissions and aiding

☼ Suggested answer

As Betty has consented and, despite her age, there is no evidence to suggest that she cannot give valid consent, Eric cannot be guilty of rape. However, he could be charged under s. 6 of the Sexual Offences Act 1956, which makes it an offence for a man to have unlawful sexual intercourse with a girl under the age of 16. There does not appear to be any general defence available to Eric, but there are two statutory defences under s. 6. The first is inapplicable as this depends upon the accused believing the girl was his wife by reason of having gone through a form of marriage ceremony. However, Eric may be able to plead the second defence under s. 6(3) if he can prove on the balance of probabilities that he honestly believed that Betty was aged 16 or over, that such a belief was reasonable, that he had not been charged with a like offence and that he is aged under 24. Obviously it depends on the circumstances as to whether Eric can prove this defence, but if he knows Betty's proper age it will fail.

Although Betty may have been a willing participant in the activity she will not be guilty of any offence. There is no crime of conspiracy arising out of their agreement, as Betty would be regarded as a victim; and under s. 2 of the Criminal Law Act 1977, there is no conspiracy if the only two parties to the agreement are the accused and the victim. The same rationale is applied to the crime of aiding and abetting. Thus in *R v Tyrrell* [1894] 1 QB 710, the accused, a girl between the ages of 13 and 16, abetted X to have unlawful sexual intercourse with her. It was held that she could not be guilty of abetting the offence committed by X, as the offence was created for the purpose of protecting women and girls. This principle has been more recently applied by the Court of Appeal in *R v Pickford* [1995] 1 Cr App R 420.

In supplying the contraceptives Dr Spock may be charged as an accessory to the offence under s. 6 of the 1956 Act. By the Accessories and Abettors Act 1861, s. 8: 'Whosoever shall aid, abet, counsel, or procure the commission of any indictable offence, whether the same be an offence at common law or by virtue of any Act passed or to be passed, shall be liable to be tried, indicted, and punished as a principal offender.'

Although the doctor may contend that he did not want to encourage unlawful sexual intercourse and that his prime purpose was to stop an unwanted pregnancy, it is by no means certain that he would be exonerated. This is because the *mens rea* for an accomplice is satisfied by proof of an intention to assist coupled with knowledge or contemplation of the type of crime committed (*DPP for Northern Ireland* v *Maxwell* [1978] 3 All ER 1140). This issue arose in the civil case of *Gillick* v *West Norfolk and Wisbech Health Authority* [1984] 1 All ER 913, where the House of Lords ruled that a doctor who supplied contraceptives in these circumstances would not be guilty of aiding and abetting unlawful sexual intercourse, as this could be part of the doctor's lawful treatment of the patient. The majority decision was that the doctor would lack the necessary *mens rea* because of a good motive, a desire to stop unwanted pregnancies. Some commentators take the view that this is an acceptance of the recognition of necessity — the doctor is choosing the lesser of two evils — although the House of Lords did not base their decision on this point.

Doris, Betty's mother, might also face an aiding and abetting charge as she was present when the unlawful sexual intercourse took place. However, as many commentators point out, a person is not guilty merely because he or she is present at the scene of a crime and does nothing to prevent it. Thus in *R v Coney* (1882) 8 QBD 534, it was held that mere presence, without more, at an illegal prize fight would not in itself be sufficient for abetting the battery committed by the contestants. Similarly, standing by, watching a rape take place, was not sufficient in *R v Clarkson* [1971] 3 All ER 344 for abetting rape, the Court of Appeal holding that the abettor must either be present in pursuance of an agreement that the crime be committed, or must give assistance or encouragement at the time of its commission. Both these ingredients were present in *Wilcox v Jeffrey* [1951] 1 All ER 1920, when the accused, a music critic, was found guilty of abetting a musician to contravene the Aliens Order 1920, when the accused attended the prohibited performances, cheered and wrote rave reviews for the music press. This was more than mere presence!

Although Doris has remained silent, as Betty's mother she does have a duty to try to control her daughter's actions. It is possible to give positive encouragement by inactivity, and it could be argued that morally she should have intervened. However, as Betty and Eric were unaware of Doris's presence, the prosecution could not contend that her inactivity positively encouraged them, and it is submitted that Doris would not be found guilty of abetting unlawful sexual intercourse.

Further reading

Clarkson, C., 'Law Commission Report No. 218' [1994] Crim LR 324.

Lacey, N., 'Beset by Boundaries: The Home Office Review of Sex Offences' [2001] Crim LR 3.

Wells, C., 'Stalking: the Criminal Law's Response' [1997] Crim LR 463.

The defences I

Introduction

The general defences to criminal responsibility are a large and important part of the criminal law syllabus. An exam paper may well contain two questions on the general defences, or one full question with an additional one involving the specific defences which reduce murder to manslaughter. Therefore it is an area that you must know comprehensively, and because it contains a vast array of diverse material this is no easy task.

The defences have been divided between two chapters, the first dealing with the defences of automatism, insanity, diminished responsibility, and intoxication; and the second covering duress, necessity, mistake, and self-defence. In some textbooks you will find the material relating to automatism and mistake in chapters covering *actus reus* and *mens rea*, but as questions on insanity usually involve consideration of automatism (and often diminished responsibility) and questions on self-defence generally involve mistake, the questions in this chapter have been formed accordingly.

It must be appreciated that many people suffering from mental disorder who commit crimes never actually stand trial but will be detained under the Mental Health Act 1983 provisions. If they are tried and are deemed fit to plead, they have the difficult decision of whether to put their mental incapacity before the court. The risk in so doing is being found not guilty by reason of insanity on application of the *M'Naghten* Rules 1843, which (despite constant criticism) remain the test for insanity in the eyes of the law. That the concept of 'disease of the mind' is no longer a medical concept has long been recognised by the Butler Committee (1975) and the Law Commission, who recommended (Draft Code, cl. 35) that the concept of mental disorder was more appropriate (thus a mental disorder verdict would be returned if the defendant was suffering from severe mental illness or severe mental handicap).

It is clear that such a change is required, if only because many defendants are loath to risk the defence being put to the jury. So in *R v Sullivan* [1983] 2 All ER 673, the accused preferred to plead guilty to assault occasioning actual bodily harm, a crime which carries a maximum sentence of five years' imprisonment, when the trial judge suggested that his epilepsy constituted a disease of the mind and his relevant defence was therefore not automatism but insanity. This problem has to some extent been alleviated as far as murder is concerned by the Homicide Act 1957, which introduced the partial defence of diminished responsibility; and most mentally disordered defendants charged with murder would now plead this defence in the knowledge that it has succeeded in a wide variety of situations not covered by insanity.

As *Sullivan* indicates, the defences of insanity and automatism are closely linked, as for both defences the accused has acted while not in control of his or her mental faculties. If automatism succeeds the accused is found not guilty with no custodial repercussions; but although an accused found not guilty by reason of insanity will not inevitably be detained since the passing of the Criminal Procedure (Insanity and Unfitness to Plead) Act 1991, there is still the stigma of being labelled insane. There is a need for a clear boundary between the defences, but unfortunately this does not exist. This is aptly illustrated by the cases of *R v Quick* [1973] 3 All ER 347 and *R v Hennessey* [1989] 2 All ER 9, both involving defendants suffering from diabetes. In the first case, it was held by the Court of Appeal that a diabetic who was in a state of hypoglycaemia as a result of taking insulin and alcohol could not be deemed insane (within the *M'Naghten* Rules). In the second case, an accused in a state of hyperglycaemia because he hadn't taken his insulin was found to be insane! Only a criminal lawyer could explain the reasoning for this outcome.

The defence of intoxication has also undergone recent review by both the Law Commission (Consultation Paper No. 127 'Intoxication and Criminal Liability', 1993; Law Com. No. 229, 1995) and the House of Lords (*R v Kingston* [1994] 3 All ER 353). It can be a defence to certain crimes (those where the prosecution must prove intention) and it is also a factor in considering the availability of other defences. Accordingly two questions have been set on this important topic.

Q Question 1

Albert and John attend a party where they have some non-alcoholic drinks. It is known that Albert has recently been experiencing dizzy spells and fainting fits, but he has not sought medical treatment. At the party Albert becomes dizzy and is given six valium tablets in an attempt to calm him down. Very shortly after taking the tablets Albert leaves the party with John. On the way home Albert repeatedly hits John over the head with a bottle, thereby killing him.

When arrested and charged with murder, Albert says: 'I cannot remember hitting him. I must have had a blackout.'

Discuss Albert's possible defences.

Commentary

Questions on mental abnormality are quite common in examinations. They are often in essay form, but this problem does require the student to take into account the alternative reasons why Albert acted as he did. If a murder has taken place and insanity is an obvious issue, a consideration of the related defences of automatism and diminished responsibility is required. The ingredients of all three defences must therefore be covered in detail with a clear demonstration of the differences between them. Sometimes voluntary intoxication must also be considered as it is easy to link relevant facts giving rise to this issue in a question of this nature.

For the sake of completeness, the non-availability of the defence of provocation is referred to briefly. However, this author would not deduct marks if this was not contained in a student's answer.

- **Automatism —** *Bratty* **[1963]**

- **Insanity —** *M'Naghten* **Rules 1843**

- **Disease of the mind —** *Burgess* **[1991]**

- **Diminished responsibility — s. 2 Homicide Act 1957**

- **Provocation**

:Q: **Suggested answer**

There are three defences that will be available to Albert — automatism, insanity and diminished responsibility — which may result in either a complete defence to murder or a reduction of murder to manslaughter.

Prima facie, the most attractive defence to Albert is automatism, as this is a complete defence to murder and the burden of proof is on the prosecution to disprove the existence of the defence. Automatism was defined by Lord Denning in *Bratty* v *Attorney-General for Northern Ireland* [1963] AC 386, as 'an act which is done by the muscles without any control by the mind such as a spasm, a reflex or a convulsion, or an act done by a person who is not conscious of what he is doing such as an act done whilst suffering from concussion or whilst sleep-walking'.

Albert will argue that he did not know what he was doing and therefore his act was involuntary. The prosecution must prove that the act was voluntary, but they are entitled to rely on the presumption that every man has sufficient mental capacity to be responsible for his act; and if the defence wish to displace this presumption they must give some evidence from which the contrary may reasonably be inferred.

The medical evidence presented on Albert's behalf may indicate that he so acted either because he had taken the valium, or because of the medical condition producing the dizziness and fainting fits. If Albert had taken alcohol or non-prescribed hallucinatory drugs, automatism will not succeed (*R* v *Lipman* [1969] 3 All ER 410). However, Albert has taken valium, a soporific drug, and in the leading case of *R* v *Sullivan* [1983] 2 All ER 673, Lord Diplock recognised that non-insane automatism would be the appropriate defence 'in cases where temporary impairment not being self induced by consuming drink or drugs results from some external physical factor such as a blow on the head causing concussion or the administration of an anaesthetic for therapeutic purposes'. Further, in *R v Hardie* [1984] All ER 848, the Court of Appeal recognised that the accused who caused criminal damage was not at fault when he did not realise that he would become uncontrollable and aggressive after taking five valium. His conviction was quashed as a majority of the public would not appreciate the danger of taking this substance, and the trial judge was therefore wrong to direct the jury that this was to be regarded as reckless conduct.

It is therefore submitted that if the medical evidence stating that the taking of the valium was the cause of Albert's conduct was accepted, the defence of automatism would succeed. There would also be no risk of Albert being found 'not guilty by reason of insanity' under the *M'Naghten* Rules 1843, as in *R v Quick and Paddison* [1973] 3 All ER 347 Lawton LJ in the Court of Appeal stated: 'A malfunctioning of the mind of transitory effect caused by the application to the body of some external factor such as violence, drugs, including anaesthetics, alcohol and hypnotic influences cannot fairly be said to be due to disease'.

If, on the other hand, the condition responsible for the dizziness and the fainting was the cause of Albert's conduct, different considerations apply. When the defence of automatism is raised the judge has first to decide if a proper evidential foundation for the defence has been made out so that it can be left to the jury. If it has, is this a case which falls within the defence of insanity under the *M'Naghten* Rules 1843. Under these rules, which determine the accused's sanity (for legal purposes) at the time he committed the *actus reus*, everyone is presumed sane until the contrary is proved. However, it is a defence for the accused to show that he was labouring under such defect of reason due to disease of the mind as either:

(a)   not to know the nature and quality of his act; or

(b)   if he did know this, not to know that what he was doing was wrong.

The trial judge must first decide if Albert was suffering from a disease of the mind, and if so, the jury will then decide if the other ingredients of the defence have been satisfied. The judicial pronouncements on insanity are certainly at variance with medical practice, and the question of public safety is a factor which the judiciary obviously take into account. In *Bratty*, Lord Denning stated that 'any mental disorder which has manifested itself in violence and is prone to recur is a disease of the mind' and this was reiterated by Lord Diplock in *R v Sullivan*, where the House of Lords upheld the trial judge's decision to label epilepsy 'a disease of the mind', when he stated:

> if the effect of a disease is to impair these facilities [of reason, memory and understanding] so severely as to have either of these consequences referred to in the latter part of the rules, it matters not whether the aetiology of the impairment is organic, as in epilepsy, or functional, or whether the impairment itself is permanent or is transient and intermittent, provided that it subsisted at the time of the commission of the act.

Thus arteriosclerosis (*R* v *Kemp* [1956] 3 All ER 249), diabetes (*R* v *Hennessey* (1989) 89 Cr App R 10), and violent sleepwalking (*R* v *Burgess* [1991] 2 All ER 769) have all been deemed diseases of the mind.

The most recent case of *Burgess* demonstrated how judicial attitude has hardened in recent years. The Court of Appeal decided that many people sleepwalk, but that if an accused uses violence while sleepwalking, that must be due to a disease of the mind. So the accused who while sleepwalking violently assaulted the victim was found 'not guilty by reason of insanity' as he was plainly suffering from a defect of reason from some sort of failure of the mind causing him to act as he did without conscious motivation. The Court of Appeal upheld the trial judge's decision to label it a disease of the mind, on the basis that it was due to an internal factor which had manifested itself in violence.

If the judge was to rule that the medical condition was not a disease of the mind, Albert would still face two problems concerning automatism. The first is that for automatism to succeed the court must accept that there was a total loss of control. In *Attorney-General's Reference (No. 2 of 1992)* [1993] 4 All ER 683, the Court of Appeal ruled that the trial judge was wrong to direct the jury that a syndrome known as 'driving without awareness' could amount to automatism. Impaired, reduced or partial control is not enough. So the prosecution could argue that as Albert had enough control to pick up a bottle and repeatedly hit John over the head, automatism should not apply.

The second problem concerns the fact that Albert has not sought medical treatment for his condition. The prosecution could argue that therefore the automatism was self-induced and that Albert was blameworthy in not seeking treatment. It is uncertain after *R* v *Hardie* whether the prosecution must show that Albert realised he might be dangerous if he did not seek treatment, or whether it would be sufficient that a reasonable man would have so realised. As Lawton LJ stated in *R* v *Quick and Paddison*, automatism is a 'quagmire of law seldom entered nowadays save by those in desperate need of some kind of defence'.

If Albert is found 'not guilty by reason of insanity', he has the right to appeal under s. 1 of the Criminal Procedure (Insanity) Act 1964; and if the appeal succeeds because the judge wrongly directed the jury, the accused will be entitled to a 'not guilty' verdict with no custodial repercussions or attached conditions for treatment (Criminal Procedure (Insanity and Unfitness to Plead) Act 1991).

Whereas automatism and insanity are complete defences, diminished responsibility is only a partial defence which reduces murder to manslaughter. The defence was introduced by s. 2(1) of the Homicide Act 1957, which provides:

> Where a person kills or is a party to the killing of another, he shall not be convicted of murder if he was suffering from such abnormality of mind (whether arising from a condition of arrested or retarded development of mind or any inherent causes or induced by disease or injury) as substantially impaired his mental responsibility for his acts or omissions in doing or being a party to the killing.

Since this defence has been introduced, many accused plead it rather than insanity on a murder charge; and it has succeeded in a wide variety of circumstances, including mercy killings, crimes of passion and killings as a result of irresistible impulse. Professor Andrew Ashworth has pointed out that in 80 per cent of cases where it is raised the prosecution are prepared to accept the plea. In two recent cases involving 'battered women's syndrome' — *R* v *Ahluwalia* [1992] 4 All ER 889 and *R* v *Thornton (No. 2)* [1996] 1 WLR 1174 — although the juries had convicted the accused of murder, in the retrials different juries found that the accused had established the defence of diminished responsibility on the balance of probability and were guilty of manslaughter.

Although the taking of valium (unless there was evidence of uncontrollable addiction) could not constitute an abnormality of the mind, it is possible that the medical condition could be so regarded and that this defence could succeed in Albert's case.

It is submitted that on the facts, as there is no evidence of it, provocation could not succeed as a partial defence. This has been illustrated by *R* v *Acott* [1997] 1 All ER 706, where the House of Lords confirmed that some evidence of provocation had to be raised for the judge to be under an obligation to put it to the jury.

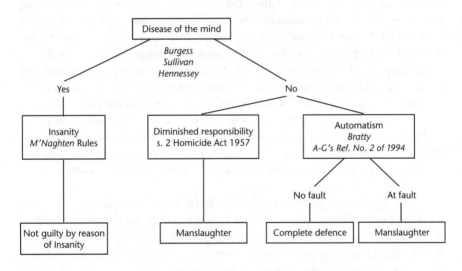

Q Question 2

Diane is a black West Indian aged 17, with a very fiery temper. Two years ago she was involved in a car accident which caused her some brain damage; which, although it cannot be classified as a disease of the mind, causes her to become very irritable on occasions. Partly as a result of the accident she has become a glue-sniffer.

One day she was playing cards with her friend Olly, a diabetic who had taken his insulin but in breach of his doctor's instructions had not eaten and had taken one small brandy. Olly had done this on previous occasions with the result that he would become aggressive and lose control. While they were playing, Diane's uncle, Victor, who had lived with Diane for three years, entered the room and, annoyed that they were playing cards, called Diane 'a no-good black whore'. This caused Diane and Olly to grab knives and, intending to kill him, continually stab Victor until he died.

When arrested for murder, Olly said, 'The last thing I can remember is playing cards and having a drink'.

Discuss the criminal responsibility of Diane and Olly.

Commentary

This question is specifically set to test knowledge of two partial defences to murder: provocation and diminished responsibility. These defences will often be found in the same question as, amongst other things, it tests knowledge of the burden of proof.

The question is a little artificial as it has been made clear from the facts that the defence of insanity is unavailable and that Olly's automatism is self-induced.

Further, as we have already had three questions involving murder, detailed discussion of malice aforethought has been eliminated by stating that Diane and Olly intended to kill and continually stabbed Victor. Other questions on these topics will often leave these issues open.

- Murder

- Provocation — s. 3 Homicide Act 1957

  - the subjective condition

  - the objective condition

  - *Camplin* [1978]

  - *Morhall* [1995]

  - *Smith* [2000]

- Diminished responsibility — s. 2 Homicide Act 1957

- Automatism

ːỌː **Suggested answer**

Diane and Olly will be charged with murder, the unlawful killing of a human being within the Queen's peace with malice aforethought. Since the introduction of the Law Reform (Year and a Day Rule) Act 1996, it is not necessary to prove that the death followed the unlawful act or omission within a year and a day. In many murder cases there is dispute as to whether the accused possessed malice aforethought, an intention to kill or cause grievous bodily harm (*R* v *Moloney* [1985] 1 All ER 1025). However, as the question states that Diane and Olly intended to kill Victor, the prosecution prima facie will be able to establish *mens rea*.

Diane will raise the defence of provocation, a common law defence which is defined in s. 3 of the Homicide Act 1957:

> Where on a charge of murder there is evidence on which the jury can find that the person charged was provoked (whether by things done or things said or by both together) to lose his self-control, the question whether the provocation was enough to make a reasonable man do as he did shall be left to be determined by the jury; and in determining that question the jury shall take into account everything both done and said according to the effect which, in their opinion, it would have on a reasonable man.

The first condition to be considered is: Was the accused provoked and did she lose her self-control? In recent cases involving women who kill this has sometimes been a problem; and in *R* v *Thornton* [1996] 2 All ER 1023 two separate juries rejected this defence as, because the accused had already armed herself with a kitchen knife, they could not conclude that there had been a 'sudden and temporary loss of self-control' (*R* v *Duffy* [1949] 1 All ER 923). However, this does not seem to be a problem in the vast majority of provocation cases, and it is submitted that as there is some evidence of provocation here, the judge would have to leave this issue for the jury's consideration.

The second condition (i.e., the 'reasonable man') is likely to be the most difficult to apply because the original objective test now has subjective elements. The starting point for this analysis is the House of Lords' decision in *DPP* v *Camplin* [1978] 2 All ER 168, where Lord Diplock said that:

> the reasonable man referred to is a person having the power of self-control to be expected of an ordinary person of the sex and age of the accused, but in other respects sharing such of the accused's characteristics as they think would affect the gravity of the provocation to him and whether such a person would in like circumstances be provoked to lose his self-control but would also react to the provocation as the accused did.

In *Camplin*, the House of Lords stated that the jury should have put themselves in the position of a reasonable 15-year-old. However, in *R* v *Ali* [1989] Crim LR 736, the Court of Appeal held that the judge was not wrong in failing to direct the jury that the accused's age of 20 was a relevant consideration; but in *R* v *Humphreys* [1995] 4 All ER 1008 the Court of Appeal held that the judge should have directed the jury to consider what effect the provocation would have had on a young woman who had the accused's traits of immaturity and attention seeking. It is therefore submitted that Diane's youth must be taken into account.

A more difficult issue is the effect of Diane's glue-sniffing. It would seem that the fact that she may have been sniffing glue at the time of the incident cannot be taken into account as the 'reasonable person' is sober. However, in *R* v *Morhall* [1995] 3 All ER 659, the House of Lords, reversing the decision of the Court of Appeal, held that the jury in considering the 'objective test' should have been directed to take into account the fact that the accused was a glue-sniffer. Nevertheless, the court could distinguish *Morhall*, as in that case the accused was taunted about the fact that he was a glue-sniffer. In Diane's case the taunts do not relate to this fact, and it is therefore submitted that her glue-sniffing would not be taken into account.

The third factor that could be considered is Diane's ethnicity. In the Court of Appeal decision in *R* v *Morhall*, Lord Taylor CJ said that 'physical deformity, whether from birth or by accident, colour, race, creed, impotence, homosexuality are examples, but not an exhaustive list of characteristics which are clearly consistent with the concept of the reasonable man'. This is a problem which so far our courts have not had to analyse, but in the New Zealand case of *R* v *Tai* [1970] NZLR 102, the Court of Appeal noted that the ordinary person 'is not one of exclusively British blood or background but one who could be expected to react in the way people who commonly accept current New Zealand standards react'. Similarly, the Australian case of *Masciantonio* v *R* (1995) 129 ALR 598 decided that ethnicity could be relevant in assessing the gravity of the provocation to the reasonable man, but not in determining how a reasonable man would have reacted to provocation of that strength. It is submitted that the fact that Diane is a black West Indian should be deemed a characteristic to be taken into account by the jury, although it would not appear to be a significant fact.

The question of whether brain damage can be taken into account in the objective test has recently been answered by the Privy Council in *Luc Thiet Thuan* v *R* [1997] 2 All ER 1033, where it was held that the accused's mental infirmity, which impaired or reduced the accused's powers of self-control below those to be expected of an ordinary person, was not a factor to be attributed to the ordinary person for the purpose of determining whether an ordinary person having the accused's characteristics would have acted as the accused did. The reasoning behind this was that such mental disability could be taken into account when considering the defence of diminished responsibility. However, the House of Lords in *R* v *Smith* [2000] 3 WLR 654, refused to follow *Luc* when they held by a 3–2 majority that the jury could take into account the accused's severe depression when assessing not only the gravity of the provocation, but also the powers of self-control of the reasonable man under the objective test. Lord Hoffman, stated that the judge should 'be able simply to tell the jury that the question of whether the defendant's behaviour fell below the standard which should reasonably have been expected of him was entirely a matter for them'.

Lastly, it is clear that Diane's fiery temper would not be taken into account as this is incompatible with the reasonable man. In *R* v *Newell* (1980) 71 Cr App R 331, the Court of Appeal stated that 'a disposition to be unduly suspicious or to lose one's temper readily will not suffice, nor will a temporary or transitory state of mind such as a mood of depression, excitability or irascibility'. Thus in *R* v *Humphreys* (above), although the jury were allowed to take into account the accused's immaturity and attention seeking, they could not deem her fiery temper to be a characteristic. This principle was recognised by the House of Lords in *R* v *Smith* where Lord Hoffmann stated that a tendency to violent rages or childish tantrums is a defect in character rather than an excuse.

The third condition to be satisfied is whether such a person would also react to the provocation as the accused did. Although in assessing this the jury can take into account the whole history of the relationship, and words alone can constitute provocation, it is submitted that it will be very difficult for Diane to succeed on this point as the mode of her resentment does seem out of all proportion to the nature of the provocation.

One of the advantages of pleading provocation is that the burden of proof remains on the prosecution; as Lord Steyn stated in *R* v *Acott*: 'If there is such evidence [of provocation] the judge must leave the issue to the jury'. If, on the other hand, Diane raised the defence of diminished responsibility, which it is submitted she would, the defence will have to prove it on the balance of probabilities. Under s. 2(1) of the Homicide Act 1957:

> Where a person kills or is party to the killing of another, he shall not be convicted of murder if he was suffering from such abnormality of mind (whether arising from a condition of arrested or retarded development of mind or any inherent causes or induced by disease or injury) as substantially impaired his mental responsibility for his acts or omissions in doing or being a party to the killing.

The effect of the defence (if successful) is to reduce murder to manslaughter.

It is the responsibility of the trial judge to explain the effect of s. 2(1) to the jury, who must then decide if the conditions are fulfilled (*R* v *Terry* [1961] 2 All ER 569). The defence is often accepted by the prosecution and has been liberally interpreted. Thus in *R* v *Reynolds* [1988] Crim LR 679, post-natal depression and pre-menstrual tension were accepted as within s. 2; and the Court of Appeal in *R* v *Tandy* [1989] 1 WLR 350 recognised that alcoholism could be, although voluntary intoxication is not. As Diane is a glue-sniffer, this may be equated with alcoholism and diminished responsibility may succeed. Certainly it is more likely than provocation to be successful on these facts.

It is submitted that as Olly has admitted that he cannot remember the incident, it will be very difficult (after the House of Lords' decision in *R* v *Acott* [1997] 1 All ER 706) for him to convince the trial judge to leave the defence of provocation to the jury. He would also face difficulties with the defence of automatism, an act done by the muscles without control by the brain.

Although the court could not hold that this is the defence of insanity, because the decision in *R* v *Quick* [1973] 3 All ER 347 states that the effect of applications of external substances will not constitute a disease of the mind, the defence of automatism is also likely to fail because the automatism is self-induced (*R* v *Lipman* [1969] 3 All ER 410). Olly has failed to follow his doctor's instructions, and as he has fallen into this state on other occasions he could certainly be deemed reckless and blameworthy (see *R* v *Hardie* (1984) 80 Cr App R 157). However, the evidence may convince the jury that he did not form the malice aforethought for murder and he would therefore be convicted of manslaughter.

If the jury did decide that Olly had formed the intention to kill or cause grievous bodily harm, Olly might be able to prove that his condition amounted to an abnormality of the mind which substantially impaired his mental responsibility. In this case the defence of diminished responsibility would apply and he would be found guilty of manslaughter.

Q Question 3

Martin got so drunk that he did not know what he was doing. While in this state he killed Vernon, and held down Walter while he was killed by Oswald. He then hit Zoro over the head causing him serious injury, and took his wallet. Lastly, he broke into Ray's house, mistakenly believing it was his own house.

Discuss the criminal liability of Martin.

Commentary

This question requires knowledge of and an ability to apply the principles concerning the defence of intoxication. This question is slightly artificial because it informs the student that Martin is drunk and leaves little room for discussion about the ingredients of the offences that have been committed. Many exam questions will leave these issues in doubt, and they will therefore require much more consideration.

For this reason the author has abandoned the usual technique of dealing first with the offences in detail, and then considering possible defences.

- Consider relevant offences

- Intoxication and *Majewski*

- Specific and basic intent

- Aiding and abetting — *Powell and English* [1997]

- Robbery and burglary

- Criminal damage — *Jaggard and Dickinson* [1980]

:Q: Suggested answer

Martin could be charged with murder, aiding and abetting murder, robbery, aggravated assault, burglary and criminal damage, arising out of the incidents that have taken place. As he was drunk at the time he will be able to raise the issue of intoxication which can negative the *mens rea* of certain offences and therefore act as a defence.

The leading case on intoxication is *DPP* v *Majewski* [1976] 2 All ER 142, where the House of Lords decided that intoxication can be a defence to crimes of specific intent but not to those of basic intent. Not all judges and commentators agree on the precise definition of these terms, but it is generally considered that a crime of specific intent is one where the prosecution must prove actual intention on behalf of the accused, whereas recklessness is sufficient *mens rea* for a crime of basic intent. Thus if an accused is charged with murder, a crime of specific intent, his defence of intoxication could succeed as in *R* v *Lipman* [1969] 3 All ER 410, where the accused, 'on a bad trip' after taking a non-prescribed hallucinatory drug, wrongly believed he was being attacked by snakes and strangled his girlfriend. The prosecution in *Lipman* could not prove that the accused intended to kill or cause grievous bodily harm (malice aforethought) and therefore he could not be convicted of murder. However, he was convicted of manslaughter as — manslaughter being a crime of basic intent, where the prosecution do not have to prove intention — intoxication is no defence.

The rationale for this approach is questionable, but it appears to be that if you are reckless enough to get so drunk in the first place that you do not know what you are doing, this takes the place of the recklessness that would otherwise have to be established at the time of the *actus reus*. The Law Commission's Consultation Paper No. 127 ('Intoxication and Criminal Liability', 1993) pointed out that this approach is a rough form of justice and conflicts with many of the established principles of criminal responsibility. In particular, it conflicts with the general principle of contemporaneity, i.e., the fact that the *actus reus* and *mens rea* must be present at the same time, and is another example of constructive crime, as the deemed recklessness relates only to the risk of becoming drunk, not to the specific harm prohibited. Further, although traditionally the burden of proof remains on the prosecution if the offence is one of basic intent, an accused, by putting forward intoxication as a defence, is in reality pleading guilty.

However, despite recognising these anomalies, the Law Commission in their final report (No. 229, 1995) recommended following the approach adopted by the US Model Penal Code 1962, which is very similar to the approach in *Majewski*. This is another example of the criminal law applying principles not of strict logic, but of public policy. The House of Lords in *Majewski* recognised that if voluntary intoxication by drink or drugs can negative the special or specific intention necessary for the commission of crimes such as murder or theft, how can you justify in strict logic the view that it cannot negative a basic intent crime? The answer is that in strict logic this view cannot be justified. But this is the view that has been adopted by the common law which is founded on common sense and experience rather than strict logic.

Turning to the offences that Martin has committed, it is clear with regard to Vernon's death that Martin will be guilty of manslaughter, not murder, unless the prosecution can prove (as they were able to in *R v Moloney* [1985] 1 All ER 1025) that despite the drinking he did form the necessary malice aforethought. The position regarding Walter is not so straightforward. Unless Martin is charged as a co-principal, the relevant offence will be aiding and abetting murder. The *mens rea* requirement for this offence is an intention to assist, contemplating death or grievous bodily harm as a possible consequence (*Chan Wing Siu v R* [1984] 3 All ER 877), or a realisation that the primary party might kill with intent to do so, or with intent to cause grievous bodily harm — *R v Powell and English* [1997] 4 All ER 545. There is no binding authority as to whether intoxication is a defence to this crime, but it could be argued that as the *mens rea* requires more than recklessness it is not a crime of basic intent and therefore intoxication is a complete defence. However, it is submitted that as policy plays a major part in determining the applicable principles in this topic, the court would look first at the principal offence to decide if intoxication was a defence, and then apply this principle to determine the accomplice's responsibility. Thus as intoxication would reduce the murder charge to a manslaughter conviction, Martin would be guilty of aiding and abetting manslaughter. It would be most odd if Oswald was found guilty of manslaughter because of his drunkenness, whereas Martin was completely acquitted because of his.

The third incident involves both a crime against the person and a crime against property. Martin could be charged with offences under the Offences Against the Person Act 1861 as he has caused Zoro serious (i.e., grievous) bodily harm. The most serious offence is s. 18 (wounding or causing grievous bodily harm with intent), but as intention is required (*R v Belfon* [1976] 3 All ER 46) intoxication is a defence. However, the less serious offence under s. 20 (malicious wounding or inflicting grievous bodily harm) is a crime of basic intent (*Majewski*) and therefore intoxication would not succeed as a defence.

As Martin has taken Zoro's wallet he could be charged with robbery. This is defined under s. 8(1) of the Theft Act 1968: 'A person is guilty of robbery if he steals, and immediately before or at the time of doing so, and in order to do so, he uses force on any person or puts or seeks to put any person in fear of being then and there subjected to force'. However, Martin can be convicted of robbery only if he is guilty of theft, and as theft is an offence of specific intent, his defence of intoxication can succeed and he would therefore not be guilty.

When he broke into Ray's house, Martin could be committing the crimes of burglary and criminal damage. Burglary is defined by s. 9 of the Theft Act 1968 and requires the accused to enter a building or part of a building as a trespasser with intent to commit certain substantive offences, or to have actually committed or attempted to commit certain offences. However, even if the prosecution could prove that Martin had the necessary *mens rea* to be a trespasser (*R* v *Collins* [1972] 2 All ER 1105), there is no evidence of an intention to commit a substantive offence as Martin wrongly believes that he is entering his own house.

Lastly, Martin could be guilty of criminal damage under s. 1(1) of the Criminal Damage Act 1971:

> A person who without lawful excuse destroys or damages any property belonging to another intending to destroy or damage any such property or being reckless as to whether any such property would be destroyed or damaged shall be guilty of an offence.

Metropolitan Police Commissioner v *Caldwell* [1981] 1 All ER 961 clearly establishes that this is a crime of basic intent and therefore intoxication could not generally be a defence. However, in *Jaggard* v *Dickinson* [1980] 3 All ER 716, an accused who while drunk mistakenly broke into X's house, believing it to be Y's house, where Y had given him consent to break in, was held by the Court of Appeal to have the defence of lawful excuse under s. 5(2)(a) of the Criminal Damage Act 1971. Further in *R* v *Smith* [1974] 1 All ER 632, the Court of Appeal quashed the conviction of a tenant of a flat who had damaged his landlord's property in the mistaken belief that it was his own. The prosecution would argue, though, that following *R* v *O'Grady* [1987] 3 All ER 420, a mistake caused by drunkenness cannot negative *mens rea*, and as the principles applicable to intoxication are often governed by policy, this argument is likely to succeed and Martin's defence may fail.

Q Question 4

Alfred is an alcoholic. He has a grudge against Victor and decides that he is going to kill him. He then drinks 12 pints of strong beer and, while in a drunken stupor, mistakenly believing that Victor is about to attack him, stabs Victor with a knife causing his death.

Discuss Alfred's possible defences to a charge of murder.

Commentary

In many examination papers there will be a full question involving murder and manslaughter in detail. In order to avoid duplication of answer material, another question in which a murder has taken place will simply require the student to discuss possible defences. This is such a question.

It is slightly unusual, because generally you would expect to cover two or three defences in detail. This question, however, requires the student to consider a number of defences, some of which are not always closely related to each other. In this sense it is similar to a mixed question (see Chapter 10). With the constraints of time, an in-depth analysis of all the relevant defences is not possible, so recognition of all the defences and conciseness are essential.

- **Mistake and self-defence**

    - *Williams* [1984]

    - *O'Grady* [1987]

- **Provocation** — *Thornton* [1996]

- **Diminished responsibility** — *Tandy* [1987]

- **Insanity** — *M'Naghten* Rules 1843

- **Automatism** — *Lipman* [1969]

- **Intoxication**

    - *Majewski* [1977]

    - *Gallagher* [1963]

⌖ Suggested answer

There are a number of possible defences available to Alfred, but *prima facie* the most favourable would be self-defence, as this is a complete defence to a murder charge. Alfred has the evidential duty to raise self-defence, but the burden of proof remains on the prosecution to prove that the force used was not necessary or reasonable. The fact that an accused has made a mistake will not necessarily rule out the defence, as in *R v Williams* (1984) 74 Cr App R 276, the court held that the accused is to be judged on the facts as the accused believed them to be. Therefore, if an unreasonable mistake as to the facts has been made, this will not in itself cause the defence to fail, provided the mistake was honestly made. However, according to *R v O'Grady* [1987] 3 All ER 420, a mistake arising from voluntary intoxication cannot be relied upon for self-defence. Therefore as Alfred was drunk this defence will fail.

Alfred might next turn to provocation which (if successful) would reduce murder to manslaughter under s. 3 of the Homicide Act 1957:

> Where on a charge of murder there is evidence on which the jury can find that the person charged was provoked (whether by things done or by things said or by both together) to lose his self-control, the question whether the provocation was enough to make a reasonable man do as he did shall be left to be determined by the jury; and in determining that question the jury shall take into account everything both done and said according to the effect which, in their opinion, it would have on a reasonable man.

Although the jury could take into account the fact that Alfred was an alcoholic when assessing whether a reasonable man with the accused's characteristics would have done as he did (*R* v *Morhall* [1995] 3 All ER 659), they cannot take into account the fact that he was drunk at the time. However, the main problem facing Alfred is convincing the judge that he did lose his self-control and that this is a case of provocation. Despite cases such as *R* v *Ahluwalia* [1992] 4 All ER 889 and *R* v *Thornton* [1996] 2 Cr App R 108 recognising the fact that women suffering from 'battered women's syndrome' may react on a slower fuse, the courts still insist that there must be a sudden and temporary loss of self-control. As Alfred has a grudge against Victor, it is likely that his conduct will be regarded as a cold-blooded act of revenge, rather than retaliation in the heat of the moment to provocation.

However, Alfred might have more chance of success with another defence under the Homicide Act 1957 which reduces murder to manslaughter, i.e., diminished responsibility under s. 2:

> Where a person kills or is party to the killing of another, he shall not be convicted of murder if he was suffering from such abnormality of mind (whether arising from a condition of arrested or retarded development of mind or any inherent causes or induced by disease or injury) as substantially impaired his mental responsibility for his acts or omissions in doing or being a party to the killing.

For diminished responsibility, unlike provocation, Alfred would have to prove the existence of the defence on the balance of probabilities. If he killed because he was drunk, this in itself would not amount to an abnormality of the mind. On the other hand, several cases (including *R* v *Tandy* (1987) 87 Cr App R 45) make it clear that an alcoholic's craving for drink, if irresistible, can constitute such an abnormality. In *Tandy*, the accused, an alcoholic, after a heavy drinking session, killed her daughter. Medical evidence called on her behalf stated that when she awoke in the morning she had to have an alcoholic drink, and this triggered a mechanism which meant she carried on drinking. However, the prosecution medical evidence, while accepting that when she had taken one alcoholic drink she had to continue drinking, contended that the accused could on some days resist the first drink so that her urge to drink was *not* irresistible. The jury accepted the prosecution evidence and the defence of diminished responsibility failed, with the Court of Appeal ruling that the trial judge's direction to the jury was correct and dismissing the appeal.

It is therefore unlikely that, on the facts, this defence would succeed; and by raising diminished responsibility, Alfred runs the risk of being found 'not guilty by reason of insanity'. This is because once an accused puts his lack of mental capacity before the court in the form of a plea of automation or diminished responsibility, the trial judge can direct the jury to consider the defence of insanity under the *M'Naghten* Rules 1843, by reason of s. 6 of the Criminal Procedure (Insanity) Act 1954.

Under the rules, Alfred would have the defence of insanity if, at the time of committing the act, he was labouring under such a defect of reason, from disease of the mind, as not to know the nature and quality of the act he was doing or, if he did know it, he did not know that what he was doing was wrong. In the unlikely event of Alfred wanting this defence to succeed, he would have the burden of proving it on the balance of probabilities; whereas if the prosecution were seeking a verdict of 'not guilty by reason of insanity' (from which, incidentally, the accused has a right of appeal under the Criminal Procedure (Insanity) Act 1964), they would have to establish it beyond reasonable doubt.

In *R* v *Quick and Paddison* [1973] QB 910, the Court of Appeal stated that a condition produced by the application of extraneous substances such as alcohol or drugs, could not be regarded as a disease of the mind if it was only a temporary or transient state. However, in *R* v *Inseal* [1992] Crim LR 35, it was recognised that heavy drinking over a long period of time could have had such an effect on the mind as to amount to a disease of the mind within the meaning of the *M'Naghten* Rules. Surprisingly, this is a question of law for the trial judge, and if the judge resolves that a disease of the mind exists then the jury must decide if the other elements of the defence have been made out.

It is submitted that Alfred would not raise the defence of insanity; and if the trial judge threatened to leave it to the jury, he might do the same thing as many accused in this position and change his plea to guilty, in the hope that the judge's conduct might be sufficient for a successful appeal (as was the case in *R* v *Quick*).

Alfred could also claim that as he was so drunk and did not know what he was doing, he has the defence of automatism, defined by Lord Denning in *Bratty* v *Attorney-General for Northern Ireland* [1963] AC 386 as 'an act which is done by the muscles without any control by the mind such as a spasm, a reflex or a convulsion; or an act done by a person who is not conscious of what he is doing such as an act done whilst suffering from concussion or whilst sleep-walking'. However, *R* v *Lipman* [1969] 3 All ER 410 makes it quite clear that this defence cannot succeed if the state has been induced by the accused voluntarily taking alcohol or non-prescribed hallucinatory drugs.

The related defence of intoxication would be Alfred's final argument, as it is accepted that intoxication can be a defence to crimes of specific but not basic intent (*DPP* v *Majewski* [1977] AC 443). Murder is a crime of specific intent and therefore, in theory, on the application of this principle, Alfred could only be guilty of manslaughter, a crime of basic intent. However, it would appear that Alfred would fall foul of the principle established in *Attorney-General for Northern Ireland* v *Gallagher* [1963] AC 349, that if you form the *mens rea* of the offence and then deliberately get drunk to give yourself 'Dutch courage', so that you do not know what you are doing when you perform the *actus reus*, the defence will fail.

In conclusion, one can see that there are serious weaknesses surrounding all the defences that Alfred would consider. His best hope of success would be diminished responsibility, reducing murder to manslaughter. Even on this defence, he could not be confident of success.

Further reading

Gough, S., 'Surviving Without Majewski' [2000] Crim LR 719.

Griew, E., 'The Future of Diminished Responsibility' [1988] Crim LR 75.

McKay, R.D., 'The Abnormality of Mind Factor in Diminished Responsibility' [1999] Crim LR 117.

Virgo, G., 'The Law Commission Consultation Paper on Intoxication' [1993] Crim LR 415.

Ward, T., 'Magistrates, Insanity and the Common Law' [1997] Crim LR 796.

The defences II

Introduction

In this chapter questions have been set on duress by threats, duress of circumstances, necessity, self-defence, and mistake. (Reference has been made elsewhere in the book to entrapment and superior orders, which are not recognised as defences (see *R v Sang* [1979] 2 All ER 1222 and *R v Clegg* [1995] 1 All ER 334).) You therefore need to know and understand many interesting and diverse principles and cases on these defences in order to answer the inevitable exam question(s).

Although duress by threats has existed as a defence for many years, uncertainty regarding the correct principles to be applied has recently been highlighted by the Law Commission's Consultation Paper No. 122, which identified the following five questions as requiring discussion:

(a) Against whom must the threat be directed?

(b) If the actor might resort to police or other official protection, is it relevant that such resort is likely to prove, or that the actor thinks it is likely to prove, ineffective?

(c) Must the actor's belief in the existence or nature or seriousness of the threat, or in the impossibility of avoiding the threatened harm, be reasonably held?

(d) Is the defence to be denied to one who is incapable of mounting the resistance to the threat that would be put up by a person of 'reasonable firmness' or steadfastness?

(e) Should the defence be available on a charge of murder or attempted murder?

It is, of course, this last question which has demonstrated the difference of opinion between the Law Commission and the Law Lords. On two occasions the Law Commission have recommended that duress should be available as a defence to murder, but in both *R v Howe* [1987] 1 All ER 771 and *R v Gotts* [1992] 1 All ER 832, the House of Lords refused to so recognise it. This issue is fully explored in Question 4.

The development of the defence of necessity has always been hampered by the decision in *R v Dudley and Stephens* [1881–5] All ER Rep 61 that it was not available on a murder charge. The effect of this case for many years was that when a defendant chose the lesser of two evils, the defence would not be considered. Thus in *R v Kitson* (1955) 39 Cr App R 66, a defendant who while drunk steered a car in which he was a passenger to a halt, having woken up and noticed that the driver was no longer driving, was refused the defence of necessity and his conviction for driving under the influence of alcohol was upheld. Fortunately, in recent years the courts have recognised the similar defence of duress of circumstances, which will now be accepted in the same way as duress by threats (*R v Pommell* [1995] 2 Cr App R 607).

Many commentators believed that duress of circumstances was the defence of necessity in disguise, but the Law Commission have recognised that there is a difference between the two concepts, by recommending that whereas duress by circumstances should be defined by statute, necessity should be allowed to develop through judicial decision (see cl. 43 of the Draft Code, and the Draft Criminal Law Bill). Necessity was recognised as a defence by the House of Lords in *F v West Berkshire Authority* [1989] 2 All ER 545, where Lord Brandon said that 'it will not only be lawful for doctors, on the ground of necessity to operate on or give other medical treatment to adult patients disabled from giving their consent, it will also be their common law duty to do so'.

Further recognition of the defence of necessity was made by the Court of Appeal in *Re A (Children) (Conjoined Twins: Surgical Separation)* [2000] 4 All ER 961, when they authorised an operation to separate conjoined twins, which was necessary to save the life of the stronger twin, although it would inevitably cause the death of the weaker twin. Brooke LJ stated that the three necessary requirements for the application of the defence of necessity were satisfied; namely

(a) the act was needed to avoid inevitable and irreparable evil;

(b) no more should be done than was reasonably necessary for the purpose to be achieved; and

(c) the evil inflicted was not disproportionate to the evil avoided.

Dudley and Stephens was distinguished, and although *Re A* is a civil case, it is clear that the defence of necessity could be developed to apply to all offences.

An issue that often affects the defences of duress and self-defence is mistake. The defendant has made a mistake, and viewed objectively the conditions for the defence have not been satisfied. However, the defence would be made out if he or she were judged on the facts as he or she believed them to be. Which approach should prevail? Fortunately, the courts when considering self-defence have followed the House of Lords' decision in *DPP v Morgan* [1975] 2 All ER 347 and applied the subjective test (see *R v Williams* (1983) 78 Cr App R 276). On the other hand, with duress an objective approach has been required. Thus in *R v Martin* [1989] 1 All ER 652, CA, Simon Brown J said that 'the jury . . . should be directed to determine, was the accused or may he have been impelled to act as he did because as a result of what he reasonably believed to be the situation'. This principle has recently been doubted by the Court of Appeal in *R v Martin* [2000] Crim LR 615 where the court held that for the defence of duress, the accused should be judged on the facts as he believed them to be, not on what he reasonably believed them to be. Yet a differently constituted Court of Appeal in *R* v *Abdul-Hussain and others* [1999] Crim LR 570 approved the principle that the accused cannot rely on an unreasonable belief of fact in order to found a defence of duress. This once again demonstrates the lack of consistency throughout the criminal law.

The other major controversy relating to self-defence is the House of Lords' decision in *R* v *Clegg* [1995] 1 All ER 334, concluding (against the recommendations of the Law Commission, 14th Report, Cmnd 7844) that a defendant entitled to use force in self-defence but who kills the attacker by using unreasonable force, will be guilty of murder instead of manslaughter. Perhaps the defendant in these circumstances lacks the culpability of a murderer, but as Australia recognised (*Zecevic* v *DPP (Victoria)* (1987) 162 CLR 645), in practical terms the defendant is generally in a better position if the prosecution's case is weak and the jury only have the options of murder or acquittal (as opposed to a third option of manslaughter). The problem of course for Clegg was that he was tried by a 'Diplock court' with no jury; but even if there is a jury, it is often difficult to predict the outcome.

This was aptly demonstrated by *R v Martin* [2002] 2 WLR 1, where a jury rejected the accused's defence of self-defence and convicted him of the murder of a burglar who he had shot while protecting his property. Although his conviction for murder was reduced by the Court of Appeal to manslaughter on the grounds of diminished responsibility, they confirmed that any change in the law to make an accused who used excessive force in self-defence guilty of manslaughter instead of murder would have to be made by Parliament.

Q Question 1

Mary, an unmarried mother aged 17, suffers from anxiety and panic attacks. She is a member of a protest group, 'Free West Country TV from Welsh Influence', and is told by Alan, the leader of the group, that unless she takes part in an attack on the local TV station her young daughter will be killed.

As a result, Mary takes part in the raid. She accosts Sid, a motorist, takes his car and causes him slight injuries. Then she collects Alan and drives him to the TV station where he murders a night-watchman, Bill.

Discuss the criminal liability of Mary.

Commentary

The question concerns the conditions surrounding the defence of duress. There have been many recent developments regarding this defence, and the debate as to whether duress should be a defence to murder is still on going (see Law Com. No. 83 and Working Paper No. 55). So it is always likely to crop up in an examination question.

As always with problem questions concerning defences, the facts disclose certain offences, which can generally be covered quite quickly, although this answer requires a fairly comprehensive discussion on aiding and abetting murder. Most of the marks however, are awarded for coverage of the defence of duress.

Note: you are not required to discuss Alan's criminal responsibility.

- **Consider offences**
  - **assault; aggravated assault**
  - **theft: s. 12 Theft Act 1968**
  - **aiding and abetting murder**
- **Duress — definition**
- **Conditions for the defence of duress**
- **Duress and murder**

:Q: Suggested answer

Mary could be charged with a number of offences in connection with this event. When she accosts Sid, the motorist, she could be guilty of common assault under s. 39 of the Criminal Justice Act 1988. However, as she has caused him slight injuries the charge is more likely to be the more serious offence of assault occasioning actual bodily harm under s. 47 of the Offences Against the Person Act 1861. Actual bodily harm covers slight injuries such as bruising, or even psychiatric injury, which is established by expert evidence (*R* v *Mike Chan-Fook* [1994] 2 All ER 552). The *mens rea* for the s. 47 offence is the same as for assault and battery. There is no requirement for the prosecution to prove that Mary intended or foresaw the risk of actual bodily harm (*R* v *Savage and Parmenter* [1991] 4 All ER 698).

Further, when Mary takes Sid's car she could be committing theft under s. 1 of the Theft Act 1968, i.e., she 'dishonestly appropriates property belonging to another with the intention of permanently depriving the other of it'. However, when a car is taken it is often difficult to establish that the accused had an intention permanently to deprive, as the car is often dumped and traced back to its owner. Therefore, the more usual charge is under s. 12 of the Theft Act 1968, 'taking a conveyance without the owner's authority'. For this offence temporary deprivation is sufficient.

The most serious offence that Mary might face is aiding and abetting murder. An unlawful homicide has occurred and Alan is the principal offender. Mary was present at the scene of the crime, and it is clear that driving the principal offender to the murder scene satisfies the *actus reus* of being an accomplice to murder (*DPP for Northern Ireland* v *Lynch* [1975] AC 653; overruled on another point by *R* v *Howe* [1987] AC 417). Whether Mary would have the necessary *mens rea* for this offence will be discussed after consideration of the defence of duress.

Duress is a long-established general defence available when there have been 'threats of immediate death or serious personal violence so great as to overbear the ordinary powers of human resistance' (*Attorney-General* v *Whelan* [1934] IR 518). However in *R* v *Abdul-Hussain and others* [1999] Crim LR 570 the Court of Appeal in a detailed analysis decided that if there was a threat of imminent death or grievous bodily harm, as opposed to immediate, this would be sufficient for duress to succeed. Threats of lesser harm, such as false imprisonment or damage to property, are not sufficient (*R* v *Howe*) and the threat must be of immediate death or grievous bodily harm. So if an accused has an opportunity to nullify the threat by seeking police protection and fails to do so, the defence will probably fail (*R* v *Hudson and Taylor* [1971] 2 All ER 244).

The fact that the threats were to harm Mary's child, and not Mary herself, will not necessarily cause the defence to fail. The Australian case of *Hurley and Murray* [1967] VR 526, decided that threats to kill the accused's *de facto* wife amounted to duress; and threats against the life or safety of D's family and others to whom he owes a duty almost certainly will, and threats to a stranger probably will, be sufficient evidence of duress.

It is arguable whether there should be an objective requirement that the will of a reasonable person would have been overborne for the defence to succeed, since if the accused was too frightened to resist then, this should be sufficient. However, the relevance of the objective criterion was confirmed in *R* v *Graham* [1982] 1 All ER 801, where the House of Lords approved the following jury direction formulated by Lord Lane CJ:

> was (D) or may he have been, impelled to act as he did because, as a result of what he reasonably believed (E) had said or done, he had good cause to fear that if he did not so act (E) would kill him or . . . cause him serious physical injury? . . . If so, have the prosecution made the jury sure that a sober person of reasonable firmness, sharing the characteristics of (D), would not have responded to whatever he reasonably believed (E) said or did by taking part in the killing?

Mary can therefore argue that the jury should take into account her age and medical condition when considering the objective test set out by Lord Lane CJ, above. This is very similar to the objective condition in the defence of provocation, where many characteristics have been held to be relevant, including disreputable ones such as glue-sniffing (*R* v *Morhall* [1995] 3 All ER 659). Thus, by analogy with *R* v *Camplin* [1978] AC 705, the fact that Mary is aged 17 and arguably less resilient than an adult, and consequently less able to resist the threat, may be taken into account. However, the fact that she suffers from anxiety and panic attacks is less certain of being admitted. In *R* v *Hegarty* [1994] Crim LR 353, expert evidence to show that the accused was 'emotionally unstable or in a grossly elevated state' was held inadmissible; whereas in *R* v *Emery* (1993) 14 Cr App R (S) 394, the Court of Appeal stated *obiter* that it would be correct to allow expert evidence as to the causes and effects of learned helplessness. The traditional approach has always been that, as it is within the jury's experience as to how a reasonable person should react, there is no need to hear from experts.

However, as Beldam LJ pointed out in *R* v *Hurst* [1995] 1 Cr App R 82, 'we find it hard to see how the person of reasonable firmness can be invested with the characteristics of a personality which lacks reasonable firmness'. It is therefore submitted that, unless there is expert psychiatric evidence to the effect that this is a recognised psychiatric illness (in which case, in accordance with *R* v *Bowen* [1996] 4 All ER 837, the jury should consider it), the anxiety and panic should not be taken into account when considering the objective condition.

A further difficulty that Mary faces regarding the availability of duress as a defence is the fact that she is an existing member of the protest group. In *R* v *Sharp* [1987] QB 853, Lord Lane CJ stated:

> Where a person has voluntarily, and with knowledge of its nature, joined a criminal organisa-tion or gang which he knew might bring pressure on him to commit an offence and was an active member when he was put under such pressure, he cannot avail himself of the defence of duress.

Because the protection of society demands that people do not easily capitulate to the threat of violence, this principle has been strictly enforced in a number of cases, and in *R* v *Heath* [2000] Crim LR 109 the Court of Appeal held that the accused, a heroin user, could not rely on duress, because although he was not a member of any criminal organisation, he had voluntarily exposed himself to unlawful violence.

One factor in Mary's favour is that once she raises the issue of duress the prosecu-tion have to disprove the existence of the defence. On the facts, there are weaknesses, as has been pointed out, but it is submitted that the defence of duress would have a good chance of succeeding with a sympathetic jury.

Duress has been recognised as a general defence to all crimes except treason and murder. Thus, if it succeeds, Mary could not be found guilty of the offences under the 1861 or 1968 Acts. However, she could be found guilty of being an accomplice to murder, as *DPP for Northern Ireland* v *Lynch* (where the House of Lords decided that duress was a defence to an accomplice to murder) was overruled in *R* v *Howe*. The House of Lords in *Howe* decided that there is no difference between the culpability of an accomplice and that of a principal offender. They applied the traditional approach that you are never justified in taking someone else's life simply because yours is threatened, so that duress would be no defence.

Although Mary has committed the *actus reus* of aiding and abetting murder, she can be found guilty of this offence only if the prosecution prove that she contemplated death or grievous bodily harm as a possible consequence (*Chan Wing Siu* v *R* [1984] 3 All ER 877) or she realised that the primary party, Alan, might kill with intent to do so, or with intent to cause grievous bodily harm — *R* v *Powell and English* [1997] 4 All ER 545. Mary will argue that violence against the person was clearly outside the scope of the agreement; but if she pleads duress to the other charges, she is in effect admitting that she did contemplate death or grievous bodily harm. She could point out that she contemplated this consequence in respect of another victim, her daughter, in a separate attack; but for accomplice liability there is no requirement for the prosecution to prove that the accomplice knew all the details of the principal offence (*R v Bainbridge* [1959] 3 All ER 200), and the prosecution could argue that by analogy with the doctrine of transferred malice, contemplation of such violence to anyone is sufficient.

If the court accepted the prosecution's contention, Mary could fall back on the weak argument that she did not intend to assist Alan, but simply intended to save her daughter. This submission was surprisingly accepted in *R v Steane* [1947] 1 All ER 813, where the accused's conviction for doing acts likely to assist the enemy with intent to assist the enemy, was quashed on the grounds that his participation in Nazi broadcasts during the war was done with the intention of saving his wife and family from a concentration camp and not with the intention of assisting the enemy.

It is submitted that Mary should not on these facts be found guilty of aiding and abetting murder; and in practice, as was pointed out by Lord Griffith in *R v Howe* [1987] 1 All ER 771, the Crown Prosecution Service would exercise its discretion in the public interest and not prosecute her for this offence, but instead call her as leading prosecution witness in the trial of Alan for murder.

Q Question 2

Anne, who was of a nervous disposition, was approached by John who wanted to kiss her. Anne, who knew that John had a reputation for violence, wrongly believed that he had a knife and wanted to rape her. She concluded that the only way to stop him was to kill him, and so she took out a gun and repeatedly shot him. He died instantly. John was unarmed.

Discuss the criminal liability of Anne.

Commentary

This is a relatively straightforward question as it involves only one major topic, self-defence. However, there are many important principles that need to be stated and analysed, and the question is further complicated by the issue of mistake.

There have been many important cases in this area in recent years and the decisions in *DPP v Morgan* [1976] AC 182, *R v Williams* [1987] 3 All ER 411 and *R v Clegg* [1995] 1 All ER 334 must be applied. Nevertheless, if you have mastered this topic this problem would give you a great opportunity to pick up high marks.

- Murder — definition

- Self-defence — definition

  - reasonable force

- mistake — *Williams* [1987]

- excessive force — *Clegg* [1995], *Martin* [2002]

�💡 Suggested answer

Anne would be charged with murder, i.e., the unlawful killing of a human being within the Queen's peace with malice aforethought. Since the Law Reform (Year and a Day Rule) Act 1996, it is not necessary that the victim's death took place within a year and a day of the accused's act or omission. However, if the death takes place more than three years after the unlawful act or omission, the consent of the Attorney-General must be obtained in order to bring proceedings.

The prosecution will be able to establish that Anne had the necessary malice aforethought, which is intention to kill or cause grievous bodily harm (*R* v *Moloney* [1985] 1 All ER 1025); but Anne will be able to raise the defence of self-defence or s. 3 of the Criminal Law Act 1967, which states: 'A person may use such force as is reasonable in the circumstances in the prevention of crime, or in effecting or assisting in the lawful arrest of offenders or suspected offenders or of persons unlawfully at large.' Thus both defences allow persons to use reasonable force to defend themselves or others from an attack.

Traditionally, for the common law defence to succeed it would have to be established that the accused actually retreated from the offered violence. However, in *R* v *Julien* [1969] 2 All ER 856 it was stated that the accused need only demonstrate that he or she is prepared to temporise and disengage, and perhaps to make some physical withdrawal. In *R* v *Bird* [1985] 2 All ER 513 this *dictum* was disapproved, the Court of Appeal holding that in some circumstances this may be too heavy a responsibility on the accused, and the best way to deal with this issue was simply to leave it to the jury to determine whether the accused had acted reasonably.

The prosecution would argue that far from retreating, Anne was the aggressor. This in itself would not rule out self-defence succeeding, as in *Beckford* v *R* [1987] 3 All ER 425 Lord Griffith in the Privy Council stated (at p. 431): 'Furthermore a person about to be attacked does not have to wait for the assailant to strike the first blow or fire the first shot. Circumstances may justify a pre-emptive strike'. However, no jury is going to accept an accused's assertion that he or she believed he or she was about to be attacked without testing it against all the surrounding circumstances. Further, as the Court of Appeal stated in *R* v *Whyte* [1987] 3 All ER 416, the defence is not open to the accused if there was an obvious and easy way of avoiding the incident instead of using violence.

Although the courts have held that it is only in exceptional circumstances that the jury will conclude that the accused mistakenly believed an attack was impending, it is submitted that Anne on the facts might have held this belief as it is a subjective test. The jury would therefore consider whether the use of force was reasonable. The

Criminal Law Revision Committee's 14th Report, *Offences Against the Person* (Cmnd. 7844 (1980)) stated that the court 'would take into account all the circumstances, including in particular the nature and degree of force used, the seriousness of the evil to be prevented and the possibility of preventing it by other means'. Clearly if Anne was being attacked by a person with a knife who wanted to rape her, she would be entitled to use force to defend herself. However, she still faces two problems: was it reasonable to kill to prevent rape; and is she entitled to be judged on the facts as she believed them to be?

The first question was considered by Lord Diplock in *Attorney-General for Northern Ireland Reference (No. 1 of 1975)* [1976] 2 All ER 937, where the accused had shot and killed the victim mistakenly believing that he was an escaping terrorist. The court held that where the only options open to the accused were either to let the deceased escape or to shoot at him knowing that death or grievous bodily harm was probable, it would be open to the jury to take the view that it would not be unreasonable to assess the kind of harm to be averted by preventing the escape as even greater. Thus the jury would ask themselves whether they were satisfied that no reasonable person with knowledge of such facts as were known to the accused or believed by him to exist, in the circumstances and time available for reflection, would have done as the accused did. Thus if a reasonable person might have done as Anne did, shooting to kill could be reasonable self-defence.

The second problem involves the issue of mistake, which traditionally was dealt with on an objective basis. Until *DPP v Morgan* [1976] AC 182, it was considered that in order to succeed as a defence, mistake had to be honestly made on reasonable grounds. However, in *Morgan* the House of Lords controversially decided that if an accused charged with rape honestly believed that the victim was consenting, he could not be guilty even though he had no reasonable grounds for this belief. There was initial doubt as to whether this decision would apply throughout the criminal law as decisions immediately following *Morgan* sought to limit it to the crime of rape. But following *R v Williams* [1987] 3 All ER 411, it is quite clear that Anne is to be judged on the facts as she believed them to be. In *Williams*, M witnessed a youth snatching a woman's handbag, chased after him, caught him and knocked him to the ground. W, who came on the scene, was told by M that M was arresting the youth and that he was a police officer (which he was not). W asked M to produce his warrant card which he could not do. A struggle then ensued during which W punched M. In quashing W's conviction for assault occasioning actual bodily harm (s. 47 of the Offences Against the Person Act 1861), the Court of Appeal held that W would lack the necessary *mens rea* if, on the facts as he mistakenly believed them to be, he was entitled to use reasonable force either in self-defence or in the prevention of crime.

Thus the reasonableness of Anne's belief is theoretically irrelevant, although in practice the more unreasonable the mistake the more unlikely it is that the jury will accept that Anne made it. However, as Anne is of a nervous disposition and John has a reputation for violence, there is evidence to enable the jury to reach the conclusion that Anne honestly believed she was about to be attacked. Further, it is not for Anne to prove the defence. Once Anne has satisfied the evidential burden, the prosecution have the burden of proof. This is favourable for Anne as the jury has to judge her on the facts as she believed them to be, and as long as no more than reasonable force was used in those mistakenly perceived circumstances there is no criminal liability. As Lord Morris stated in *Palmer* v *R* [1977] 1 All ER 1077 (at p. 1088): 'if a jury thought that in a moment of unexpected anguish a person attacked had only done what he honestly and instinctively thought was necessary, that would be most potent evidence that only reasonable defensive action had been taken'.

If the jury concluded that Anne was entitled to use force in self-defence but had used unreasonable force, it would appear, following the House of Lords' decision in *R* v *Clegg* [1995] 1 All ER 334, that she would be convicted of murder. The Law Commission (cl. 59 of the Draft Code) have accepted the argument that a person in this situation lacks the culpability of a murderer. However, although the House of Lords agreed with this approach, their Lordships felt that it was for Parliament and not them to change the law, and Clegg's conviction for murder (as opposed to manslaughter) was upheld. This principle was recently followed by the Court of Appeal in *R* v *Martin* [2002] 2 WLR 1. Oddly the law in Australia has recently been changed (in *Zecevic* v *DPP (Victoria)* (1987) 61 ALJR 375); whereas for many years an accused who used unreasonable force in self-defence in killing the victim was guilty of manslaughter, now he would be guilty of murder.

Q Question 3

James was driving on a narrow mountain road. He came to a hairpin bend where he saw Norma sitting in her parked car. Because the road was narrow he could not go back or forward, or around the car. He saw a sign by the side of the road 'Danger — serious risk of avalanche' and noticed small rocks coming down the mountainside. Fearing an impending avalanche and believing he had no alternative, he drove into the car in front, knocking it over the mountainside. He realised that this course of action was dangerous, and it resulted in Norma (the occupant of the car) being killed and the car being badly damaged. There was in fact no avalanche.

Discuss the criminal liability (if any) of James.

Commentary

This question involves a detailed consideration of the defence of necessity/duress of circumstances. There are many uncertainties concerning the defence and this question should be attempted only if you are confident of dealing with these issues.

You must, however, guard against the risk of dealing only with this defence, as you must give due consideration to the ingredients of the offences with which James could be charged. Thus a full discussion of the concepts of intention and recklessness must be given in relation to murder, manslaughter, and criminal damage.

Note: road traffic offences have not been considered in detail.

* **Murder — definition**

* **Intention —** *Moloney* **[1985],** *Woollin* **[1998]**

* **Involuntary manslaughter**

* **Criminal damage — s. 1(1) and s. 1(2) Criminal Damage Act 1971**

* **Necessity/duress of circumstances**

  * **conditions —** *Graham* **[1982]**

  * **availability —** *Pommell* **[1995]**

·Ọ· Suggested answer

James could face charges involving unlawful homicide and criminal damage, but he would be able to raise the defence of necessity/duress of circumstances.

The most serious offence to consider is murder, i.e., the unlawful killing of a human being within the Queen's peace with malice aforethought. Following the Law Reform (Year and a Day Rule) Act 1996, the prosecution no longer have to prove that death followed the unlawful act or omission within a year and a day. Malice aforethought, the *mens rea* of murder, is satisfied by the prosecution proving that the accused intended to kill or cause grievous bodily harm (*R* v *Moloney* [1985] 1 All ER 1025). This is a question of fact for the jury; and although the general rule is that as intention is a word in common use, easily understood by the public, there is no need for the trial judge to embark on a detailed explanation of the concept, this might be such a difficult issue on the facts that a detailed direction is required.

Whereas it is clear that foresight of consequence is some evidence of intention, it is not in itself conclusive evidence. Similarly, a judge cannot direct the jury that if James foresaw the consequence and the result was a natural consequence, James intended it. No precise direction has to be given, as it is recognised that the trial judge is in the best position, after hearing all the evidence, to tailor a direction to the needs of the particular jury; but a trial judge would now probably use the direction suggested by the House of Lords in *R* v *Woollin* [1998] 4 All ER 103 that the jury was not entitled to find the necessary intention unless they felt sure that death or serious bodily harm was a virtually certain result of D's actions (barring some unforeseen intervention), and that D had appreciated that fact.

James could argue that although he foresaw this possible consequence, death or grievous bodily harm was not his purpose as his motive was to save himself. Although this argument succeeded in *R v Steane* [1947] 1 All ER 813, this was not a murder case, and it is recognised that motive is not the same as intention. Motive is the reason why one acts, whereas intention is the state of mind present when the act is committed.

If the jury decided that James lacked malice aforethought, he could still be found guilty of involuntary manslaughter, i.e., unlawful killing without malice afore-thought. There has always been uncertainty as to what should be and what is the state of mind required for this offence, but traditionally constructive, reckless and gross negligence bases are considered. Although there is some overlap between them, it is submitted that on the facts the prosecution would argue constructive manslaughter, i.e., the accused intended to do an act which was unlawful and dangerous, and caused the victim's death.

Whether an act is unlawful is a question for the judge and jury. It is not necessary for James to know it is unlawful, although the prosecution must prove that he had the necessary *mens rea* for that offence (*R v Jennings* [1990] Crim LR 588).

Traditionally there has been a reluctance to use a driving offence as the unlawful act in constructive manslaughter. Thus in *Andrews v DPP* [1937] AC 576, the House of Lords held that an accused would not automatically be guilty of manslaughter when he killed the victim as a result of careless driving. Lord Aitkin said: 'There is an obvious difference in the law of manslaughter between doing an unlawful act and doing a lawful act with a degree of carelessness which the legislature makes criminal'. How-ever, in our case James realised the risk, and it is submitted that this would be suf-ficient to constitute the unlawful act, i.e., causing death by dangerous driving under the Road Traffic Act 1991, unless the court decided that because of the defence of necessity it was not unlawful.

The second ingredient of constructive manslaughter is that the act must be danger-ous. Again, the prosecution do not have to prove that James realised the danger (*DPP v Newbury and Jones* [1977] AC 500). It is enough that all sober and reasonable people would recognise the risk of some physical harm albeit not serious harm (*R v Church* [1965] 2 All ER 72). As James recognised the risk, it is submitted that the prosecution would have no difficulty in satisfying this condition.

There are also two offences under the Criminal Damage Act 1971 that must be considered. It appears that James committed criminal damage under s. 1(1) of the Act when he damaged the car. The *mens rea* requirement is satisfied by intention or reck-lessness, and as James realised the risk, there appears to be little doubt about his guilt unless necessity/duress of circumstances could apply. There are two special defences to s. 1(1) under s. 5(2) of the Act, but it is submitted that they could not apply on the facts as s. 5(2)(a) relates to a belief in the owner's consent, and s. 5(2)(b) can apply only if the act was done with a view to protecting property (*R v Baker and Wilkins* [1997] Crim LR 497).

The more serious offence under the Act is s. 1(2), i.e., damaging or destroying property either intending that or being reckless that the life of another would thereby be endangered. Although this is a very serious offence its ingredients are easily satisfied. The prosecution do not have to prove that a life was actually endangered (*R* v *Dudley* [1989] Crim LR 57) and objective recklessness is sufficient *mens rea*. Thus as James has created a serious risk that life would be endangered, he will be found guilty if the jury conclude that either he recognised that some risk of that kind was involved, or he did not consider the possibility of there being any such risk and the risk was in fact obvious (*Metropolitan Police Commissioner* v *Caldwell* [1981] 1 All ER 961).

Where an accused is able to choose between two courses of action, one of which involves breaking the criminal law and the other some evil to himself, and he breaks the criminal law, the defence of necessity is in issue. Whether or not there should be a defence in such circumstances has been hotly debated by the judiciary and various Law Commissions on many occasions, with little agreement as to the correct approach. In 1977, the Law Commission stated (Law Com. No. 83): 'There should be no general defence of necessity and if any such general defence exists at common law it should be abolished'. However, in their most recent report (Consultation Paper No. 122) they suggest that while there should be a statutory defence of duress of circumstances, the defence of necessity should be developed as required by the judiciary.

For many years the development of the defence was hindered by the decision in *R* v *Dudley and Stephens* [1881–5] All ER Rep 61, in which two shipwrecked seaman killed and ate a cabin boy in order to survive. The court ruled that necessity could be no defence to murder and the accused were found guilty, and many commentators believed that the case was authority for the principle that necessity was not available as a general defence to other charges. It was not until the mid-1980s that the argument was renewed in a number of cases involving road traffic offences (*R* v *Willer* (1987) 83 Cr App R 225; *R* v *Conway* [1988] 3 WLR 1338; and *R* v *Martin* [1989] 1 All ER 652) and the related defence of duress of circumstances was developed.

If the defence is raised the prosecution retains the burden of proof, and according to the House of Lords in *R* v *Graham* [1982] 1 All ER 801 the jury should be directed as follows:

(a) Was the defendant, or may he have been, impelled to act as he did because as a result of what he reasonably believed to be the situation he had good cause to fear that if he did not so act death or serious physical injury would result?

(b) If so, have the prosecution made the jury sure that a sober person of reasonable firmness sharing the characteristics of the defendant would not have responded to the situation by acting as the defendant did?

There is a surprising amount of reference to the objective element in this defence, and this could be a problem for James as, although he believed there was an impending avalanche, this was not in fact the case. Although in *R* v *Williams* [1987] 3 All ER 411 it was recognised that for the defence of self-defence, the accused should be judged on the facts as he believed them to be, and an honest but unreasonable mistake would not prevent the defence succeeding, *Graham* was approved by the House of Lords in *R v Howe* [1987] 1 All ER 771. James must therefore argue that the subjective approach should also apply to necessity and duress, but unless the jury believe that he had reasonable grounds to conclude there was an impending avalanche, the defence will fail.

Despite the recent recognition by the Court of Appeal (Civil Division) in *Re A (Children) (Conjoined Twins: Surgical Separation)* [2000] 4 All ER 961, that necessity could be a defence to murder in relation to medical treatment to separate conjoined twins, it is most unlikely that the defence could help James if he possessed the necessary *mens rea* for murder. Although in this case *R v Dudley and Stephens* was distinguished, it has been approved by the House of Lords in *R v Howe*. However, in *R v Pommell* [1995] 2 Cr App R 607 it was recognised that the defence, being closely related to the defence of duress by threats, appears to be general, applying to all crimes except murder, attempted murder and some forms of treason. Thus if the jury accepted that James lacked malice aforethought and he had reasonable grounds to believe that his life was in danger, he would be acquitted of all charges.

Q Question 4

The uncertainties surrounding the defence of duress by threats justify the House of Lords' decisions in *R v Howe* [1987] 1 All ER 771 and *R v Gotts* [1992] 1 All ER 832, rejecting duress as a defence to murder.
Discuss.

Commentary

This is one of the most controversial topics within the criminal law, the Law Commission's views being the opposite of two recent House of Lords' decisions.

The question requires an analysis of the defence of duress with reference to the uncertainties concerning its ingredients. There are many arguments justifying an extension of the defence to murder and these must be covered in detail, together with the counterarguments of the House of Lords found mainly in *R v Howe* [1987] 1 All ER 771.

Because there is so much to cover you must avoid the pitfall of covering the facts of the key cases in detail. They are not important and you simply do not have enough time.

- **Duress — definition**

- **Threats against whom?**

- **Types of threats**

- Subjective and objective tests

- Availability of *Howe* [1987]

- Gang membership — *Sharp* [1987]

- Law Commission No. 122

:Ọ: Suggested answer

The defence of duress is available when the accused has been forced to commit a crime against his will. This is because 'threats of immediate death or serious personal violence so great as to overbear the ordinary power of human resistance should be accepted as a justification for acts which would otherwise be criminal' (*Attorney-General* v *Whelan* [1934] IR 518, *per* Murnaghan J). However, despite the fact that the defence has been recognised for many years, Lord Keith stated in *R* v *Gotts* [1992] 1 All ER 832, that 'the complexities and anomalies involved in the whole matter of the defence of duress seem to me to be such that the issue is much better left to Parliament to deal with in the light of broad considerations of policy'.

Lord Mackay also referred to these uncertainties in the leading House of Lords' decision in *R* v *Howe* [1987] 1 All ER 771, and used this argument in refusing to extend this defence to murder: 'I question whether the law has reached a sufficiently precise definition of that defence to make it right for us sitting in our judicial capacity to introduce it as a defence for an actual killer for the first time in the law of England.' There are many such uncertainties as was recently demonstrated in *R* v *Abdul Hussain and others* [1999] Crim LR 570 where the Court of Appeal decided that if there was a threat of imminent death or grievous bodily harm as opposed to immediate, duress was established. Nevertheless it is submitted that they could have been easily clarified by the House of Lords.

First, must the threat be against the accused, or is it sufficient if it is directed against a third party? In *Hurley* v *Murray* [1967] VR 526, the Supreme Court of Victoria held that threats to kill or seriously injure D's *de facto* wife amounted to duress; and as self-defence is available as a defence if D uses force against an attacker of a third party (*R* v *Duffy* [1966] 1 All ER 62), it is submitted that following the Law Commission's Draft Code such threats against a member of D's family should be sufficient.

Secondly, will threats of harm less than death or grievous bodily harm be sufficient? In *R* v *Graham* [1982] 1 All ER 801 and in *R* v *Conway* [1988] 3 All ER 1025, the Court of Appeal required death or grievous bodily harm to be threatened; and more recently in *R* v *Baker and Wilkins* [1997] Crim LR 497, the Court of Appeal rejected serious psychological injury as being sufficient for duress of circumstances. The defence will not succeed if the threats are to damage property or cause financial loss.

Thirdly, as it was recognised in *R* v *Graham* that the defence fails if the prosecution prove that a person of reasonable firmness sharing the characteristics of the defendant would not have given way to the threats as did the defendant, what characteristics can the jury take into account? Although there is an analogy on this point with the defence of provocation, as both are recognitions of human frailty, with duress the courts have not been prepared to accept that characteristics of an accused are generally relevant for the jury to consider. Thus in *R v Hegarty* [1994] Crim LR 353, the Court of Appeal stated that 'as the test predicted a sober person of reasonable firmness, there was no scope for attributing to that hypothetical person as one of the characteristics of the accused a pre-existing mental condition of being emotionally unstable or in a grossly elevated neurotic state'. As Beldam LJ pointed out in *R v Hurst* [1995] 1 Cr App R 82, 'we find it hard to see how the person of reasonable firmness can be invested with the characteristics of a personality which lacks reasonable firmness'. However, more recently in *R v Bowen* [1996] 4 All ER 837, the Court of Appeal stated that if the accused was suffering from a recognised psychiatric illness, this characteristic could be taken into account.

Perhaps it is contrary to principle to require the fear to be a reasonable one. Because of the difficulties of applying the test (for example, in *R v Emery* [1993] 14 Cr App R(S) 394, where the test was a woman of reasonable firmness suffering from a condition of dependent helplessness), it is submitted that a purely subjective test is justified.

Traditionally, duress has never been recognised as a defence to murder, *Blackstone's Commentaries of the Law of England* (1857) stating that a man under duress 'ought rather to die himself than escape by the murder of an innocent'. However, in *DPP for Northern Ireland* v *Lynch* [1975] AC 653, the House of Lords made an inroad into this blanket rule by holding that duress was available as a defence to an accused charged as an accomplice to murder, and shortly afterwards Lords Wilberforce and Edmund-Davies, in a much acclaimed minority judgment in the Privy Council decision in *Abbott* v *R* [1976] 3 All ER 140, concluded that the decision in *Lynch* should be extended to cover a principal offender. The Law Commission (Law Com. No. 83) also recommended this approach, but this trend was abruptly halted by the House of Lords in *R v Howe* where their Lordships not only confirmed the traditional approach, but also, using the Lord Chancellor's Practice Note [1966] 3 All ER 77, overruled their earlier decision in *Lynch*.

A number of reasons were given for this decision, although there are equally strong reasons for recognising the defence. First, Lord Hailsham pointed out that following superior orders is not a defence to murder (Article 8 of the chapter of the International Military Treaty series no. 26 of 1946), and *R v Dudley and Stephens* [1881–5] All ER Rep 61 also ruled out the similar defence of necessity. It is submitted that both necessity and duress should be a defence to murder and that the analogy with superior orders is inappropriate.

Secondly, the principle underlying the denial of both defences (duress and necessity) is the special sanctity that the law attaches to human life and which denies a person the right to take an innocent life even at the price of his own or another's life.

However, in more recent years the Suicide Act 1961 and the House of Lords' decision in *Airedale NHS Trust* v *Bland* [1993] 1 All ER 821 have recognised that life does not have to be preserved at all costs, and it is not beneficial simply to adopt a blanket rule without good reason. Thus an accused should have the defence of duress considered if he or she was forced to take one life but in doing so save more.

Thirdly, Lord Hailsham stated in *R* v *Howe* (at p. 579): 'I do not at all accept in relation to the defence of murder it is either good morals, good policy or good law . . . that the ordinary man of reasonable fortitude is not to be supposed to be capable of heroism if he is asked to take an innocent life rather than sacrifice his own'. However, as the Law Commission have recognised (Law Com. No. 122), it is not fair to expect the standard of the reasonable person to be one of heroism and it should be for the jury to decide if the threat was one which an accused could reasonably be expected to resist.

The fourth argument, one often raised by traditionalists, was put by Lord Griffith. Now is not an appropriate time for change. The law must stand firm against a rising tide of violence and terrorism, and terrorists should not be able to rely on a defence of duress, which would be easy to raise but difficult to resist. However, the defence is not available to a member of a criminal or terrorist organisation (*R* v *Sharp* [1987] 3 All ER 103), and the question of whether the accused was a terrorist or an innocent tool is a proper question for the jury.

Two other weak arguments were also advanced for maintaining the *status quo*: first, Parliament has made no attempt to change the law despite the recommendations of the Law Commission, and therefore Parliament must be taken to agree with the present principle; and, secondly, any injustice that might result from application of the present law would be alleviated by the exercise of executive discretion not to prosecute or to release on licence a person serving a life sentence. It is submitted that reliance on executive discretion is not an adequate response in principle or practice; and as no Bill has been introduced proposing that duress be available as a defence to murder, Parliament has never had the opportunity of expressing an opinion on the matter.

Although in *R* v *Kingston* [1994] 3 All ER 353, Lord Mustill in the House of Lords stated that 'the Court should when faced with a new problem acknowledge the justice of the case and boldly create a new common law defence', their Lordships again refused so to do in *R* v *Gotts* where duress was held to be not available as a defence to attempted murder. This approach continues to fly in the face of the Law Commission's recommendation (No. 122), the Commission believing that all uncertainties surrounding the defence could be removed by a clear statutory definition.

Shifting the burden of proof to the accused is another safeguard against unmeritorious pleas succeeding; but leaving the law as it is, it is submitted, is the least satisfactory solution. This has been recognised by the Law Commission, who state: 'If however it were decided that duress should not be available as a complete defence, we would regard its statutory recognition as a partial defence reducing murder to man-slaughter as the second best option.' Unsurprisingly, this view had already been rejected by the House of Lords in *Howe*.

Further reading

Douglas, G.R., '*Dudley and Stephens* — Revisited and Updated', Justice of the Peace (Vol. 166) 40.

Douglas, G.R., 'Self-defence in the Light of *R* v *Martin*', Justice of the Peace (Vol. 166) 368.

Elliott, D.W., 'Necessity, Duress and Self-defence' [1989] Crim LR 611.

Rogers, J., 'Necessity, Private Defence and the Killing of Mary' [2001] Crim LR 515.

Smith, K.J.M., 'Duress and Steadfastness' [1999] Crim LR 363.

Inchoate offences and accessories

Introduction

How far from the actual substantive offence should the criminal law go to protect the public from people disposed to commit crime? This is essentially the key question in deciding on the appropriate basis for the criminal responsibility required for commission of the inchoate offences of incitement, conspiracy and attempt. It is submitted that it is virtually impossible to formulate principles in this area that will satisfy the correct balance between nipping crime in the bud and simply punishing criminal thoughts. Thus in *R v Cromack* [1978] Crim LR 217, it was held that an accused who wrote to his friend in prison asking him to instruct his wife to commit perjury at the accused's trial could be guilty of an attempt to incite perjury (even though the prisoner took no further action). In *R v Geddes* [1996] Crim LR 894, however, the Court of Appeal quashed the conviction for attempted false imprisonment, where an accused was found lurking near a boys' school with a rucksack containing a kitchen knife, rope and masking tape. The court held that the entire evidence was not sufficient in law to support a finding that the accused had done an act which was more than merely preparatory to wrongfully imprisoning a person unknown. Once again we are faced with the lack of a uniform approach and a common starting point. Incitement is a common law offence, whereas conspiracy is largely statutory, governed by the Criminal Law Act 1977, although there remain the common law conspiracies to defraud, corrupt public morals and outrage public decency. Attempt is governed by the Criminal Attempts Act 1981, which rules out the defence of impossibility on charges of attempt and statutory conspiracy, but not on charges of common law conspiracy and incitement (see *R v Fitzmaurice* [1983] 1 All ER 189).

Similarly when we look at accomplice responsibility, although there is a foundation — an Act which applies to an accomplice's conduct before or at the time of the substantive offence — it is an Act dating back to 1861 (the Accessories and Abettors Act 1861); and the differences between counselling, procuring, aiding and abetting were only revealed by the Court of Appeal's decision in *Attorney-General's Reference (No. 1 of 1975)* [1975] 2 All ER 684.

To some extent problems have been hidden by the prosecution's policy of charging all accomplices as principal offenders; but more recently the uncertainty in the law has been recognised by the points of law of public importance certified by the Court of Appeal in many decisions. The need for reform has been recognised by the Law Commission (Law Com. No. 131 — 'Assisting and Encouraging Crime'), but it appears unlikely that these recommendations will be implemented.

Rather than spending hours searching for coherent principles, your time might be better employed seeking answers to the following questions:

(a) What is the *mens rea* of incitement?

(b) Is recklessness sufficient *mens rea* for conspiracy?

(c) Is impossibility a defence to a statutory conspiracy?

(d) Is intention to cause grievous bodily harm sufficient *mens rea* for attempted murder?

(e) Who decides, on a charge of attempt, if the accused has done more than a merely preparatory act?

(f) What is the *mens rea* required for an accomplice to murder?

(g) Can an accomplice be guilty of a more serious offence than the principal offender?

(h) Is the defence of withdrawal available to —

   (i) an accomplice,

   (ii) a conspirator?

The questions in this chapter cover all the problem areas of these topics, and are quite demanding. If you read the answers thoroughly you will find the answers to the questions posed above. Remember, it is very easy for an examination question which is based on another topic (e.g., unlawful homicide) to include reference to accomplices or related inchoate offences, so they are subjects which you must know well at exam time.

Q Question 1

Amy, Betty, Claire, and Debbie plan to break into X's warehouse in order to steal. Amy, Betty, and Claire know that there will be a nightwatchman on the premises, but Debbie does not know this fact. Amy gives Betty a loaded revolver, telling her not to hesitate to use it if the occasion should so require. When they set off to X's warehouse, Debbie knows that Betty has a revolver in her possession but Claire does not. The four are interrupted by the nightwatchman, Victor. As Betty is in the act of firing the revolver, Amy, recognising Victor as her cousin, knocks Betty's hand to one side crying out 'Don't shoot'. Amy's act causes the bullet to miss Victor, but it strikes and kills a police officer who is entering the room.

Discuss the criminal liability of the parties.

Commentary

There are many points to cover in the answer, and it is therefore important to plan and to concentrate your efforts on the most important topic, accomplice liability. It is best to dispose of the two minor offences, conspiracy and burglary, quickly and then to cover the most serious offence, murder. In a typical exam paper, in addition to this question you could expect a full question on murder, so this answer does not require a detailed analysis of all aspects of that crime. Most of your answer will be taken up dealing with the intricacies of accomplice liability. You must, after stating the principles clearly, emphasise the difference between Claire and Debbie, as Debbie's knowledge of the gun puts her in a much worse position. Full consideration of the possible defence of withdrawal is also required when considering Amy's responsibility.

- Conspiracy — s. 1 Criminal Law Act 1977

- Burglary — s. 9 Theft Act 1968

- Murder/manslaughter

- Accomplice liability

    - *mens rea* — *Powell and Daniels* [1997]

    - withdrawal — *Becerra* [1975]

    - scope of agreement

:Q: Suggested answer

Even before the four parties enter the warehouse, they would be guilty of the crime of conspiracy to burgle under s. 1 of the Criminal Law Act 1977, as they have agreed to pursue a course of conduct which would necessarily involve a criminal offence. Similarly, as soon as they enter the warehouse, they will be guilty of burglary under s. 9 of the Theft Act 1968, as they are entering a building or part of a building as trespassers with intent to steal. As Betty is in possession of a gun when she enters the building, she could be charged with aggravated burglary under s. 10 of the Theft Act 1968; and if Amy and Debbie are deemed to be in joint possession of it, they too will be guilty of this offence.

Betty would be charged with murder, the unlawful killing of a human being within the Queen's peace with malice aforethought. Since the Law Reform (Year and a Day Rule) Act 1996, death does not have to follow the unlawful act within a year and a day. Malice aforethought, the *mens rea* of murder, is satisfied by the prosecution proving that Betty intended to kill or intended to cause grievous bodily harm (*R v Moloney* [1985] 1 All ER 1025). Betty may argue that she did not intend to harm the victim, but the court will apply the doctrine of transferred malice. Thus if the accused has the necessary *mens rea* of the offence, but the actual victim is different from the intended victim, the *mens rea* will be transferred and the accused will be guilty (*R v Mitchell* [1983] 2 All ER 427).

Betty may be able to argue that she was simply firing a warning shot and that it was Amy's act of hitting her arm which caused her aim to alter resulting in the victim's death. In the unlikely event of this argument being accepted, Betty would still be guilty of involuntary manslaughter on the constructive basis. The prosecution could prove that she intended to do an act which was unlawful and dangerous (*R v Newbury and Jones* [1976] 2 All ER 365): simply drawing and pointing a gun at someone would be unlawful, i.e., assault; and as the test for dangerous is objective ('the unlawful act must be such as all sober and reasonable people would inevitably recognise must subject the other person to at least the risk of some harm resulting therefrom, albeit not serious harm' *per* Edmund Davies J in *R v Church* [1965] 2 All ER 72), Betty would be guilty.

The other three participants would face charges of abetting murder. While it is clear that the prosecution must prove that the accomplice intended to assist, there has always been controversy about what other mental awareness has to be established to satisfy the *mens rea* requirement. In *DPP for Northern Ireland v Maxwell* [1978] 3 All ER 1140, the House of Lords stated that it was enough for the accomplice to contemplate the type of crime committed; and in respect of murder, the Privy Council in *Chan Wing Siu v R* [1984] 3 All ER 877 confirmed that contemplation of death or grievous bodily harm as a possible consequence is sufficient. As Sir Robin Cooke stated in *Chan Wing Siu*, the principle of liability 'turns on contemplation. It meets the case of a crime foreseen as a possible incident of the common unlawful enterprise. The criminal culpability lies in participating in the venture with that foresight'. This principle has been applied in many subsequent cases, in particular *R v Hyde* (1991) 92 Cr App R 131 and *Hui Chi Ming v R* [1991] 3 All ER 897, although the House of Lords recently recognised the severity of a principle which allows an accomplice to be guilty of murder on less *mens rea* than the malice aforethought required by a principal offender (in *R v Powell and Daniels* [1997] 4 All ER 545). Nevertheless, the court did apply *Chan Wing Siu* to uphold the accused's conviction, and rejected the argument that the House of Lords' decisions in *R v Moloney* and *R v Hancock and Shankland* [1986] AC 455, applied to accessories to murder. The House of Lords recognised that the criminal law exists to control crime and a prime function of that system must be to deal justly but effectively with those who join with others in criminal enterprises.

Thus the House applied *Chan Wing Siu* to uphold A's conviction stating that, to found a conviction for murder, it was sufficient for a secondary party to have realised, in the course of a joint enterprise, that the primary party might kill with intent to do so or with intent to cause grievous bodily harm. This principle was applied in *R* v *Uddin* [1998] 2 All ER 744 where the Court of Appeal took the opportunity to explain in detail the principles to be applied for accessory liability.

Initially, when Amy gives Betty the gun with the instructions 'not to hesitate to use it' she would be committing the crime of incitement to murder, mere encouragement to commit the crime with the appropriate contemplation being sufficient. However, as Betty has committed the offence this makes Amy an abettor. From the facts she cannot argue that the unlawful homicide was not contemplated or outside the scope of the agreement, but she could contend that she had effectively withdrawn before the murder took place. The key case on withdrawal is *R* v *Becerra and Cooper* (1975) 62 Cr App R 212, where before the principal offender in the course of a burglary killed the victim, the accomplice had said 'Come on let's go' and had left the building. The Court of Appeal, in upholding his conviction for murder, held that something vastly more substantial and effective was required to constitute a valid withdrawal, such as shouting a warning or physical intervention. Amy would argue that in shouting 'Don't shoot' and knocking Betty's hand, she had done all that she reasonably could to prevent the crime, but it is likely that the jury will conclude that her actions were too little too late. The prosecution could also argue that withdrawal should not be available as a defence as Amy does not have a good motive. However, in keeping with the general principle that motive is irrelevant in criminal law, this is not a requirement for the defence to succeed.

If Betty was found guilty of manslaughter, Amy might contend that she could not be found guilty of the more serious offence of abetting murder. This point arose in the Privy Council case of *Hui Chi Ming* v *R* [1991] 3 All ER 897, where the court upheld the conviction of the accused for murder even though the principal offenders had in an earlier trial been found guilty of manslaughter only. The principle is that if the *actus reus* has been committed, the court will look at the *mens rea* of the individual participants in order to ascertain their criminal responsibility.

Claire could argue that she cannot be guilty of abetting murder as she did not know that Betty had a gun, and therefore Betty's actions were outside the scope of the agreement. In *Davies* v *DPP* [1954] AC 378, the court stated that if there was a fight where the participants agreed to use fists only, but the principal offender stabbed the victim to death with a knife, the other gang members would not be guilty of abetting murder. Although they had agreed to use violence and may have contemplated death or serious injury, the court recognised that there was a difference between an agreement to use fists and an agreement to use weapons. Thus, if death was caused by the first blow, this would be an unforeseen consequence but within the scope of the agreement and the gang members would have been guilty of abetting murder. The scope of the agreement is all important, and if the prosecution cannot prove that Claire knew Betty had a gun, she cannot be guilty of abetting murder.

However, the prosecution could still contend that as Claire knew that there was a nightwatchman, she would have contemplated the risk of some physical violence; and that as there was an unlawful and dangerous act causing death, she should be found guilty of the lesser offence of abetting manslaughter. This is a point on which the authorities appear equally divided. In *R v Dunbar* [1995] 1 All ER 781, the Court of Appeal quashed an abettor's conviction for manslaughter on the basis that even though she contemplated some physical harm, she was exonerated of all criminal responsibility regarding the victim's death when the principal offender deliberately killed the victim. This decision followed a principle established in *R v Anderson and Morris* [1966] 2 All ER 644. However, in *R v Stewart and Schofield* [1995] 1 Cr App R 441 (following *R v Reid* (1975) 62 Cr App R 109) the Court of Appeal stated that in such circumstances the abettor could be guilty of abetting manslaughter, although this was certified as a point of law of public importance for the House of Lords to resolve. Unfortunately this point was not considered by the House in *Powell* and *English*, but more recently the Court of Appeal in *R v Gilmour* [2000] 2 Cr App R 407, upheld the conviction of an accessory to manslaughter although the principal offender was guilty of murder.

Because Debbie knows that Betty has a gun she is in a much worse position than Claire, as it appears that Betty is acting within the scope of their agreement. Debbie would be forced to use the weak argument that although she knew that they had a gun, she did not contemplate that they would actually use it. In *R v Baldessare* (1930) 22 Cr App R 70, the court held that an accused who agreed to take and drive away a car was guilty of abetting manslaughter when the principal offender drove so negligently as to cause a pedestrian's death, as although this consequence was unforeseen it arose when the principal offender was acting within the scope of the agreement. It is submitted that Debbie will be found guilty of abetting murder.

Q Question 2

Alf planned to beat up Steve, and Barry, Chris and Desmond told Alf that they would help him. On the appointed day, Barry failed to turn up, but Chris and Desmond held Steve while Alf hit him causing some minor bruising. Chris then said 'I can't do this anymore' and walked away to the other side of the room. Shortly after, Desmond said 'Come on let's go' and he left with Chris. Alf then hit Steve again, breaking his jaw.

Discuss the criminal responsibility of the parties.

Commentary

The criminal responsibility of accessories appears to be an area of the law which is in a state of transition. The Court of Appeal has recently certified many points of law of public importance on this topic which have remained unanswered, and the Law Commission have produced a consultation paper (No. 131) with proposals to change the nature of accomplice liability.

All this does not lead to certainty, and therefore this is a good area for an examination question. A good answer will deal with the *mens rea* required for an accomplice, but will then concentrate on the question of withdrawal, another topic where there has been a spate of cases. In addition you must deal with the criminal responsibility of Alf for offences under the Offences Against the Person Act 1861.

- **Conspiracy to assault**

- **s. 47 Offences Against the Person Act 1861**

- **s. 18 Offences Against the Person Act 1861**

- **Accomplice liability — *Powell* [1997]**

  - ***Stewart and Schofield* [1995]**

  - **Withdrawal — *Rook* [1993], *Baker* [1994]**

:Q: Suggested answer

Although there is a possibility that all four participants could be charged with conspiracy to assault under s. 1 of the Criminal Law Act 1977, as the court might consider that there is an agreement between them, it is more likely that Alf will be charged as a principal offender and the other three as accessories.

Alf, when he deliberately hits Steve causing him some bruising, would be guilty of assault occasioning actual bodily harm under s. 47 of the Offences Against the Person Act 1861. This offence is very easily established by the prosecution who only need to prove that an accused had the *mens rea* for common assault in order to satisfy the *mens rea* requirement under s. 47 (*R v Savage and Parmenter* [1991] 4 All ER 698). However, as Alf hit Steve again breaking his jaw, he would be charged under s. 18 of the 1861 Act with wounding or causing grievous bodily harm with intent. Whether this constitutes grievous bodily harm is a question of fact for the jury, but in *R v Wood* (1830) 1 Mood CC 278, a broken collar bone was held to constitute grievous bodily harm. The prosecution also must establish that Alf intended to cause grievous bodily harm, but it appears from the facts of the question that either this was Alf's purpose, or he knew that grievous bodily harm was a virtual certainty, and this would be sufficient. The House of Lords stated in *R v Moloney* [1985] 1 All ER 1025 that as 'intention' is a word in common use, the trial judge should simply leave it to the jury without giving them an involved direction unless the issue on the facts of the case is complicated. It is submitted that the jury would not require guidance on these facts and would be most likely to convict Alf under s. 18.

In the unlikely event of the prosecution not being able to establish intention, Alf would be convicted under s. 20 of the 1861 Act (wounding or inflicting grievous bodily harm maliciously); 'maliciously', the *mens rea*, can be satisfied by the prosecution proving that Alf intended or foresaw the risk of some physical harm (not necessarily grievous bodily harm: *R v Savage and Parmenter*).

Barry, Chris and Desmond could therefore be charged with abetting an offence under s. 18 of the Offences Against the Person Act 1861. The Accessories and Abettors Act 1861, s. 8 provides: 'Whosoever shall aid, abet, counsel or procure the commission of any indictable offence shall be liable to be tried, indicted, and punished as a principal offender.' The prosecution must also prove that the accused intended to assist with knowledge of the type of crime intended (*DPP for Northern Ireland v Maxwell* [1978] 3 All ER 1140). However, difficulties arise when the crime committed by the principal offender is more serious than initially envisaged by the abettors. Thus if the principal offender deliberately exceeds the scope of the agreement, the accomplices may be exonerated (*Davies v DPP* [1954] 1 All ER 507). Nevertheless, if the court concludes that they were all acting with a common purpose and as part of a joint enterprise, the accomplices may be guilty if they contemplated the consequence (provided it was more than a fleeting thought) or gave tacit authorisation to the principal offender (*Chan Win Siu v R* [1984] 3 All ER 877). Thus accomplices would be guilty of murder if they realised that the primary party might kill with intent to do so or with intent to cause grievous bodily harm (*R v Powell and English* [1997] 4 All ER 545).

The difficulties are illustrated by the case of *R v Wan and Chan* [1995] Crim LR 295. D1 and D2 were alleged to have arranged for V to be beaten up. They were convicted of abetting an offence under s. 20, but were acquitted of abetting an offence under s. 18; and their appeal against conviction for abetting the s. 20 offence succeeded on the basis that the jury (in acquitting them of abetting the s. 18 offence) must have concluded that the principal offender exceeded the scope of the agreement and therefore D1 and D2 should be exonerated in respect of the charge of abetting an offence under s. 20. The Court of Appeal did, however, certify the following point of law of public importance: 'If two people have agreed to assault another, and in the course of the assault one of them causes grievous bodily harm and intends to do so, can the other be guilty of section 20 of the Offences Against the Person Act 1861 even if he was not present and did not intend to cause grievous bodily harm or contemplate that it might be used?'

However, in *R v Stewart and Schofield* [1995] 3 All ER 159, the Court of Appeal held that if the participant in a joint enterprise contemplates that the victim will suffer bodily harm, but the principal offender with malice aforethought kills the victim, the participant can still be convicted of manslaughter. This was also the outcome in the recent Court of Appeal decision in *R v Gilmour* [2000] 2 Cr App R 407, where the agreement was to post an incendiary bomb through a letter box. The principal offender was guilty of murder, but as the accessory foresaw only minor physical harm, he was guilty of aiding and abetting manslaughter.

It is submitted that, on the facts, the jury would most likely decide that Barry, Chris and Desmond did contemplate some physical harm, and this would appear sufficient for a conviction of at least abetting a s. 20 offence. However, the accused may be able to use the defence of withdrawal. Barry would appear to have the strongest argument because he was not present when the crime was committed. Nevertheless, his earlier involvement is enough to constitute counselling (*Attorney-General's Reference (No. 1 of 1975)* [1975] QB 773); and in *R v Rook* [1993] 2 All ER 955, the Court of Appeal on similar facts stated that 'his absence on the day could not possibly amount to an unequivocal communication of his withdrawal'. As Rook knew that there was a real risk that the murder would take place, his conviction was upheld.

In order to constitute a valid withdrawal there must be evidence that the accomplice has taken all reasonable steps unequivocally to abandon the enterprise. This will depend on the accomplice's involvement. Thus in *R v Whitefield* (1984) 79 Cr App R 36, where the accomplice had given the principal offender information that would enable him to commit burglary, the Court of Appeal recognised that a valid withdrawal could be effected by the accomplice simply telling the principal offender that he was no longer prepared to assist. On the other hand, in *R v Becerra* (1975) 62 Cr App R 212, the leading case on withdrawal, the Court of Appeal stated that something vastly more substantial and effective was required than simply saying 'Come on let's go' and leaving, where the accomplice had given the principal offender a weapon, which he later used to kill a nightwatchman who interrupted their burglary. The court stated that to be an effective withdrawal, the accomplice should have tried to recover the weapon, shouted a warning to the victim, or physically intervened to prevent the attack. Similarly in *R v Baker* [1994] Crim LR 444, the Court of Appeal, in upholding a murder conviction, stated that an accomplice who had moved a few feet away from the spot where the victim was killed, uttering words 'I'm not doing it', had given far from unequivocal notice that he was wholly disassociating himself from the entire enterprise and had not effected a valid withdrawal.

Applying these principles, it appears that there is no difference between the responsibility of the three accomplices. Although they can argue that they were not actually present when the accused committed the s. 18 offence, it is submitted that they would all be found guilty of abetting this offence.

Q Question 3

Alvin contacted Bernard suggesting that they kill Zac because he had refused to pay them a debt. After hearing Alvin's proposals, Bernard secretly decided that he would not do anything to help Alvin, but he told Alvin that he would do anything he could to assist. Their conversation was overheard by Ceri and Desmond, who both agreed to help. Ceri obtained a loaded revolver and gave it to Alvin, and Desmond agreed to drive them in his car to Zac's house.

On the appointed day, Bernard failed to arrive; and after Desmond had taken them to their destination he telephoned the police in time to stop Alvin shooting at Zac.

Discuss the criminal responsibility of the parties.

Commentary

This is a relatively straightforward question concerning the inchoate offences and accomplice liability. The two areas often overlap, but in practice if the substantive offence was attempted or committed the Crown Prosecution Service would usually charge the participants as accomplices. If not, they will be charged with the inchoate offences.

This question requires you to consider incitement, conspiracy and attempt with regard to Alvin, although, as there is little factual information surrounding the attempted shooting, you cannot deal with this topic in great detail. The others could be guilty of conspiracy, and for Bernard you must consider the troublesome House of Lords' decision in R v Anderson [1985] 2 All ER 961 as interpreted by the Court of Appeal in R v Siracusa (1989) 90 Cr App R 340.

Lastly, the position of the parties' liability for abetting must be considered, in particular whether there is an offence of aiding and abetting an attempt.

- **Incitement**

- **Conspiracy to murder**

    - *Anderson* [1985], *Siracusa* [1989]

- **Attempted murder**

    - **s. 1(1) Criminal Attempts Act 1981**

- **Accomplice liability**

ː<u>Q</u>ː **Suggested answer**

There are a number of inchoate offences with which Alvin could be charged. His initial action in contacting Bernard suggesting that they kill Zac could amount to the crime of incitement to murder. An inciter is one who reaches and seeks to influence the mind of another by suggestion, request, proposal, argument, persuasion or inducement. Thus in *Invicta Plastics Ltd* v *Clare* [1976] Crim LR 131, a company who simply advertised the sale of a device 'Radatec' which could be used to detect police radar traps, was found guilty of incitement of an offence under s. 1(1) of the Wireless Telegraphy Act 1949. The prosecution must prove that Alvin knew of or was wilfully blind to the circumstances of the act incited which constitutes the crime. This includes knowing that the person incited will act with the appropriate *mens rea* of the crime in question. It is submitted that Alvin's conduct clearly satisfies the *actus reus* of incitement, and the prosecution should be able to establish *mens rea*. The old common law offence of inciting a conspiracy was abolished by s. 5(7) of the Criminal Law Act 1977, but incitement to incite is still an offence (*R* v *Sirat* (1986) 83 Cr App R 41).

All four participants could be charged with conspiracy to murder under s. 1 of the Criminal Law Act 1977. Formerly conspiracy was a common law offence, but since 1977 the only remaining common law conspiracies are conspiracy to defraud, conspiracy to corrupt public morals, and conspiracy to outrage public decency (see *Shaw* v *DPP* [1961] 2 All ER 446). In order to establish a statutory conspiracy, it must be shown that two or more persons agreed that a course of conduct should be pursued which, if the agreement were to be carried out in accordance with their intentions, either:

(a) would necessarily amount to or involve the commission of any offence or offences by one or more of the parties to the agreement; or

(b) would do so but for the existence of facts which render the commission of the offence or any of the offences impossible.

The prosecution must prove that an agreement existed between the parties, and if they are still in the course of negotiations this would not be sufficient. It is submitted that there is an agreement on the facts and, as they intend that death will result, the parties could be guilty of conspiracy to murder. However, Bernard will argue that as he had no intention to assist, and did nothing to assist, he cannot be guilty. The key case on this point is the House of Lords' decision in *R* v *Anderson* [1985] 2 All ER 961. In this case the accused was convicted of conspiring with a number of people to help one of them escape from jail. He had agreed to supply wire to cut the prison bars, but said he never intended the plan to be put into effect and believed that it could not possibly succeed. However, his conviction was upheld as he had agreed that the criminal course of conduct should be pursued, and it was not necessary to prove that he intended that the offence be committed. In this case Lord Bridge also stated (at p. 965) that the *mens rea* of conspiracy is established 'if and only if it is shown that the accused when he entered into the agreement, intended to play some part in the agreed course of conduct in furtherance of the criminal purpose which the agreed course of conduct was intended to achieve'. On this basis Bernard would have a defence, but unfortunately for him Lord Bridge's *dictum* was clarified by the Court of Appeal decision in *R* v *Siracusa* (1989) 90 Cr App R 340, where O'Connor J stated that 'participation in a conspiracy is infinitely variable: it can be active or passive. There is no need for the prosecution to prove an intention on each accused's part in the carrying out of the agreement'. It is submitted that Bernard would therefore be found guilty of conspiracy to murder.

Desmond may also be able to argue that he lacked the *mens rea* for conspiracy to murder, as his informing the police demonstrated that he had an intention to frustrate the intention of the conspiracy. In *R v McPhillips* [1990] 6 BNIL, Lord Lowry CJ in the Court of Appeal of Northern Ireland, held that an accused who had joined in a conspiracy to plant a bomb, timed to explode on the roof of a hall of a disco, was not a party to a conspiracy to murder because he intended to give a warning in time for the hall to be cleared. However, in *Yip Chiu Cheung* v *R* [1994] 2 All ER 924, the Privy Council held that an undercover police officer posing as a drug dealer would have the necessary *mens rea* for conspiracy, when he deliberately carried drugs to entrap other drug dealers. Neither his good motive nor the instructions of his superiors would have been a valid defence.

As withdrawal is recognised as a defence for an accomplice, it is submitted that a conspirator should have a similar defence, if only to provide an incentive for a conspirator to make efforts to stop the conspiracy succeeding. It is submitted that Desmond should not be found guilty of conspiracy. Perhaps the Crown Prosecution Service would decide it is not in the public interest to prosecute Desmond, and instead make him chief prosecution witness!

Alvin may also be guilty of attempted murder. Clearly he has the necessary *mens rea*, an intention to kill (*R* v *Whybrow* (1951) 35 Cr App R 141), but has he committed the *actus reus* of attempt? The test the prosecution must satisfy under s. 1(1) of the Criminal Attempts Act 1981 is that the accused has done an act which is more than merely preparatory to the offence. This is a question of fact for the jury after the trial judge has decided that there is sufficient evidence to be left to them to support such a finding. Thus in *R* v *Jones* (1990) 91 Cr App R 356, the Court of Appeal upheld the jury's decision that the accused had done more than a merely preparatory act for attempted murder in pointing a sawn-off shotgun at the victim, even though he had still to remove the safety catch. Whether Alvin would be guilty of attempted murder would therefore purely depend on what precise point the plan had reached before he was stopped.

Bernard, Ceri and Desmond may also face charges under the Accessories and Abettors Act 1861 of counselling, procuring, aiding and abetting. It is often difficult to identify precisely the specific involvement (see *R* v *Richards* [1974] 3 All ER 1088), but counselling and procuring are acts done before the principal offence whereas aiding and abetting take place at the time of its occurrence. Clearly, as they intended to assist and contemplated the type of crime (*Chan Wing Siu* v *R* [1984] 3 All ER 877) they appear to have the necessary *mens rea*. Desmond would argue that he had validly withdrawn by contacting the police in time for them to stop the murder (*R* v *Becerra* (1975) 62 Cr App R 212), and Bernard would contend that his failure to arrive constituted a withdrawal. It is submitted that whereas Desmond's argument would succeed, Bernard's would fail as in *R* v *Rook* [1993] 2 All ER 963, the Court of Appeal held merely not turning up to be insufficient, suggesting that a positive act may be required. Ceri does not appear to have any defence available, and his act of giving Alvin a loaded gun satisfies the ingredients of this offence.

Thus, Ceri and Bernard could be found guilty of abetting an attempted murder. Although the offence of attempt to aid and abet was abolished by s. 5 of the Criminal Law Act 1977, there is an offence of attempting to abet (see *R* v *Dunnington* [1984] 1 All ER 676).

Q Question 4

(a) Oliver and Pam, his wife, decide to remedy their financial problems by trying to obtain money fraudulently from Oliver's life assurance company. Oliver fakes his death by disappearing, while Pam (after informing the company that Oliver has died) asks for and receives a claims form to complete. However, before she returns the completed form Pam breaks down under the insurance company's agent's questioning.

   Discuss the criminal responsibility of Oliver and Pam.

(b) Norman encouraged Ray to kill Violet. Norman gave Ray a substance which both believed to be a deadly poison capable of killing Violet. Ray went to Violet's house with a drink containing the poison, intending to make Violet drink it. However, when Ray knocked on the front door he was told that Violet had died one week earlier. Ray in a fit of remorse confessed to the police, who analysed the drink and discovered it was incapable of causing death.

   Discuss the criminal responsibility of Norman and Ray.

Commentary

This two-part question concentrates on the inchoate offence of attempt, but also requires reference to conspiracy (in (a)) and incitement (in (b)). Both parts require consideration of whether the *actus reus* of attempt has been completed, and although the test is clearly stated in the Criminal Attempts Act 1981, the recent cases demonstrate that it is difficult to apply in practice. The most important of these decisions are covered in the answer.

The other troublesome aspect of attempt, impossibility, must also be covered in answering (b). Again, reference to the provisions of the Criminal Attempts Act 1981 must be made, together with the contrast for incitement. The two key cases on this point — *R* v *Fitzmaurice* [1983] 1 All ER 189 and *R* v *Shivpuri* [1985] 1 All ER 143 — must be covered.

(a)

• s. 15 Theft Act 1968 — consider

- **Attempt — s. 1 Criminal Attempts Act 1981**

  - *Campbell* [1990]

  - *Widdowson* [1985]

(b)

- **Incitement to murder**

- **Impossibility** — *Fitzmaurice* [1983]

- **Attempted murder**

  - **s. 1(1) Criminal Attempts Act 1981**

  - **impossibility** — *Shivpuri* [1985]

�💡 Suggested answer

(a) If Oliver and Pam had succeeded in obtaining the insurance money, they would have been guilty of obtaining property by deception under s. 15 of the Theft Act 1968. Although there was a clear agreement to defraud the company, they cannot be found guilty of conspiracy because s. 2 of the Criminal Law Act 1977 prevents husbands and wives conspiring with one another when there is no other person involved (*R v Chrastny* [1992] 1 All ER 189). This controversial rule has been criticised by the Law Commission, and its continued existence is surprising in view of the fact that spouses can conspire with one another for the tort of conspiracy. Oliver and Pam would therefore be charged with an attempt to obtain property by deception under s. 1 of the Criminal Attempts Act 1981. Although recklessness can suffice for the substantive offence, intention as to consequence (but not necessarily circumstances) must be established for attempt. In *R v Pearman* (1984) 80 Cr App R 259, this was defined as 'a decision to bring about, in so far as it lies within the accused's power, the commission of the offence which it is alleged the accused attempted to commit, no matter whether the accused desired that consequence of his act or not'. Clearly the prosecution will have no problem in establishing the parties' *mens rea*.

However, the situation is less clear in applying the test for *actus reus*. Under s. 1(1) of the Criminal Attempts Act 1981, it must be shown that the accused has done an act which is more than merely preparatory to the commission of the offence. This is a question to be determined by the jury after the trial judge has decided that there is sufficient evidence for them to consider (s. 4(3)). It can sometimes produce surprising results. Thus in *R v Campbell* (1990) 93 Cr App R 350, a jury convicted an accused of attempted robbery, when he was arrested on the entrance steps of a post office armed with an imitation gun and a ransom demand which he intended to give to the cashier. Nevertheless, the Court of Appeal quashed his conviction on the ground that there was insufficient evidence for the trial judge to leave the question of attempt to the jury!

Before the 1981 Act many different tests had been suggested for determining the *actus reus* of attempt. In *DPP* v *Stonehouse* [1977] 2 All ER 909, Lord Diplock, commenting on the proximity test, stated that only acts immediately connected with the offence could be attempts: 'In other words the offender must have crossed the Rubicon and burnt his boats'. However, this was rejected in *R* v *Gullefer* [1990] 3 All ER 882, where Lord Lane referred to an alternative test formulated by Stephen (*Digest of Criminal Law*, 5th edn, 1894): 'an attempt to commit a crime is an act done with intent to commit that crime and forming part of a series of acts which constitute its actual commission, if it were not interrupted'.

The pre-1981 Act tests no longer apply, but it is likely that juries in applying the statutory test are likely to reach the same decisions as their predecessors. Thus Oliver is likely to be found guilty on analogy with *DPP* v *Stonehouse*. In this case the House of Lords upheld the conviction of the accused in similar circumstances to Oliver's. Stonehouse had faked his death by appearing to drown off the coast of Miami, knowing his death would be reported and that his wife would make a claim on his life assurance policy. Although he argued that merely disappearing could not constitute the *actus reus* of attempt, the House of Lords stated that as he had done the last act he had to do, knowing that the ensuing chain of events (if successful) would result in the money being paid to his wife, this was enough.

On the other hand, on analogy with *R* v *Robinson* [1915] 2 KB 342, Pam might escape conviction. In this case a jeweller, who was insured against theft, faked a burglary intending to make a fraudulent insurance claim. However, before he submitted the claims form he broke down under police questioning and admitted his plan. His conviction was quashed. Similarly, the accused in *Comer* v *Bloomfield* (1970) 55 Cr App R 305, who in similar circumstances had actually obtained a claims form but had not submitted it, was acquitted. Both these cases are pre-1981, and although in *Stonehouse* the House of Lords suggested that they might be too favourable to the accused, the Court of Appeal in *R* v *Widdowson* (1985) 82 Cr App R 314 quashed a conviction of attempt to obtain services by deception, where an accused had written to a finance company, giving a false name and salary, requesting information on credit facilities. The court held that such conduct could amount to mere preparation only and was not sufficient to constitute an attempt.

It is therefore submitted, in the light of similar decisions, that Oliver would be found guilty of attempting to obtain property by deception; but Pam would not have committed more than a merely preparatory act and would therefore be not guilty.

(b) Norman, in encouraging Ray to kill Violet, could be committing the crime of incitement to murder; and Ray, in going to Violet's house in this way, could be guilty of attempted murder. The mere incitement of another to commit an offence is a crime, whether the incitement is successful or not. Clearly the *actus reus* of the offence has been committed, and as Norman intends to bring about Violet's unlawful death the *mens rea* is satisfied. However, Norman will argue that as Violet had already died, he has the defence of impossibility.

The House of Lords in *DPP* v *Nock* [1978] 2 All ER 654, decided that impossibility is a general defence at common law, and this was confirmed by the Court of Appeal decision in *R* v *Fitzmaurice* [1983] 1 All ER 189. In this case the defence failed, as it was possible on the facts for the actual crime incited to take place. However, Neill J said:

> If B and C agree to kill D and A, standing beside B and C, though not intending to take any active part whatever in the crime, encourages them to do so, we can see no satisfactory reason, if it turns out later that D was already dead, why A should be convicted of incitement to murder whereas B and C at common law would be entitled to an acquittal on a charge of conspiracy.

It is submitted, therefore, that if at the time when Norman encouraged Ray, Violet was actually dead, Norman could not be guilty of incitement; but if Violet was then alive but died later, impossibility would not succeed and Norman would be guilty.

Although Ray would have the same argument of impossibility, he will be in a worse position as he will be charged with attempted murder under s. 1(1) of the Criminal Attempts Act 1981. The prosecution must prove that he has done more than a merely preparatory act and that he had an intention to kill; an intention to cause grievous bodily harm is not sufficient for attempted murder (*R* v *Whybrow* (1951) 35 Cr App R 141). It is a question of fact for the jury whether the accused's acts are more than merely preparatory, but most juries given such evidence normally conclude that they are, even if the Court of Appeal later disagrees. See, for example, the surprising case of *R* v *Campbell* (1990) 93 Cr App R 350.

Ray has two arguments regarding impossibility, the first being that Violet could not have been killed even if she had taken the drink. This point on impossibility of means, arose in the case of *R* v *White* (1910) 4 Cr App R 257, where the accused put potassium cyanide into a drink with intent to murder his mother. Although medical evidence established that she died not as a result of taking the drink, but of heart failure, the accused was convicted of attempted murder. There was some dispute as to whether the quantity of poison in the drink was in fact capable of killing the victim, but the court suggested that even if this was the case the accused would still be found guilty.

Ray's second argument, that Violet was already dead, might well have succeeded under the old common law provisions (*Haughton* v *Smith* [1973] 3 All ER 1109), but the position is now governed by s. 1(2) and s. 1(3) of the 1981 Act. Section 1(2) states that 'a person may be guilty of attempting to commit an offence to which this section applies even though the facts are such that the commission of the offence is impossible'; and s. 1(3) has the effect that the accused is to be judged on the facts as the accused believed them to be.

These provisions were analysed in great detail by the House of Lords in *R* v *Shivpuri* [1985] 1 All ER 143, where the House overruled its earlier decision in *Anderton* v *Ryan* [1985] 2 All ER 355. In *Shivpuri* the House of Lords upheld the accused's conviction for attempt to import a controlled drug. He had believed that he was in possession of heroin, which proved on analysis to be a harmless substance akin to snuff. However, the fact that he believed it was a prohibited drug was sufficient for a conviction of attempt. Thus, on application of these provisions, Norman and Ray are guilty of conspiracy to murder and Ray of attempted murder.

In respect of Ray's criminal responsibility, it is therefore irrelevant whether Violet was already dead when he was incited by Norman, or whether she died afterwards. In either case, on application of the Criminal Attempts Act 1981 and the House of Lords' decision in *R* v *Shivpuri*, provided the jury are satisfied that Ray's conduct constitutes more than a merely preparatory act, he will be guilty of attempted murder.

Q Question 5

Fred decides to take his family and friends for a meal at an expensive restaurant. However, as he is penniless he informs them of a plan to enable them to leave without paying, and they agree to it.

Thus Fred, his wife Bonnie, their sons Clive (aged 13) and Dave (aged nine), together with Eric, their friend (who is, unknown to them, a police informer), go to a restaurant, consume a meal and tell their waitress they have already paid their bill, which is untrue. Then they all walk out without paying. Eric immediately contacts the police and they are all arrested.

Discuss the criminal liability of the parties.

Commentary

The question involves conspiracy and the Theft Act 1978. Both are difficult topics which are generally disliked by students, although questions involving these topics can usually yield high marks to the well-prepared candidate. You must consider statutory and common law conspiracy to defraud, and consider the status of the participants. This involves the question whether infants and police informers can be regarded as 'other persons' for the purpose of conspiracy.

There is some overlap between the three offences contained in the 1978 Theft Act, and the answer mentions them all: (i) obtaining services by deception under s. 1; (ii) evasion of liability by deception under s. 2; and (iii) making off without payment under s. 3. The cases of *R* v *Holt* [1981] 2 All ER 584 and *R* v *Brooks and Brooks* (1982) 76 Cr App R 66 are very relevant in this context. All three offences contain the ingredient of dishonesty which is a question of fact for the jury. The pressure of time prevents a detailed analysis of this important issue, but the test under *R v Ghosh* [1982] 2 All ER 689 should be stated.

- **Conspiracy**
  - **s. 1 Criminal Law Act 1977**
  - **s. 2 Criminal Law Act 1977**
  - *Anderson* [1985]
  - *Yip Chiu* [1994]
- **Entrapment —** *Sang* [1979]
- **Theft Act 1978**

⋮Ọ̈⋮ **Suggested answer**

At the outset the parties are clearly involved in a conspiracy, i.e., 'an agreement of two or more to do an unlawful act, or a lawful act by unlawful means' (Willis J in *Mulchay* v *R* (1868) LR 3 HL 306). Most charges of conspiracy are under s. 1 of the Criminal Law Act 1977, i.e., where a person agrees with any other person or persons that a course of conduct be pursued which, if their agreement is carried out in accordance with their intentions, will necessarily amount to or involve the commission of an offence, or would do so but for the existence of facts which render the commission of the offence impossible. However, three common law conspiracies still remain: corrupting public morals; outraging public decency; and (the one that might be charged in this situation) conspiracy to defraud. This last was widely defined in *Scott* v *Metropolitan Police Commissioner* [1974] 3 All ER 1032 as 'an agreement by one or more by dishonesty to deprive a person of something which is his or to which he is or might be entitled'.

After difficulties arising from the House of Lords' decision in *R* v *Ayres* [1984] 1 All ER 619, it is now clear that as a result of s. 12 of the Criminal Justice Act 1987, an agreement to commit a crime involving fraud is both a statutory conspiracy and a conspiracy to defraud. So it would be for the Crown Prosecution Service to decide with which type of conspiracy to charge the parties.

However, s. 2 of the Criminal Law Act 1977 states that a person will not be guilty of conspiracy if the only other person with whom he agrees is: (i) a spouse, (ii) a person under the age of criminal responsibility, or (iii) the intended victim of the offence. Fred could therefore argue that Bonnie, as his wife, would not be 'another person', nor would Dave as (being under 10) he is irrebutally presumed to be incapable of committing a crime. In the past, Fred would also have contended that Clive (who is between the ages of 10 and 14) is *doli incapax* and therefore cannot be 'another person'. The

House of Lords in *C* v *DPP* [1995] 2 All ER 43 confirmed this principle, but it was abolished by s. 34 of the Crime and Disorder Act 1998. Thus Clive could be guilty of conspiracy.

Eric, the police informer, could be regarded as 'another person'. This is not free from doubt as Lord Bridge in *R* v *Anderson* [1985] 2 All ER 961, in an attempt to stop undercover police operatives and informers being charged with conspiracy, stated that the *mens rea* of conspiracy is established 'if and only if, it is shown that the accused when he entered into the agreement intended to play some part in the agreed course of conduct'. Similarly, Smith and Hogan, *Criminal Law*, 8th edn, suggest (at p. 282) that 'an intention to frustrate the object of a conspiracy is a special defence'. On the other hand, the Court of Appeal in *R* v *Siracusa* [1989] Crim LR 712, stated that participation in a conspiracy can be active or passive; and in *Yip Chiu Cheung* v *R* [1994] 2 All ER 924, the Privy Council held that an undercover police officer who, with his superior's authorisation, transported prohibited drugs in order to entrap other drug dealers, did have the *mens rea* for conspiracy and was 'another person' with whom a co-conspirator (whose conviction was upheld) agreed.

It is therefore submitted that Fred would be guilty of conspiracy as he has agreed with another person, and there is no defence of entrapment available in English law (*R* v *Sang* (1979) 69 Cr App R 282). The criminal responsibility of Eric (in the unlikely event of his being charged) is uncertain, but Betty would be guilty, even though she might have only agreed with her husband Fred, if she knew that there were other parties also involved in the conspiracy (*R* v *Chrastny* [1992] 1 All ER 189).

The parties would also face charges under the Theft Act 1978. Section 1 provides that a person who by any deception dishonestly obtains services from another shall be guilty of an offence. There has clearly been a deception as when Fred ordered a meal at a restaurant he impliedly represented that he would pay for it (*DPP* v *Ray* [1973] 3 All ER 131). However for s. 1, the prosecution must prove that the deception preceded the obtaining of services, and if the accused formed the intention to deceive after consuming the meal s. 1 will not apply. They may therefore be charged under s. 2 (evasion of liability by deception). They are clearly liable to pay, and in representing to the waitress that they have already paid they are practising a deception. There are three subsections in s. 2 which probably create three separate (but overlapping) offences. In the identical case of *R* v *Holt* [1981] 2 All ER 854, the accused was convicted under s. 2(1)(b), i.e., 'with intent to make permanent default in whole or in part on any existing liability to make a payment or with intent to let another do so, dishonestly induces the creditor to wait for payment or forgo payment'.

Lastly, an offence under s. 3 would seem to have been committed as the parties have, knowing that payment on the spot for goods supplied or services done was required, dishonestly made off without having paid as required, with intent to avoid payment of the amount due. Whether or not the accused 'makes off' is a question of fact for the jury, but the words are to be given their ordinary meaning. Thus in *R* v

Brooks and Brooks (1982) 76 Cr App R 66, the accused — who had left a restaurant without paying the bill, but who had voluntarily returned to the restaurant when requested by the manager — were deemed to have made off because they had passed the point where payment was expected.

All three offences require the prosecution to prove that the accused had acted dishonestly. Again, this is a word in common use and a question of fact for the jury (*R v Feely* [1973] 1 All ER 341). However, following *R v Ghosh* [1982] 2 All ER 689, the jury must consider two questions:

(a) Was what was done dishonest according to the ordinary standards of reasonable and honest people? If not, the accused is not guilty.

(b) If it was, did the accused realise that reasonable and honest people regard what he did as dishonest? If so, he is guilty; if not, he is not guilty.

It is submitted that Fred would be held to be dishonest, but both Betty and Clive could argue either that they were under no liability to make payment (the liability being Fred's) or that they honestly believed that Fred was treating them. Such belief does not have to be on reasonable grounds (*R v Small* [1987] Crim LR 777), although in view of their criminal agreement, it is submitted that this argument is unlikely to succeed. Dave, being under the age of criminal responsibility, will not be guilty.

Further reading

Clarkson, C., 'Complicity, Powell and Manslaughter' [1998] Crim LR 556.

Dennis, I.H., 'The Rationale of Criminal Conspiracy' [1997] 93 LQR 39.

Law Commission Consultation Paper No. 131 — 'Assisting and Encouraging Offenders'.

Smith, J.C. [1998] Crim LR 231.

Smith, K.J.M., 'Withdrawal in Complicity' [2001] Crim LR 769.

Theft and criminal damage

Introduction

I have criticised our criminal law system for lack of a code, and therefore I should report that there is a marked improvement for theft and theft-related offences, for here we have the Theft Act 1968 which is as near as the criminal law gets to a criminal code. The old larceny laws were very complicated, and according to Lord Diplock in *R v Treacey* [1971] AC 537, 'the Theft Act 1968 makes a welcome departure from the former style of drafting in criminal statutes. It is expressed in a simple language as used and understood by ordinary literate men and women. It avoids as far as possible those terms of art which have acquired a special meaning understood only by lawyers in which many of the final enactments which it super-cedes were couched'. However, one only has to examine the problems the courts have had with the concept of consensual appropriation (in particular *DPP v Gomez* [1993] 1 All ER 1) to appreciate that problems still remain.

This is partly the draftsmen's fault, but also stems from the fact that the law of theft is dependent on civil concepts of ownership, possession and passing of property — complicated topics which are constantly being analysed and altered by the civil courts (for example, does a bribe received by an employee belong to the employer: *Attorney-General for Hong Kong v Reid* [1994] 1 All ER 1), of which the public have little or no knowledge. As Lord Lane recognised in *Attorney-General's Reference (No. 1 of 1985)* [1986] 2 All ER 219: 'There are topics of conversation more popular in public houses than the finer points of the equitable doctrine of the constructive trust'. Yet knowledge of this topic is essential in determining if the accused is under a legal obligation to retain and deal with property in a particular way.

The uncertainty has again surfaced with three Court of Appeal decisions concerning gifts and theft. In particular, can a person who receives an indefeasible title to property be guilty of theft of that property? No, according to the Court of Appeal in *R v Mazo* (1997) 2 Cr App R 518, but yes according to *R v Kendrick and Hopkins* (1997) 2 Cr App R 524 and *R v Hinks* [2000] 3 WLR 1590. The effect of these later decisions means that a civil court may declare that there was a valid gift of property from V to A, and therefore A has become the owner of that property, but this will not prevent a criminal court from holding that he had still dishonestly appropriated that property and is therefore guilty of stealing it. When you consider that theft is a property offence and ownership of property is a civil law issue, it is remarkable that the Court of Appeal have produced this outcome and even more remarkable that the House of Lords has confirmed this approach.

So, the following points should be born in mind when studying theft:

(a) Gaps in the 1968 Act have had to be filled by the passing of the Theft Act 1978, creating additional offences, and the Theft Amendment Act 1996 to amend the law after the House of Lords' decision in *R* v *Preddy* [1996] 3 All ER 481.

(b) There has been an inconsistent approach to the relevance of pre-1968 cases. Some judges rule that the provisions of the 1968 Act are the starting point for consideration of the law, while in other areas pre-1968 decisions are still applied.

(c) Similarly, there has been uncertainty as to how deeply the courts should analyse civil concepts in determining criminal responsibility, e.g., Sachs LJ in *R* v *Baxter* [1971] 2 All ER 359: 'when that Act [the Theft Act 1968] is under examination this Court deprecates attempts to bring into close consideration the finer distinctions in civil law as to the precise moment when contractual communications take effect or when property passes'. However, the contrary view was put by Bingham LJ in *Dobson* v *General Accident Fire and Life Assurance Corporation plc* [1989] 3 All ER 927, when he recognised that the question of whether property belongs to another 'is a question to which the criminal law offers no answer and can only be answered by reference to civil law principles'.

(d) Decisions are often based not on general concepts of blameworthy or culpable conduct, but on the precise interpretation of technical terms within the Act. Thus in *Low* v *Bleaze* [1975] Crim LR 513, it was held that as electricity was not property capable of appropriation, the accused could not be convicted of burglary where he entered premises as a trespasser and made an unauthorised telephone call. If he had used a gas appliance, that would have been appropriating property, theft, and therefore burglary. Similarly, if the court concluded that the accused should be found guilty of an offence, but the Crown Prosecution Service have not charged him with the appropriate offence, it will sometimes make the facts fit the offence actually charged. Thus in both *Lawrence* v *Metropolitan Police Commissioner* [1971] 2 All ER 1253, and *DPP* v *Gomez*, the House of Lords were quite prepared to uphold convictions for theft where the appropriate charge was obtaining property by deception under s. 15 of the Theft Act 1968.

Virtually all criminal law exam papers will contain at least two questions on theft or theft-related offences, and although copies of the Acts are often supplied for the exam, this is a difficult area of the syllabus, where an understanding of the precise boundaries of the offences is essential.

Criminal damage is governed by the Criminal Damage Act 1971, which replaced the Malicious Damage Act 1861. The Criminal Damage Act has been analysed by the House of Lords on three occasions:

- Metropolitan Police Commissioner v *Caldwell* [1981] 1 All ER 961;

- *R* v *Miller* [1983] 1 All ER 978;

- *R* v *Steer* [1987] 2 All ER 833;

although the first two decisions concentrated on the general principles of recklessness and omissions, rather than specific points of the Act. Many of the important cases and principles should already be familiar to you.

There are five offences under the Act, but by far the two most important for exam purposes are s. 1(1) (criminal damage) and s. 1(2) (aggravated criminal damage). An important point to remember regarding the offence of criminal damage under s. 1(1) is the fact that in addition to the general defences there are two specific defences contained in s. 5(2) and there are many interesting cases interpreting these provisions. Aggravated criminal damage is an odd offence as it is a combination of an offence against property and an offence against the person. It is very useful for the prosecution, as its ingredients are very easily satisfied. These points are emphasised in the two questions on criminal damage in this chapter.

Q Question 1

Brian visits his local store to complete his weekly shopping. He takes a bottle of wine from the shelf and places it in the store's wire container. He intends to find a lower price tag and substitute it for the price tag on the bottle of wine but, fearing he is being watched by the store detective, puts the wine back on the shelf. He does, however, swap price tags on a bottle of brandy which he puts in the container; but when he comes to pay for it at the checkout point, the cashier Shirley notices the discrepancy and Brian pays the correct amount.

Shirley, instead of ringing up the money on her till as she is required to do, simply places it in her till, as she intends to take it for herself at the end of her shift.

Doris, another cashier, in breach of the store's instructions, had taken a £20 note from her till, as she needed the money to pay her hairdresser. She paid another £20 note to the till the day after.

Discuss the criminal responsibility of Brian, Doris and Shirley.

Commentary

In a balanced examination paper, you could expect only one question on theft. However, as that question could cover many different aspects of the crime, another 'pure' theft question has been included in this chapter. There is always the issue of dishonesty to be covered, but this question concentrates on the concept of appropriation.

There was much debate on the conflict between certain aspects of the House of Lords' decisions in *Lawrence* v *Metropolitan Police Commissioner* [1971] 2 All ER 1253 and *R* v *Morris, Anderson* v *Burnside* [1983] 3 All ER 288. In particular, did appropriation involve doing an act adverse to the owner's interest? This conflict has been decided in favour of *Lawrence* by the House of Lords' decision in *DPP* v *Gomez* [1993] 1 All ER 1, although *Morris* was not overruled and *Gomez* can be distinguished on the facts of this problem. Thus a full discussion of this issue is required.

In addition you must also consider s. 6 of the Theft Act 1968 (intention permanently to deprive) and the case of *R* v *Velumyl* [1989] Crim LR 299.

- **Theft — s. 1 Theft Act 1968**

- **s. 3 Theft Act 1968 — appropriation**

  - *Lawrence* [1971]

  - *Morris* [1983]

  - *Gomez* [1993]

- **s. 2 Theft Act 1968 — dishonesty**

  - *Ghosh* [1982]

:Ọ: Suggested answer

Brian could be charged with theft under s. 1 of the Theft Act 1968 for his activities within the store. A person is guilty of theft if he or she dishonestly appropriates property belonging to another with the intention of permanently depriving the other of it. The key issue in this problem is the concept of appropriation, and although it is defined under s. 3 of the 1968 Act as 'any assumption of the right of an owner', its application has caused great difficulty, especially when consent of the owner has been obtained.

In the first House of Lords' decision on this point, *Lawrence* v *Metropolitan Police Commissioner* [1971] 2 All ER 1253, their Lordships decided that a taxi driver had appropriated an Italian tourist's money when, at the request of the tourist, who did not understand our monetary system, the taxi driver took too much money from the victim's wallet for the taxi ride. Arguably, as informed consent had not been obtained, the tourist still retained some proprietary interest (within the meaning of s. 5(1) of the Act) in the money. However, the Law Lords indicated that there would still be an appropriation even if the victim's entire proprietary interest had passed to the defendant.

The second case *R* v *Morris* [1983] 3 All ER 288, involved a completely different scenario but the same legal principle. In this case the defendant had taken a bottle of wine from the supermarket shelf and substituted a lower price label for the correct one. As a result, he paid a lower price for the goods at the checkout point. Another defendant had been stopped before paying. They were charged with theft but argued that this was a s. 15 case (obtaining property by deception) and that the two offences were mutually exclusive. In particular, as one defendant had not paid, this could amount only to a preparatory act for the s. 15 offence and therefore could not constitute the full offence of theft. These arguments were rejected by the Law Lords, who decided that as soon as the defendants had changed the price labels, they had appropriated the property by assuming the rights of an owner. However, difficulties arose because Lord Roskill stated that appropriation involved an act of adverse interference with or assumption of the rights of an owner. It was this point that formed part of the certified questions for the House of Lords to consider in *DPP* v *Gomez* [1993] 1 All ER 1.

In this case, the defendant, who worked as an assistant in a firm selling electrical goods, had enabled his co-defendants to take goods from the firm by telling his employer that the cheque they gave him was good. He knew that the cheque would bounce, and at first instance he was convicted of theft. The Court of Appeal decided this was a classic case of obtaining property by deception, but as the owner had consented there was no appropriation and therefore no theft. They certified the following questions as points of law of public importance:

> when theft is alleged and that which is alleged to be stolen passes to D with the consent of the owner, but that consent has been obtained by false representation has —
>
> (a) an appropriation within the meaning of section 1(1) of the Theft Act 1968 taken place? or
>
> (b) must such a passing of property necessarily involve an element of adverse interference with some right of the owner?

In the House of Lords the majority answered 'Yes' to (a) and 'No' to (b), and reinstated the defendant's conviction for theft. Lord Keith said that '*Lawrence* must be regarded as authoritative and correct and there is no question of it now being right to depart from it'.

Smith and Hogan maintain that the effect of *Gomez* is that anyone doing anything whatever to property belonging to another, with or without the consent of the owner, appropriates it; and if he does so dishonestly and with intent (by that or any subsequent act) permanently to deprive, he commits theft, unless the effect of the appropriation is that he acquires an indefeasible right to the property.

As their Lordships stated in *Gomez* that an appropriation could take place on the accused assuming any one of the owner's rights, it would seem that Brian would be guilty of theft of the brandy when he swaps price labels, and possibly at the earlier stage when he takes the wine bottle from the shelf with the intention of swapping labels. The prosecution must of course prove the necessary *mens rea* of dishonesty and intention permanently to deprive, but it is submitted that this would not be difficult on the facts.

Ironically, if Brian was also charged with attempting to obtain property by deception under s. 1 of the Criminal Attempts Act 1981, it is probable that the trial judge would not leave the issue to the jury regarding the wine on the basis that Brian's actions could not be deemed more than merely preparatory (*R* v *Campbell* (1991) 93 Cr App R 350). However, regarding the brandy, he has done his last act to bring about the completed offence and it is submitted that this would amount to attempt.

It is submitted that Shirley would also be deemed to have appropriated property belonging to another in not ringing up the money on her till. Clearly the money belongs to her employer, and even before the House of Lords' decision in *Gomez*, such conduct was regarded as an appropriation (*R* v *Monaghan* [1979] Crim LR 301).

In Doris's case, there clearly was an appropriation of property when she took the £20. However, she would argue that she cannot be guilty of theft, because she lacked the necessary *mens rea*. First, the prosecution must prove that there was an intention permanently to deprive the owner of the £20; and as another £20 note has been returned, this element is lacking. However, as the store has been deprived permanently of its original property, the fact that the economic equivalent has been returned does not rule out theft (*R* v *Velumyl* [1989] Crim LR 299). This is recognised by the wording of s. 6(1) of the 1968 Act, which states a person's appropriation 'is nevertheless to be regarded as having the intention of permanently depriving the other of it if his intention is to treat the thing as his own to dispose of regardless of the other's rights; and a borrowing or lending of it may amount to so treating it'.

Generally, returning the economic equivalent would be strong evidence of lack of dishonesty, but s. 2(2) of the Act states that a person's appropriation may be dishonest notwithstanding that he is willing to pay for the property. Doris might refer to s. 2(1)(b), which provides that D will not be dishonest if D believes he has the consent of the owner. However, as Doris knows that cashiers are expressly prohibited from taking money from the till, the prosecution may succeed in establishing dishonesty.

In all three cases, the question of dishonesty will be one of fact for the jury who will decide the issue in accordance with the test in *R* v *Ghosh* [1982] 2 All ER 689:

(a) Was D's conduct dishonest according to the standards of ordinary reasonable people? If not, D must be acquitted.

(b) If it was, then was D aware that his conduct would be regarded as dishonest by ordinary reasonable people? If so, D is guilty; if not, he is not guilty.

Q Question 2

Mats and Stefan are the sole shareholders and directors of Happy Tours Ltd, a travel agency. Anders is employed by the company and is unhappy that this year he has not received his annual £200 bonus.

Carol, a customer, pays a deposit for a holiday in Italy to Mats. Instead of using

this money to pay for the holiday, Mats uses it to pay Anders' wages. The holiday for Carol is never booked.

Dave, another customer, wanted to go on a Spanish bullfighting tour, but was told by Anders that the tour was fully subscribed. He offered Anders a bribe of £200 to put him to the front of the queue and Anders did this, keeping the £200 himself on the basis that it represented his 'lost' bonus.

As the business is not going very well, Mats and Stefan agree to transfer £1,000 from Happy Tours Ltd account to their own personal accounts. Shortly after this, the company goes into liquidation and there is not enough money to pay the creditors.

Discuss the criminal responsibility of Mats, Stefan and Anders.

Commentary

There is only one crime to concentrate upon in this question, but as theft contains many diverse elements, there are a lot of points to analyse. The first concept to consider is whether the recipients of the deposit and the bribe are under a legal obligation to retain and deal with that property for the benefit of another within the meaning of s. 5(3) of the 1968 Act. If so, they have committed the *actus reus* of theft. The answer must therefore refer to the key cases on this point, in particular *R v Hall* [1972] 2 All ER 1009 and the recent developments with the Privy Council case of *Attorney-General for Hong Kong v Reid* [1994] 1 All ER 1 concerning bribes.

There is also the issue of whether Mats and Stefan are guilty of theft from their company, Happy Tours Ltd. At first this proposition might seem odd, but you can be guilty of stealing your own property. See *R v Turner (No. 2)* [1971] 2 All ER 441. However, a company is a separate legal entity distinct from its members, and even before *DPP v Gomez* [1993] 1 All ER 1, the courts had accepted that this could be an appropriation of property belonging to another (*R v Phillipou* (1989) 89 Cr App R 290).

Lastly — and this is inevitably the case with theft questions — the concept of dishonesty must be analysed.

- **Theft — s. 1 Theft Act 1968**

- **Belonging to another — s. 5 Theft Act 1968**

  - *Hall* [1972]

  - *Reid* [1994]

- **s. 2 Theft Act 1968 — dishonesty**

  - *Ghosh* [1982]

- **Appropriation**

- *Phillipou* [1989]

- *Gomez* [1993]

⋮Ọ̈⋮ Suggested answer

All three parties could be charged with theft, defined by s. 1 of the Theft Act 1968 as dishonestly appropriating property belonging to another with an intention of permanently depriving the other of it.

When Mats receives the deposit from Carol he is clearly appropriating property. The only dispute regarding the *actus reus* of theft is the question of property belonging to another. Section 5(1) of the 1968 Act provides that property shall be regarded as belonging to any person having possession or control of it, or having any proprietary right or interest in it. However, the key provision in this case is s. 5(3), as Mats has received the deposit for the specific purpose of booking a holiday for Carol. Section 5(3) provides:

> When a person receives property from or on account of another, and is under an obligation to the other to retain and deal with that property or its proceeds in a particular way, the property or proceeds shall be regarded (as against him) as belonging to the other.

For this provision to be satisfied the prosecution must prove that Mats was under a legal obligation to deal with the deposit in a particular way. It is not sufficient that he was under a legal obligation to supply a service or product under a contract. A legal obligation may arise as a result of statute, for example, the Estate Agents Act 1979, placing a duty on estate agents who receive deposits on behalf of clients in respect of house transactions to put these deposits in a specific account; or as a result of a trust. Thus in *R v Wain* (1995) 2 Cr App R 660, D, who collected money from sponsors to be paid over to a charity, was guilty of theft when he kept that money as he was under a legal obligation to deal with that property in a particular way, i.e., to pay it to the charity. Whether a trustee–beneficiary, as opposed to a creditor–debtor relationship has been created is a question for the jury, who must be directed by the judge that if they find the necessary facts proved they must conclude there is an obligation (*R v Dunbar* [1995] 1 All ER 781).

The most relevant case to Mats' situation is *R v Hall* [1972] 2 All ER 1009. A customer of a travel agent wished to travel to America and gave the agent a deposit for the purpose of booking the appropriate flights. The agent spent the money on other expenses, the deposit was not returned and the flights were not provided. The court held that when money is paid to a business it is not generally allocated for specific purposes. It goes into a general fund and is used to pay various expenses regardless of its source. On this basis there was no legal obligation on the agent to retain and deal with the property in a particular way, and he was therefore not guilty of theft. The court stated that the conversation between the parties could have been enough to impose a duty, but although the customer made it very clear what he wanted done with his deposit, on the facts this was not sufficient. Therefore, unless Carol specified that the money could not be used for any other purpose, and it was accepted by Mats on this basis, there will be no criminal responsibility. It is surprising that there is not a Travel Agents Act imposing such a legal obligation.

If Mats never had any intention of supplying the holiday he could be guilty of obtaining property by deception under s. 15 of the 1968 Act (and after *DPP v Gomez* [1993] 1 All ER 1, presumably theft). However, it must be proved that the deception preceded the obtaining (*R v Coady* [1996] Crim LR 518).

Section 5(3) is also relevant in considering Anders' criminal responsibility. The prosecution will argue that he is guilty of theft as, applying s. 5(3), the bribe is property belonging to another as he is under a legal obligation to give it to his employer. Quite clearly, Anders is acting in breach of his contract in accepting a bribe and his employer will have various remedies in respect of this. However, whether the actual bribe itself belongs to the employer is uncertain. This is a civil law issue, and until recently it was considered that the actual bribe did not belong to the employer (*Lister v Stubbs* (1890) 45 Ch D 1). Thus in *Powell v Macrae* [1977] Crim LR 571, a Wembley turnstile operator who accepted a bribe in return for allowing entrance to a ticketless football fan, did not commit theft from his employer by keeping the money. However, the Privy Council in *Attorney-General for Hong Kong v Reid* [1994] 1 All ER 1, in a civil action, held that the bribe did belong to the employer. This demonstrates the inherent uncertainty within certain areas of the criminal law. *Reid* is a civil case, and being a Privy Council decision is persuasive only. However, if it were followed, Anders would have committed the *actus reus* of theft.

The prosecution would then seek to show that Anders was dishonest. He certainly intended permanently to deprive his employer of the money, but would claim that he is not dishonest because of s. 2(1)(a) of the Act. This provides that a person's appropriation of another's property is not to be regarded as dishonest if he believes that he has the right in law to deprive the other of it. Anders would argue that he believed he had the right to this money as he was wrongly deprived of his annual bonus. The Act refers to a right in law, although this does not necessarily exclude a belief in a merely moral right.

The question of dishonesty is one of fact for the jury (*R v Feely* [1973] 1 All ER 341) and will be dealt with under the twofold test in *R v Ghosh* [1982] 2 All ER 689:

(a) Was what was done dishonest according to the ordinary standards of reasonable and honest people? If not, D is not guilty.

(b) If it was, did D realise that reasonable and honest people regard what he did as dishonest? If so, he is guilty; if not, he is not guilty.

The third charge of theft arises from Mats' and Stefan's action of taking £1,000 from Happy Tours Ltd. If a sole proprietor or partners in a firm take money from the business account they will not be appropriating property belonging to another. However, the position is different with a company, as this is a separate legal entity whose property is distinct from that of its directors and members. The main difficulty in making this activity theft — apart from the fact that until a company goes into liquidation its creditors have no proprietary interest (within the meaning of s. 5(1)) in its property — is the fact that if the sole directors and shareholders consent to the company's actions, can there be said to be an appropriation? In *R* v *McHugh and Tringham* (1988) 88 Cr App R 385, the Court of Appeal said that 'an act done with the authority of the company cannot in general amount to an appropriation. Such authority may be express or implied'. However, a different view was taken in *R* v *Phillipou* (1989) 89 Cr App R 290, where a differently constituted Court of Appeal upheld a director's conviction for theft in these circumstances. This was also the view unanimously taken by the Law Lords in *DPP* v *Gomez* who were anxious that dishonest directors who plundered their company's assets to the detriment of company creditors should not escape a theft conviction on the ground that they consented to such action. Lord Browne-Wilkinson stated (at p. 40):

> where a company is accused of a crime the acts and intentions of those who are the directing minds and will of the company are to be attributed to the company. That is not the law where the charge is that those who are the directing minds and will have themselves committed a crime against the company.

As Mats and Stefan completely own the company, they may argue that this cannot be a dishonest appropriation; but as dishonesty is a question of fact for the jury, it is submitted that the jury would take into account the fact that the creditors are being deprived of funds, and could therefore convict Mats and Stefan of theft.

Q Question 3

Dave entered a betting shop and placed a £10 bet on a horse to finish in the first three. His horse came second, but the bookmaker, mistakenly believing that Dave had bet on the winner, instructed his cashier to pay Dave £100, which was £40 more than he was entitled to. In Dave's excitement, he forcibly grabbed the money from the cashier's grasp and then, realising that he had been overpaid, pushed over a security guard standing by the exit.

On his way home, Dave was asked by a charity worker to make a contribution to famine relief and, taking the view that they needed the money more than his bookmaker or himself, gave the charity the £100.

Discuss the criminal liability of Dave.

Commentary

This question concentrates on two offences under the Theft Act 1968: theft and robbery. Theft is a vast topic, but your answer must concentrate on the concepts of property belonging to another, with reference to s. 5 of the 1968 Act and *R* v *Gilks* [1972] 3 All ER 280, and dishonesty, negatively defined under s. 2 of the Act. On the other hand, as robbery is aggravated theft, there is not nearly as much material to consider. However, a key point is whether Dave has used force immediately before or at the time of the theft, and the cases of *R* v *Dawson* (1976) 64 Cr App R 170 and *R* v *Hale* (1978) 68 Cr App R 415 must be applied.

This is not a difficult question as the cases and principles should be very familiar to a well-prepared student. It is a question that should yield high marks.

- **Theft — s. 1 Theft Act 1968**

    - *Gomez* [1993]

- **s. 5(4) Theft Act 1968 — belonging to another**

    - *Gilks* [1972]

- **s. 2 Theft Act 1968 — dishonesty**

    - *Ghosh* [1982]

- **Robbery — s. 8 Theft Act 1968**

    - *Dawson* [1976]

    - *Hale* [1978]

:Q: Suggested answer

Dave could be charged with theft and robbery under the Theft Act 1968. Theft is defined under s. 1, and Dave will be found guilty if he dishonestly appropriates property belonging to another with the intention of permanently depriving the other of it.

The first element of the *actus reus* to consider is whether Dave has appropriated the money, as initially he does have the bookmaker's consent. Although appropriation is defined under s. 3 as any assumption by a person of the rights of an owner, and this includes the assumption of any one right (*R* v *Morris, Anderson* v *Burnside* [1983] 3 All ER 288), the courts have experienced great difficulty with this concept when the owner has consented to the property being taken. However, the House of Lords' decision in *DPP* v *Gomez* [1993] 1 All ER 1 makes it clear that anyone doing anything to property belonging to another with or without the consent of the owner appropriates it. So Dave has appropriated the money.

The second difficulty is whether this is property belonging to another, as Dave could argue that it becomes his property when he obtains it from the cashier. Clearly the money is property, as s. 4(1) provides that ' "property" includes money and all other property, real or personal, including things in action and other intangible property'. 'Belonging to another' is governed by s. 5, and at first sight it appears the prosecution would have to resort to s. 5(4), which provides: 'Where a person gets property by another's mistake, and is under an obligation to make restoration . . . then to the extent of that obligation the property or proceeds shall be regarded (as against him) as belonging to the person entitled to restoration'. However, for the subsection to apply there must be a legal obligation to make restoration, and on similar facts in *R* v *Gilks* [1972] 3 All ER 280, the Court of Appeal held that there was no legal obligation as the transaction between a bookmaker and punter was a betting and wagering contract and therefore illegal. In *Gilks*, the accused's conviction was upheld, as the court used s. 5(1) to decide that the punter had appropriated property belonging to another. Section 5(1) states that property shall be regarded as belonging to any person having possession or control of it, or having in it any proprietary right or interest; and in *Lawrence* v *Metropolitan Police Commissioner* [1971] 2 All ER 1253, the House of Lords decided that an owner of property who mistakenly parts with possession or ownership of it, may still have a proprietary interest in it. On application of this principle, the prosecution here can establish that Dave committed the *actus reus* of theft.

The first and most difficult element of the *mens rea* of theft is dishonesty. This is partially defined in a negative sense by s. 2 of the 1968 Act, which provides that a person's appropriation is not to be regarded as dishonest if the person:

(a) believes that he or she has in law the right to deprive the other of it; or

(b) believes he or she would have the other's consent; or

(c) believes that the person to whom the property belongs cannot be discovered by taking reasonable steps.

Dave might argue that he honestly believed that the charity had a better moral right to the money than the bookmaker, but a moral right is not the same as a legal right. It would therefore be difficult for s. 2(1)(a) to be satisfied. However, the question of dishonesty is one of fact for the jury, and the Court of Appeal in *R* v *Feely* [1973] 1 All ER 341 held that it is for the jury to decide not only what the defendant's state of mind was, but also whether that state of mind was dishonest.

Feely also decided that as dishonesty is a word in common use, the jury do not need the help of the judge to tell them what amounts to dishonesty. However, conflict emerged as to whether the jury had to ascertain if the accused considered the conduct dishonest (the subjective approach favoured in *Boggeln* v *Williams* [1978] 2 All ER 1061), or if it was sufficient if the jury considered the conduct dishonest regardless of the accused's belief (the objective approach favoured in *R* v *Gilks*). The uncertainty has now been resolved by the Court of Appeal decision in *R* v *Ghosh* [1982] 2 All ER 689, which gives a twofold test. Thus the jury must ask themselves:

(a) Was what was done dishonest according to the ordinary standards of reasonable and honest people? If not, D is not guilty.

(b) If it was, did D realise that reasonable and honest people regard what he did as dishonest? If so, he is guilty; if not, he is not guilty.

Although the test has been criticised as it may allow a 'Robin Hood' defence (and has not been applied in Australia), it does seem to operate fairly and Dave could not escape simply because in his opinion bookmakers were fair game. He would have to bring some evidence to show that he honestly believed that other people would not consider his conduct dishonest.

The second element of the *mens rea*, intention permanently to deprive, is satisfied when Dave gives the money to charity, and s. 5(4) provides that an intention not to make restoration shall be regarded as an intention to deprive.

It is submitted that Dave could not be charged under s. 15 of the Theft Act 1968 with obtaining property by deception, as there has been no operative deception on his behalf. If Dave had represented that he had bet on the winner the position would be different. However, if he is held dishonest and guilty of theft, he could also be convicted of robbery. This offence is defined by s. 8 of the 1968 Act: 'A person is guilty of robbery if he steals, and immediately before or at the time of doing so, and in order to do so, he uses force on any person or puts or seeks to put any person in fear of being then and there subjected to force.'

The key issue here would be, has Dave used force at the time of the theft in order to steal? Force is not defined in the Theft Act, and in *R v Dawson* (1976) 64 Cr App R 170, the Court of Appeal held that it is an ordinary English word and that its meaning is for the jury to decide. Thus in *Dawson*, a nudge in the back was force; and in *Corcoran v Anderton* (1980) 71 Cr App R 104, snatching a handbag was sufficient for the accused to be guilty of robbery. In this case, however, the victim had such a strong grip on the bag that D's act of pulling it caused her to fall to the ground, whereas Dave's grab has no such effect on the cashier. Further, if Dave has not formed the *mens rea* of theft at this time, even if the jury concluded that his action constituted force, it may not be deemed 'in order to steal'.

Quite clearly, pushing over the security guard would constitute force, and as Dave then realised that he had been overpaid, this would seem to constitute robbery. However, the courts have drawn a distinction between force used at the time of and in order to steal (robbery), and force used in order to escape (not robbery). The key question, therefore, is whether Dave was still in the act of appropriating the property when he pushed the security guard. This was also the problem before the court in *R v Hale* (1978) 68 Cr App R 415, where D, in the victim's bedroom, put some jewellery into his pocket shortly before his accomplice downstairs tied up the victim. The Court of Appeal, in upholding the conviction, decided that it was open to the jury to conclude that the appropriation was still continuing. Thus as the guard is in the shop, it is likely that this condition will be satisfied and Dave will be found guilty of robbery. If it was deemed to be force after the theft had taken place, Dave would not be guilty of robbery; but in addition to theft, he could be convicted of common assault under s. 39 of the Criminal Justice Act 1988.

Q Question 4

Jerry is the managing director of, and majority shareholder in, Barnham Ltd who own an old people's home. Mike is an employee of Barnham who works at the home. The business is going badly and the home is deteriorating rapidly. This fact has been noted by Ben, an eccentric resident, who has complained on many occasions that the fire-fighting equipment is totally inadequate and that the residents and the adjoining local church are in danger from the risk of fire. Jerry instructs Mike to start a fire, so that Barnham Ltd will be able to make a claim for damage to the home on their insurance policy. Mike starts a small fire.

At the same time, and independently of Mike, Ben decides to test his theory and also starts a fire. Both fires spread, the home is badly damaged and, although nobody is injured, the residents have to be evacuated.

Before Jerry submits an insurance claims form, the police arrest the three of them.

Discuss the criminal liability of the parties.

Commentary

This question involves a detailed analysis of a number of issues under the Criminal Damage Act 1971. In particular, the offences under s. 1 and the two specific defences to s. 1(1) contained in s. 5(2) must be analysed in detail. These principles have been applied in a number of recent decisions which have emphasised the peculiarities of the law on this topic.

No answer on criminal damage can afford to omit some discussion of *Metropolitan Police Commissioner* v *Caldwell* [1981] 1 All ER 961, and this is no exception. In addition, there are the two inchoate offences to consider briefly: incitement and attempt. The question has been framed in such a way so as to avoid considering the other inchoate crime, conspiracy.

- Incitement

- Criminal damage

  - s. 1(1) Criminal Damage Act 1971

  - s. 5(2) Criminal Damage Act 1971

  - *Denton* [1982]

  - *Appleyard* [1985]

- Aggravated criminal damage

  - s. 1(2) Criminal Damage Act 1971

- Recklessness — *Caldwell* [1981]

- Attempt — Criminal Attempts Act 1981

  - *Widdowson* [1985]

- *Ben*

  - Criminal damage

  - s. 1(1) Criminal Damage Act 1971

  - s. 5(2) Criminal Damage Act 1971 — *Hunt* [1977]

:Q: Suggested answer

When Jerry instructs Mike to start a fire, he is probably guilty of the crime of incitement. An inciter 'is one who reaches and seeks to influence the mind of another to the commission of a crime'. The machinations of criminal ingenuity being legion, the approach to the other's mind may take various forms, such as suggestion, proposal, request, exhortation, gesture, argument, persuasion or inducement.

Thus, although Jerry could be charged with inciting Mike to commit criminal damage under s. 1(1) of the Criminal Damage Act 1971, it is more likely that they will both be charged as principal offenders under that section: 'A person who without lawful excuse destroys or damages any property belonging to another intending to destroy or damage any such property or being reckless as to whether any such property would be destroyed or damaged shall be guilty of an offence.' As they have used fire, the charge may be arson under s. 1(3) of the 1971 Act as the maximum sentence is greater (life as opposed to 10 years).

Clearly, both Jerry and Mike have the necessary *mens rea* for these offences as they intend to damage the property. However, they may have a defence under s. 5(2) of the Act:

> A person charged with an offence to which this section applies shall, whether or not he would be treated for the purposes of this Act as having a lawful excuse apart from this subsection, be treated for those purposes as having a lawful excuse —
>
> > (a) if at the time of the act or acts alleged to constitute the offence he believed that the person or persons whom he believed to be entitled to consent to the destruction of or damage to the property in question had so consented, or would have so consented to it if he or they had known of the destruction or damage and its circumstances. . . .

Although their positions may seem identical, on analysis of the two leading cases on this section (*R* v *Denton* [1982] 1 All ER 65, *R* v *Appleyard* (1985) 81 Cr App R 319) there may be a difference in Jerry's and Mike's criminal responsibility. In *R v Denton*, an employee (D), had been instructed by his employer (X), to damage X's property by fire, so that X could make a fraudulent insurance claim. At D's trial, the judge ruled that s. 5(2) of the 1971 Act could not provide D with a lawful excuse, as he knew that his employer had consented to his starting the fire and damaging the property for fraudulent purposes only. The consent, ruled the trial judge, was therefore invalid. However, D's conviction was quashed on appeal, the court holding that no offence was committed under s. 1(1) or s. 1(3) of the Act by a person who burnt down his own premises; neither could that act become unlawful because of the intent to defraud the insurers.

On application of *Denton*, Mike would have a defence; and it would appear that Jerry could use the same argument. However, his responsibility appears to be governed by the decision in *R v Appleyard*. In this case, A, the managing director and majority shareholder of a company, X Ltd, set fire to X Ltd's property, with a view to making a fraudulent insurance claim. A argued on authority of *Denton* that he could not be guilty of damaging his own property, but this argument was rejected on the basis that the company is a separate legal entity and, as the building was owned by the company, A was damaging property belonging to another. A also contended that, as he was in control of the company and could make decisions on the company's behalf, he had the defence under s. 5(2) as he had the consent of the company. Again, the court rejected the argument on the basis that company decisions must be made for a proper purpose and in the company's best interests. As this was clearly not the case, there was no consent or belief in the owner's consent. A's conviction was upheld by the Court of Appeal.

It is therefore submitted on authority of these cases that whereas Mike would be acquitted of these charges, Jerry would be convicted.

Jerry and Mike would also be charged under s. 1(2) of the 1971 Act:

A person who without lawful excuse destroys or damages any property whether belonging to himself or another —

(a) intending to destroy or damage any property or being reckless as to whether any property would be destroyed or damaged; and

(b) intending by the destruction or damage to endanger the life of another or being reckless as to whether the life of another would be thereby endangered;

shall be guilty of an offence.

The facts demonstrate that as the home was evacuated, life may have been endangered; it is only necessary that the prosecution show that life could have been (not actually was) endangered (*R v Dudley* [1989] Crim LR 57).

Jerry and Mike may argue that they lacked the *mens rea* for this offence because they did not foresee this consequence. However, it is submitted that this argument would fail as the objective recklessness test from *Metropolitan Police Commissioner* v *Caldwell* [1981] 1 All ER 961 applies. As Lord Diplock stated:

> a person . . . is 'reckless as to whether or not any such property would be destroyed or damaged' if (1) he does an act which in fact creates an obvious risk that property will be destroyed or damaged and (2) when he does the act he either has not given any thought to the possibility of there being any such risk or has recognised that there was some risk involved and has nonetheless gone on to do it.

As Lord Diplock also stated that s. 1(2) must be approached in the same way, and the specific defences under s. 5(2) have no application to a charge under s. 1(2), it is quite clear that Jerry and Mike would be guilty of this offence.

Lastly, Jerry may be charged under s. 1(1) of the Criminal Attempts Act 1981 with an attempt to obtain property by deception. Had Jerry's plan succeeded, this would have been a clear case of the full offence under s. 15 of the Theft Act 1968, as the money paid by the insurance company is regarded as property and they would have been deceived if Jerry had stated that the fire was an accident. However, for the prosecution to establish the offence of attempt, it must be shown that Jerry did more than a merely preparatory act with the appropriate *mens rea*; and whether an act is more than merely preparatory is a question of fact for the jury (Criminal Attempts Act 1981, s. 4(3)). Each case depends on its own particular facts, but in the similar case of *R* v *Robinson* [1915] 2 KB 341, D's conviction for attempting to obtain money by false pretences was quashed on the basis that as D had not actually submitted the fraudulent claims form, his conduct had not amounted to the *actus reus* of attempt. Although this case was before 1981 and therefore did not apply the present test, *R* v *Widdowson* (1985) 82 Cr App R 314 was decided in the same way, and it is therefore submitted that Jerry has not done more than a merely preparatory act and could not be found guilty of attempted deception.

Ben would appear to be guilty of criminal damage under s. 1(1) of the 1971 Act, but he could argue that the defence of lawful excuse is available under s. 5(2)(b), i.e., if he destroyed or damaged the property in question . . . in order to protect property belonging to himself or another, and at the time of the act he believed:

(a) that the property was in immediate need of protection; and

(b) that the means of protection adopted or proposed to be adopted were or would be reasonable having regard to all the circumstances.

At first sight, this subsection appears to offer a defence in many circumstances, as it is written in subjective terms. However, an objective element has been imported by the cases, and in *R* v *Hill and Hall* (1988) 89 Cr App R 74, the Court of Appeal ruled that the trial judge has to decide whether the evidence submitted by D is sufficient to enable this defence to be left to the jury. In *R* v *Hunt* (1977) 66 Cr App R 105, the court, on similar facts to the problem, held that D's act in setting fire to property was not done in order to protect the property — which was not in any case in immediate need of protection, until D started the fire! Further, in *Blake* v *DPP* [1993] Crim LR 586, it was held that s. 5(2) is not satisfied by D's belief that God is the owner of all property and that God consents to the damage.

Consequently, Ben would also be guilty under s. 1(2) of the 1971 Act on the same basis as Jerry and Mike.

Q Question 5

Tracey, aged 14, often played in a small wood above concealed waste ground. She and her friends were in the habit of throwing stones down on to the waste ground, in the knowledge that as nobody ever went on that ground there was no risk of injury.

One day a sign was erected by the woods: 'New greenhouses, do not throw stones'. However, although Tracey saw the sign, as she could not read, being of very low intelligence, she disregarded it and threw a stone to the waste ground. The stone smashed a pane of glass in a greenhouse and narrowly missed Bill the gardener. Bill was so shocked by the incident that he became depressed and suffered headaches for a month.

Discuss the criminal responsibility (if any) of Tracey.

Commentary

There are many interesting areas within the Criminal Damage Act 1971, a statute that has also attracted a number of odd cases (*Jaggard* v *Dickinson* [1980] 3 All ER 716, for example). It is difficult to set a question which is exclusively related to criminal damage, and examiners will often involve an offence against the person to test the students' awareness of the different *mens rea* requirements. This question, like many others on criminal damage, requires an analysis of objective recklessness and knowledge of the principles from the leading case of *Metropolitan Police Commissioner* v *Caldwell* [1981] 1 All ER 961.

Section 47 of the Offences Against the Person Act 1861 must also be considered; in particular, can psychiatric injury constitute actual bodily harm?

- **Criminal damage — s. 1(1) Criminal Damage Act 1971**

- **Recklessness**

  - *Caldwell* [1981]

  - *Elliot* v *C* [1983]

- **Aggravated criminal damage — s. 1(2) Criminal Damage Act 1971**

  - *Steer* [1987]

- *Webster and Warwick* [1995]

• **s. 47 Offences Against the Person Act 1861**

- *Chan Fook* [1994]

- *Savage and Parmenter* [1991]

☀ Suggested answer

Tracey could face charges under the Criminal Damage Act 1971 and the Offences Against the Person Act 1861, although she will be able to contend that she did not possess the necessary *mens rea* for these offences.

Under s. 1(1) of the Criminal Damage Act 1971, a person who without lawful excuse destroys or damages any property belonging to another, intending to destroy or damage any such property or being reckless as to whether any such property would be destroyed or damaged, shall be guilty of an offence. There are specific defences to s. 1(1) in s. 5 of the Act, but as they relate either to a belief in the owner's consent, or to a necessary and reasonable act to prevent further damage to property, Tracey will be unable to use them. However, although she has clearly committed the *actus reus* of the offence, she can argue that she lacked the *mens rea*, on the basis that as she did not foresee the consequence, she neither intended it nor was reckless as to its occurrence.

The key case concerning recklessness under the Criminal Damage Act 1971 is *Metropolitan Police Commissioner* v *Caldwell* [1981] 1 All ER 961, where the accused, with a grievance against the proprietor of an old people's home, set fire to the property while drunk. He was convicted under both s. 1(1) and s. 1(2) of the 1971 Act. Section 1(2) states:

A person who without lawful excuse destroys or damages any property whether belonging to himself or another —

(a) intending to destroy or damage any property or being reckless as to whether any property would be destroyed or damaged; and

(b) intending by the destruction or damage to endanger the life of another or being reckless as to whether the life of another would be thereby endangered;

shall be guilty of an offence.

Caldwell appealed to the House of Lords, who considered whether an accused who had not foreseen the risk of damage to property could be considered reckless. In a controversial and heavily criticised judgment, Lord Diplock said:

a person . . . is 'reckless as to whether any such property would be destroyed or damaged' if (1) he does an act which in fact creates an obvious risk that property will be destroyed or damaged and (2) when he does the act he either has not given any thought to the possibility of there being any such risk or has recognised that there was some risk involved and has nonetheless gone on to do it.

Lord Diplock also stated that s. 1(2) must be approached in the same way.

Thus, although Tracey could argue that she did not foresee the risk, the prosecution would contend that it was an obvious risk and, as she gave no thought to the possibility of any such risk, she is reckless and therefore guilty. Tracey might contend that the risk would not have been obvious to her even if she had considered all the circumstances, as she lacked the capacity to foresee the consequence and it would be unfair to label her blameworthy simply because she has failed to reach the standard of the reasonable person. However, this argument was rejected in *Elliott* v *C (A Minor)* [1983] 2 All ER 1005. C was a 14-year-old remedial school girl who, while hungry and exhausted, set fire to a garden shed by throwing two lighted matches on to the carpeted floor after she had poured white spirit on to it. She contended that because of her characteristics the risk of fire was not obvious to her, and therefore she was not reckless. Although this argument appealed to the Queen's Bench Division of the High Court, it was rejected on the basis that the doctrine of precedent must be applied and *Caldwell* was clear on this point. The test is, 'Was this an obvious risk to a reasonable person' and there was no scope for taking into account the personal characteristics of the accused.

Although the same view was taken by the Court of Appeal in *R* v *R (Stephen Malcolm)* (1994) 79 Cr App R 344, another House of Lords' decision on recklessness (*R* v *Reid* [1992] 3 All ER 673) suggests a softening of the *Caldwell* approach. Lord Keith suggested that an accused would not be reckless 'where he acted under some excusable and understandable mistake or where his capacity to appreciate risks was adversely affected by some condition, not involving fault on his part'. Thus there is the possibility that the *Caldwell* test would not be automatically applied to criminal damage offences and the court might recognise that as Tracey lacks the capacity to foresee the consequence, her conduct is not blameworthy. However, *Reid* is a case involving causing death by reckless driving and *Elliot* v *C* is likely to be followed in this instance.

Section 1(2) of the Criminal Damage Act 1971 is the most serious offence facing Tracey; and although there is the possibility of a life sentence if the accused is found guilty, the ingredients of the offence can be easily satisfied by the prosecution. It is not necessary to show that someone's life was actually endangered, simply that it could have been endangered (*R* v *Dudley* [1989] Crim LR 57); and *mens rea* can be satisfied by *Caldwell* recklessness. So Tracey may not have foreseen either the risk of criminal damage or the risk of endangering life, but if both are obvious risks then she may be found guilty.

However, the limitation in the accused's favour is that the endangerment to life must arise as a result of the criminal damage. This was confirmed by the House of Lords in *R* v *Steer* [1987] 2 All ER 833, where the accused fired bullets, which narrowly missed V, through the window of a house. The prosecution contended that as the accused had caused criminal damage and V's life had been endangered, the offence under s. 1(2) had been established. However, the House of Lords stated that this offence was committed only if the life had been or could have been endangered by the criminal damage.

It will sometimes be difficult on the facts to make this key distinction. Thus in *R v Webster and Warwick* [1995] 2 All ER 168, where the accused threw bricks at a moving police car, smashing a window and causing glass to fall over the officers, the court held that this ingredient for s. 1(2) could be satisfied, as the driver might lose control as a result of being showered with glass. Thus, if the gardener was endangered by the stone thrown by Tracey, she would not be guilty; but if endangerment was caused by the splintering glass, she would be!

Tracey might also be charged under s. 47 of the Offences Against the Person Act 1861: 'Whosoever shall be convicted upon an indictment of any assault occasioning actual bodily harm shall be liable . . . to [imprisonment for five years]'. Although Bill has not suffered direct physical injury, psychiatric injury can amount to actual bodily harm (*R v Mike Chan-Fook* [1994] 2 All ER 552); and in *R v Ireland* [1997] 4 All ER 225, the Court of Appeal and the House of Lords held that psychiatric injury can amount to grievous bodily harm for the purpose of s. 20 of the 1861 Act. However, minor emotional harm (such as fear or mild hysteria) will not be sufficient, and the prosecution must call expert psychiatric evidence to establish that Bill's depression and headaches constitute actual bodily harm.

Assault can be defined as intentionally or recklessly putting a person in fear of being then and there subjected to unlawful force (*Fagan v Metropolitan Police Commissioner* [1968] 3 All ER 442). It is quite clear that objective recklessness does not apply to

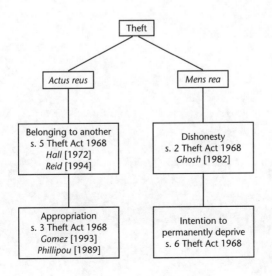

common assault or s. 47 of the 1861 Act (*R v Savage and Parmenter* [1991] 4 All ER 698); and although the *mens rea* for s. 47 is satisfied by proving the *mens rea* of common assault (i.e., the prosecution do not have to prove that the accused foresaw the risk of actual bodily harm: *R v Roberts* (1971) 56 Cr App R 95), it is submitted that as Tracey was unaware of any danger to the person, she could not be found guilty of this offence.

Further reading

Griew, E., 'Dishonesty — the Objections to Feely and Ghosh' [1985] Crim LR 341.

Elliott, D.W., 'Directors' Thefts and Dishonesty' [1991] Crim LR 732.

Heaton, R., 'Deceiving Without Thieving' [2001] Crim LR 712.

Shute, S., 'Appropriation and the Law of Theft' [2002] Crim LR 445.

Smith, J.C., 'Stealing Tickets' [1998] Crim LR 723.

Q&A 9

Other Theft Act offences

Introduction

Many criminal law syllabuses will cover only a few other theft-related offences, such as robbery, burglary and deception. Professional courses (e.g., the Common Professional Exam) will also set questions on blackmail, handling, taking a conveyance and going equipped. There are many other offences under the Theft Act 1968, such as forgery and false accounting, but only specialist bodies would set questions on these crimes.

The questions included in this chapter are typical examination problems. It is rare that essay questions are set on these offences, as the rationale of the criminal law is best explored in other areas of the syllabus, such as *actus reus* and *mens rea*. Because there is not such a vast amount of material to cover on these offences as, for example, on causation or recklessness, the questions will often involve consideration of three or four offences. Some questions are set simply to test a student's ability to differentiate between closely related offences (for example, Question 2 concerning deception). Others may require detailed analysis of cases and concepts on one crime only — burglary and handling stolen goods lend themselves to this type of question.

Because of the diverse material, and the fact that studying theft and theft-related offences almost seems like studying a separate subject from criminal law, many students are very apprehensive about tackling questions on these topics. You should not be intimidated, however, as questions tend to be set on the well-known areas of difficulty which have been discussed in leading cases. A well-prepared student should be confident of scoring high marks on these questions, which may often be easier to answer than those from other parts of the syllabus.

Q Question 1

One afternoon Sara entered a department store to buy some clothes. She purchased some articles paying for them with a cheque supported by a credit card, although she knew that there was no money in her account. However, as the sales assistant followed the correct procedure the store was eventually paid by Sara's bank.

Sara noticed that the security in the store was very lax, and she decided to hide in the store until after closing time. She did this and then, while the store was closed, she saw a till behind a three-sided counter under a sign marked 'Staff only'. She started to climb over the counter in order to empty the till, but as she was doing so she was arrested by the store detective.

Discuss the criminal responsibility of Sara.

Commentary

This is a typical question requiring knowledge of offences under the Theft Act 1968. There are four offences to be considered, but the majority of the marks are awarded for correctly applying the principles and cases concerning burglary and, to a lesser extent, obtaining by deception. There is an overlap between many Theft Act offences, and whenever you discuss s. 15 of the Theft Act 1968 you must also mention theft under s. 1 as a result of *DPP* v *Gomez* [1993] 1 All ER 1.

There are many important cases interpreting the various components of the relevant offences, and an ability to apply them correctly is the key to obtaining a good mark.

- **s. 15 Theft Act 1968**

  - *Lambie* [1981]

- **s. 16 Theft Act 1968**

  - *Waites* [1982]

- **s. 1 Theft Act 1968**

- **s. 9 Theft Act 1968**

  - *Collins* [1972]

  - *Jones and Smith* [1976]

  - *Walkington* [1979]

  - *Brown* [1993], *Ryan* [1996]

⚡ Suggested answer

Although the store has been paid for the goods obtained by Sara, she might still be guilty of various offences under the Theft Act 1968. The first offence to consider is obtaining property by deception under s. 15 of the Act, although as the store has been paid, Sara could argue that there has been no deception. This point has been before the House of Lords on two occasions — in *Metropolitan Police Commissioner* v *Charles* [1976] 3 All ER 112, where a cheque was supported by a cheque card; and in *R* v

Lambie [1981] 2 All ER 776, where a credit card was used, and this case is therefore directly in point.

Lambie knew that there were insufficient funds in her account to pay for goods she wanted to purchase from Mothercare. She also knew that she did not have the bank's authority to issue cheques when her account was overdrawn. Nevertheless, she paid for the goods by cheque, supported by a credit card; and as the assistant followed the correct procedure, the bank paid the store the appropriate amount. Lambie argued that the store was not deceived, as the only representation made by paying with a cheque supported by a credit card, is that the recipient will be paid, which is what happened. This argument was accepted by the Court of Appeal, but the House of Lords, in reinstating Lambie's conviction, held that there is another representation made by the credit card user in this situation, i.e., that he or she has the authority of the bank to use the card. As Lambie did not have this authority there was a deception. The accused argued that it was not an operative deception as the store assistant had said 'All I was concerned about was that the shop was paid'. However, the House of Lords stated that the public are honest, and would not take part in schemes to defraud banks; so had the assistant known the true position, she would not have allowed the transactions to proceed.

The House of Lords confirmed that Lambie could be guilty under s. 15 of the Theft Act 1968 (obtaining property by deception), although she was in fact found guilty under s. 16 of obtaining a pecuniary advantage by deception. Although this was under the old s. 16(2)(a) (which was abolished by the Theft Act 1978), Sara could be convicted under s. 16(2)(b). This provides that a person is obtaining a pecuniary advantage if he or she is allowed to borrow by way of overdraft, or to take out any policy of insurance or annuity contract, or obtain an improvement of the terms on which he is allowed to do so. Thus in *R v Waites* [1982] Crim LR 369, where D made no arrangement with her bank to overdraw but used her cheque card when there was no money in her account, whereby the bank guaranteed to meet a cheque up to £50, her conviction under s. 16(1)(b) was upheld by the Court of Appeal.

The court decided that there was no proper doubt as to the meaning of the verb 'allow' in the circumstances of s. 16(2)(b). Permission to use the card carried with it the power of the cardholder, albeit in breach of contract with the bank, to use the card beyond the limits imposed knowing that the bank would be obliged to meet the debt created with the shopkeeper. This surprising decision was followed in *R v Bevan* (1986) 84 Cr App R 143, and it is therefore submitted that Sara could be convicted of offences under both s. 15 and s. 16 of the 1968 Act.

In theory she might also be guilty of theft under s. 1 of the Act, as the House of Lords in *DPP v Gomez* [1993] 1 All ER 1 decided that even if the owner has consented to D taking the goods, there will still be an appropriation. Thus Sara will have dishonestly appropriated property belonging to another with the intention of permanently depriving the other of it. However, despite *Gomez* the Crown Prosecution Service have so far not charged theft when s. 15 is the appropriate offence.

In relation to her later activities in the store, Sara will be charged with burglary. Under s. 9 of the Theft Act 1968, she will be guilty of this offence if she has entered a building or part of a building as a trespasser with intent to commit theft or, having entered a building or part of a building as a trespasser, she attempted to steal anything therein. The concepts of 'trespass' and 'enters' must therefore be analysed to ascertain if the full offence has been committed.

Although trespass is a civil concept and belongs to the law of tort, the criminal law requires *mens rea* on the part of the accused to be established before this ingredient of burglary is satisfied. In *R v Collins* [1972] 2 All ER 1105, the Court of Appeal held that D must know the facts that caused him to be a trespasser, or at least be subjectively reckless whether those facts existed. So D, who believed that the houseowner's daughter had permission to invite him into the house, lacked the *mens rea* for trespass and could not be guilty of burglary.

Although Sara has clearly become a trespasser when she decides to remain in the store after closing time, the prosecution still must prove that she entered as a trespasser. When she first entered the store, she did so intending to shop, and therefore had the store's consent; and although she later exceeded this consent, there is no concept of trespass *ab initio* in criminal law to invalidate her legitimate entry. If she had entered knowing that she would commit theft, it could then be argued that she did initially enter as a trespasser as she knew that she intended to exceed her licence to be there and was therefore entering without the store's consent. This was the situation in *R v Jones and Smith* [1976] 3 All ER 54, where a son, prohibited from using his parent's home, entered it and stole a television. Although he might have argued that he believed his parents would have consented to his using the house for certain purposes, he knew that they would not consent to his entering to steal the television and he therefore entered as a trespasser. His conviction for burglary was upheld by the Court of Appeal.

The prosecution might argue that as Sara knew her account with her bank was overdrawn and she intended to use the card in breach of the bank's authority, she entered as a trespasser and committed theft when she obtained the goods (applying *Gomez*). However, it is submitted that this would be very difficult to establish, and the prosecution should look to two other incidents to satisfy the requirement of entry as a trespasser. The first is hiding in the store until after closing time.

Although Sara becomes a trespasser when she re-emerges again, there is the problem of entering part of a building as a trespasser with intent to steal. If she hides in the public part of the shop, for example, behind a display of soap powder, Sara has not entered a different part of the building. On the other hand, if she hides in a broom cupboard, this would be a part of a building. Thus when she re-enters the store she is entering a part of a building as a trespasser intending to steal.

The second possibility is climbing over the three-sided counter. It is recognised that a building can be divided into parts, without physical demarcation, so a sign marked 'Staff only' may in itself be sufficient. In *R v Walkington* [1979] 2 All ER 716, a moveable three-sided counter in a store was held to be part of a building, so D, who entered it as a trespasser intending to steal money from the till within, was guilty of burglary. The prosecution would nevertheless need to prove that Sara's act of climbing over the counter constituted an entry, and again this is not free from doubt.

Under the old common law rules the insertion of any part of the body was sufficient to constitute an entry. However, in *R v Collins*, Edmund Davies LJ stated there must be an 'effective and substantial entry' to constitute trespass. This test was referred to in *R v Brown* [1993] 2 WLR 556, where it was held that there was a sufficient entry where D's feet were on the ground outside a shop and the top part of his body was inside the broken shop window. The Court of Appeal stated that his entry was 'effective' and analysis of 'substantial' was not required. Lastly, in *R v Ryan* [1996] Crim LR 320, D was convicted of burglary, although he had become trapped by his neck with only his head and right arm inside the building. This can hardly be said to be effective as he had to be set free by the fire brigade! But the Court of Appeal again accepted that a person can enter where only part of his body is actually within the building. Thus Sara will have entered, and it is submitted that she would be found guilty of burglary as she has the necessary *mens rea* for the ulterior offence of theft.

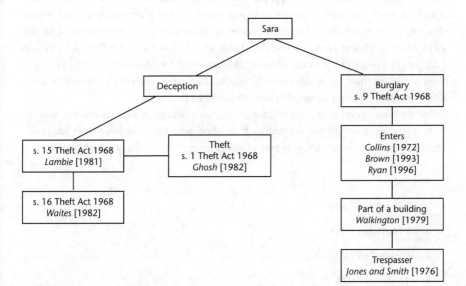

Q Question 2

Peter owed £100 in bank charges and was short of money. He went to his bank and told the manager that he would soon be inheriting £50,000 under his uncle's will and that he would pay that money into his account. This was untrue but the bank manager believed him, and as a result he offered Peter the following, which he accepted:

(a) £250 in cash to be repaid from the £50,000;

(b) overdraft facilities of up to £10,000;

(c) the removal of the £100 bank charges;

(d) free investment advice, which customers had to pay for unless they had £10,000 in their account.

There was only £10 in his account and Peter never paid any more money into it.
Discuss the criminal liability of Peter.

Commentary

This is a relatively straightforward question concerning deception. There are many offences under the Theft Acts with deception as an ingredient, and your answer must make it clear that you know which offence covers the different consequences of the deception. So you must cover ss. 15 and 16 of the Theft Act 1968, and ss. 1 and 2 of the Theft Act 1978. In addition, as a result of the House of Lords' decision in *DPP* v *Gomez* [1993] 1 All ER 1, you must also cover theft, as this offence may now be charged on every occasion (except when land is involved) where property has been obtained by deception.

There is not enough time to go into the intricacies of deception and the offences, and the facts of the question do not warrant such an approach. The question simply requires a knowledge of the relevant offences and an ability to apply them in a practical context.

- Deception

- s. 15 Theft Act 1968

- s. 16 Theft Act 1968

  - *Watkins* [1976]

- s. 2 Theft Act 1978

- s. 1 Theft Act 1978

- Dishonesty — *Ghosh* [1982]

:Q: Suggested answer

Peter could be charged with a number of offences under the Theft Acts 1968 and 1978, as he has clearly deceived his bank manager. Deception is defined under s. 15(4) of the Theft Act 1968: '"deception" means any deception (whether deliberate or reckless) by words or conduct as to fact or as to law, including a deception as to the present intentions of the person using the deception or any other person'. Further, in *Dip Kaur* v *Chief Constable for Hampshire* [1981] 2 All ER 430, the Court of Appeal confirmed that a deception is intentional if D knows that his statement is false and will or may be accepted as true by V; and a deception is reckless if D is aware that his statement may be false and will or may be accepted as true by V, or if he is aware that it is ambiguous and may be understood by V in a false sense. But carelessness or negligence is not enough (*R* v *Staines* (1974) 60 Cr App R 160). So if Peter honestly but unreasonably believed that he would inherit £50,000 and would be able to pay this sum into his bank account, he would lack *mens rea* for the deception offences; otherwise, as appears from the facts, he will have intentionally deceived the bank manager, as he has misrepresented his intentions knowing that his misrepresentation may affect the bank manager.

When Peter receives the £250, he will be guilty of obtaining property by deception under s. 15 of the 1968 Act, as by s. 4 property includes money and all other property, real or personal, including things in action and other intangible property. Further, as a result of the House of Lords' decision in *DPP* v *Gomez* [1993] 1 All ER 1, he may also be guilty of theft under s. 1, i.e., 'he dishonestly appropriates property belonging to another with the intention of permanently depriving the other of it'. Before *Gomez* it was difficult to say that there had been an appropriation of property when the owner had consented to the accused taking it. However, in this case their Lordships, in following their earlier decision in *Lawrence* v *Metropolitan Police Commissioner* [1971] 2 All ER 1253, confirmed that appropriation simply meant assuming any of the rights of an owner and did not necessarily have to involve an adverse interference with or usurpation of those rights, as had previously been suggested in *R* v *Morris*, *Anderton* v *Burnside* [1983] 3 All ER 288. Despite this recent House of Lords decision, there is no evidence as yet that the Crown Prosecution Service are charging theft in these circumstances, and it is submitted that Peter should be charged under s. 15 although he could be charged with both offences.

Although Peter may not actually use the overdraft facilities, the mere fact that he obtains them means that he might be guilty of the full offence under s. 16 of the Theft Act 1968, of by any deception dishonestly obtaining for himself or another any pecuniary advantage. Although the term 'pecuniary advantage' is potentially very wide, s. 16 is in fact very limited, covering certain specific consequences only. Thus under s. 16(2)(b), a pecuniary advantage will be obtained when Peter is allowed to borrow by way of overdraft or to take out any policy of insurance or annuity contract or obtain any improvement of the terms on which he is allowed to do so. In *R v Watkins* [1976] 1 All ER 578, where a bank agreed to grant credit facilities to the accused, he was convicted of the full offence even though he did not use those facilities.

Section 2 of the Theft Act 1978 may apply to the cancellation of Peter's bank charges. This is the offence of evasion of liability by deception, and it can be committed under three separate (but overlapping) subsections of s. 2. Section 2(1)(a) would seem to be the most appropriate, as this makes it an offence for a person, by deception, dishonestly to secure the remission of the whole or any part of any existing liability to make a payment, whether his own liability or another's. Arguably s. 2(1)(b) would also apply. This covers an accused who:

> with intent to make permanent default in whole or in part on any existing liability to make a payment, or with intent to let another do so, dishonestly induces the creditor or any person claiming payment on behalf of the creditor to wait for payment (whether or not the due date for payment is deferred) or to forgo payment.

The main difficulty in securing a conviction under s. 2(1)(b) is that the prosecution must show that when Peter made the misrepresentation he had 'intent to make permanent default'. Section 2(1)(a) merely uses the phrase 'secures the remission', and it is submitted that a charge under this subsection would be the more appropriate. (Although in *R v Holt* [1981] 2 All ER 854, the Court of Appeal was not prepared to entertain detailed defence arguments concerning the differences between the subsections. Provided that it could be established that an offence under s. 2 had been committed, the court was not concerned if the charge was brought under s. 2(1)(a) or s. 2(1)(b).)

The final relevant offence is s. 1 of the Theft Act 1978, and this could apply as Peter is given free investment advice for which he would normally have to pay. This could constitute the offence of obtaining services by deception, which under s. 1(2) involves the obtaining of services where the other is induced to confer a benefit by doing some act or permitting some act to be done, on the understanding that the benefit has been or will be paid for. Certainly the investment advice is a service, and as it is normally paid for the offence would appear to be made out. However, commentators maintain that where D induces P by deception to render for nothing a service for which P would normally charge, D commits no offences under s. 1. The essence of s. 1 is that someone has been or will be paid, and the deception has to be directly related to this consequence. Thus the more appropriate charge would again be under s. 2, as s. 2(1)(c) provides that Peter would be evading liability, if he 'dishonestly obtains any exemption from or abatement of liability to make a payment'. Thus in *R v Firth* (1990) 91 Cr App R 217, a surgeon who evaded liability by failing to disclose that certain of his patients were private patients for whom he would otherwise have had to pay hospital fees, was found guilty under this provision.

For all these offences, in addition to proving the *mens rea* for deception, the prosecution must also prove that Peter was dishonest. This should not present a problem on the facts of this case, but on authority of *R v Ghosh* [1982] 2 All ER 689 the jury must consider two questions:

(a) Was what was done dishonest according to the ordinary standards of reasonable and honest people? If not, D is not guilty.

(b) If it was, did D realise that reasonable and honest people regard what he did as dishonest? If so, he is guilty; if not, he is not guilty.

It is submitted that Peter has committed offences under s. 15 and s. 16 of the Theft Act 1968, under s. 2 of the Theft Act 1978, and under s. 1 of the Theft Act 1968.

Q Question 3

Paul is very short of money and decides to remedy the situation. He sees an open window of a house and enters with a view to stealing anything inside which he might find of value. However, after examining the contents he decides that there is nothing worth anything to him and he leaves without taking anything.

He then meets Steve, who is having an affair with a secretary. Paul tells Steve that unless Steve gives him £500 he will tell Steve's wife about the affair. Steve replies that, as his wife already knows, he will give Paul nothing.

While driving home, Paul is stopped by the police who find a crow bar and other items which could be used for burglary, and Paul admits that he intended to use them to gain access if he found an unoccupied property.

Discuss the criminal liability of Paul.

Commentary

At first glance this appears to be a question on attempt, as Paul has not succeeded in his criminal ventures. Although this topic should be mentioned briefly, the answer must concentrate on three substantive offences under the Theft Act 1968, namely: burglary (s. 9), blackmail (s. 21), and going equipped (s. 25). They do to some extent resemble the inchoate offences, as they do not require the accused to obtain anything in order to be guilty; but your answer must state that Paul will be guilty of the full offence, not merely attempt.

If you can avoid the pitfalls you should be able to obtain a high mark, as all you are required to do is demonstrate a knowledge of the basic ingredients of the three offences.

- **s. 9 Theft Act 1968**

    – *Attorney-General's References (Nos 1 and 2 of 1979)* **[1979]**

- **s. 21 Theft Act 1968 — blackmail**

- *Clear* [1968]

- *Lambert* [1972]

- s. 25 Theft Act 1968 — going equipped

- *Rashid* [1977]

- *Hargreaves* [1985]

☀ Suggested answer

As a result of entering another's property with intent to steal, Paul will be charged with burglary. This is defined under s. 9 of the Theft Act 1968, and the relevant part in this case is s. 9(1)(a), whereby a person is guilty of burglary if he enters any building or part of a building as a trespasser with intent to commit any such offence as is mentioned in s. 9(2), which includes stealing or attempting to steal anything therein. Thus it is not necessary for the prosecution to prove that Paul actually stole something, only that when he entered he intended to steal something. This will be sufficient for the full offence of burglary, not simply an attempt.

Paul has clearly entered a building as a trespasser with the requisite *mens rea* for these ingredients of the offence (*R v Collins* [1972] 2 All ER 1105), and therefore the only doubtful issue is whether his conditional intent to steal is sufficient. This particular question has caused difficulties. In *R v Easom* [1971] 2 All ER 945, where the accused had taken and then (after rifling through its contents) abandoned a ladies handbag, because there was nothing of value to him which he wanted to steal, his conviction for theft was quashed on the basis that his conditional intent was not regarded as an intention permanently to deprive for the purposes of theft. However, the position is different with burglary, as the law recognises the fact that most burglars do not intend to steal a specific thing, but will take anything they may find of value. The indictment should therefore state that Paul intended to steal 'some or all of the contents of the house'. On this basis, the Court of Appeal confirmed in *Attorney-General's References (Nos 1 and 2 of 1979)* [1979] 3 All ER 143, that the accused would be guilty of burglary. The fact that there is nothing in the building worth stealing is no bar to Paul's conviction.

Paul could also be charged with the offence of blackmail under s. 21 of the Theft Act 1968. Section 21(1) provides that a person is guilty of blackmail if:

> with a view to gain for himself or another or with intent to cause loss to another, he makes any unwarranted demand with menaces; and for this purpose a demand with menaces is unwarranted unless the person making it does so in the belief —
>
> (a) that he has reasonable grounds for making the demand; and
>
> (b) that the use of the menaces is a proper means of reinforcing the demand.

Paul has clearly made a demand, but this was not accompanied by the threat of physical violence, so can it be said that it was a demand with menaces? 'Menaces' was chosen by the Law Commission in preference to 'threats', as being the most appropriate term for blackmail, and was defined in *Thorne* v *Motor Trade Association* [1937] AC 397 as 'not limited to threats of violence but . . . including threats of any action detrimental to or unpleasant to the person addressed'. Further, it is not necessary for the prosecution to prove that the victim was affected by the demand, merely that it was of such a nature and extent that the mind of an ordinary person of normal stability and courage might be so influenced or made apprehensive as to accede unwillingly to the demand. Thus in *R* v *Clear* [1968] 1 All ER 74, an accused who demanded money from a litigant (for giving evidence) in a civil case was convicted of blackmail, although the victim was unaffected by the demand as his insurance company had agreed to settle any damages award.

A threat to tell Steve's wife could therefore be deemed a menace by the jury. Whether or not it is unwarranted depends on the accused's ability to convince the jury that he believed that he had reasonable grounds for making the demand and that the use of menaces was a proper means of reinforcing it. This is a subjective test, and in *R* v *Lambert* [1972] Crim LR 422 the trial judge directed the jury that they would find the menaces 'proper' if the accused honestly believed that they were proper. This again was a case where the accused demanded money as compensation for keeping quiet about a sexual liaison. If, on the other hand, the accused threatens to kill or harm the victim, he cannot claim that he thought this was 'proper' (*R* v *Harvey, Uylett and Plummer* (1981) 72 Cr App R 139). On the facts, it appears that Paul could not succeed with this argument; and as he has clearly made an unwarranted demand with menaces, it is submitted he will be found guilty of blackmail.

As Paul has equipment that could be used for burglary in his car, he could be charged under s. 25 of the Theft Act 1968 with 'going equipped'. Section 25 provides that a person shall be guilty of an offence if, when not at his place of abode, he has with him any article for use in the course of or in connection with any burglary, theft or cheat. From the prosecution's viewpoint, s. 25 has a great advantage over a charge of attempted burglary as for that offence the prosecution must prove that the accused has done more than a merely preparatory act (under s. 1(1) of the Criminal Attempts Act 1981). In practical terms this would require Paul to be on the very point of entering a particular property. Even this may not be sufficient, as in *R* v *Campbell* (1991) 93 Cr App R 350, the Court of Appeal quashed a conviction of attempted robbery where the accused was arrested on the entrance steps of a post office armed with an imitation gun and ransom demand, on the basis that as he was still outside the building his act was still only merely preparatory. No such difficulty arises under s. 25, and there have been convictions of British Rail stewards arrested on the way to their trains armed with sandwiches and coffee which they intended to pass off as British Rail products to passengers on the train (*R v Rashid* [1977] 2 All ER 237; *R v Corboz* [1984] Crim LR 302).

Paul would be able to argue that he lacked the necessary *mens rea* as he had not specifically formed the intention to use the equipment on a particular property. However, s. 25(3) provides that proof that the accused had with him any article made or adapted for use in committing burglary shall be evidence that he had it with him for such use; and in *R v Hargreaves* [1985] Crim LR 243, the Court of Appeal held that the prosecution had to prove only that the accused had formed the intention to use the article if a suitable opportunity arose.

Although it was recognised in *R v Bundy* [1977] 2 All ER 382 that a motor vehicle could in certain circumstances be a place of abode, it is submitted that it could not be in Paul's case as he was driving around in it at the time he was stopped. It is submitted that Paul has therefore committed all three offences: burglary, blackmail, and 'going equipped'.

Q Question 4

Ron knew that X had recently committed a serious criminal offence. He threatened to tell the police unless X gave him some property. As a result X gave Ron a watch, a ring and a lighter. Ron then gave the ring to Steve as a birthday present. He sold the watch at an undervalue to Trevor and asked William to look after the lighter for him until he wanted it returned. Steve, Trevor and William took these articles in good faith, not knowing how they had been obtained by Ron. However, three days later Ron told them the full story. Nevertheless, all three kept possession of the articles.

Discuss the criminal responsibility of Ron, Steve, Trevor and William.

Commentary

This is a difficult question requiring detailed knowledge of, and an ability to apply, the principles relating to handling stolen goods under s. 22 of the Theft Act 1968. In addition you need to be able to demonstrate an understanding of the relationship between s. 22 and theft (s. 1), with particular reference to the important protection for a bona fide purchaser for value contained in s. 3(2) of the 1968 Act. There are many important cases on these points which must be used to illustrate the application of the principles.

In addition you must also cover blackmail (Theft Act 1968, s. 21) and compounding (Criminal Law Act 1967, s. 5).

- **Blackmail — s. 21 Theft Act 1968**

- **Compounding — s. 5(1) Criminal Law Act 1967**

- Handling stolen goods — s. 22 Theft Act 1968

    - *Bloxham* [1982]

    - *Pitchley* [1972]

- Theft

    - s. 1 Theft Act 1968

    - s. 3(2) Theft Act 1968

᛫Ò᛫ Suggested answer

As a result of his dealings with X, Ron may have committed blackmail (Theft Act 1968, s. 21) and compounding (Criminal Law Act 1967, s. 5). Ron is guilty of blackmail if, with a view to gain for himself or another or with intent to cause loss to another, he makes any unwarranted demand with menaces; and for this purpose a demand with menaces is unwarranted unless the person making it does so in the belief:

(a)   that he has reasonable grounds for making the demand; and

(b)   that the use of menaces is a proper means of reinforcing the demand.

It is clear on the facts that Ron will have no defence to this charge and it appears he will also be guilty of compounding. Under s. 5(1) of the Criminal Law Act 1967:

> Where a person has committed an arrestable offence, any other person who, knowing or believing that the offence or some other arrestable offence has been committed, and that he has information which might be of material assistance in securing the prosecution or conviction of an offender for it, accepts or agrees to accept for not disclosing that information any consideration other than the making good of loss or injury caused by the offence, or the making of reasonable compensation for that loss or injury, shall be liable on conviction on indictment to imprisonment for not more than two years . . .

However, it is the possibility of charges under s. 22 of the Theft Act 1968 for handling stolen goods that will provoke the most argument. All four parties could be charged with this offence since, under s. 22(1), a person handles stolen goods 'if (otherwise than in the course of the stealing) knowing or believing them to be stolen goods he dishonestly receives the goods, or dishonestly undertakes or assists in their retention, removal, disposal or realisation by or for the benefit of another person, or if he arranges to do so'. Further, although the goods have been obtained by blackmail they are still regarded as stolen goods as a result of s. 24(4) of the 1968 Act.

Ron could be charged on the basis that he has assisted in the goods' disposal or realisation, by or for the benefit of another. As he has given the lighter to William only temporarily, to look after for Ron's benefit, this cannot constitute the offence; but his dealings with Steve and Trevor may satisfy this condition. The key case on this point is the House of Lords' decision in *R* v *Bloxham* [1982] 1 All ER 582. D had bought a car in good faith and later discovered that it had been stolen. He then sold it at an under-value to V. As he had purchased in good faith he could not be guilty of theft, as a result of s. 3(2) of the Theft Act 1968 (the protection given to a bona fide purchaser), or of handling on the basis of dishonest receipt. But he was found guilty of handling on the basis that when he sold the car at an undervalue, he was assisting in its disposal for the benefit of another, namely the purchaser. However, their Lordships, in quashing his conviction and reversing the decision of the Court of Appeal, held that a purchaser of stolen goods is not 'another person' within the meaning of s. 22. So, although the sale was at an undervalue it was not deemed to be for the benefit of another. Thus Ron would not be guilty of handling as a result of the sale of the watch to Trevor.

Ron could use this argument if he was charged with handling as a result of giving the ring to Steve. However, in *Bloxham* their Lordships were clearly influenced by the fact that as D had bought in good faith and could not therefore be guilty of theft, it would be going against the spirit of the Theft Act 1968 to convict him of handling, where the maximum sentence is greater. Ron's position differs in this respect, and also in the fact that it is hard to argue that an outright gift benefits the donor and is not for another's benefit (i.e., the donee). It is therefore submitted that *Bloxham* can be distinguished and that Ron could be found guilty of handling in this instance.

Neither Steve, nor Trevor or William could be guilty of handling on the basis that they had dishonestly received the goods, but they may be found guilty on the alternative ground involving acting by or for the benefit of another. However, as Steve is given the ring as a present and keeps it for his own use, he is not doing an act for the benefit of another and cannot be found guilty of handling.

William, on the other hand, in keeping the lighter in custody for Ron, is clearly assisting in its retention for the benefit of another. Thus as soon as he knows the true position he has the necessary *mens rea* and would therefore be guilty. This was the case in *R* v *Pitchley* (1972) 57 Cr App R 30, one of the few cases where an omission to act was sufficient for the *actus reus* of the offence. There the accused had been given a sum of money to look after for his son. He received it in good faith and placed it in his bank account, where he allowed it to remain after discovering that his son had acquired it dishonestly. The court held that this was sufficient to constitute handling, on the basis that he assisted in its retention by or for the benefit of another.

As far as the crime of handling is concerned, Trevor would appear to be in the same position as Steve as he has not done an act by or for the benefit of another. However, there is a marked difference in their criminal responsibility for theft. This is because Trevor has the protection of s. 3(2) of the 1968 Act, which provides:

> Where property or a right or interest in property is or purports to be transferred for value to a
> person acting in good faith, no later assumption by him of rights which he believed himself to

be acquiring shall, by reason of any defect in the transferor's title, amount to theft of the property.

The only way in which Trevor could be guilty is if the jury decided that as he bought the watch at an undervalue he was not acting in good faith and that s. 3(2) of the 1968 Act therefore does not apply.

Because Steve is not a purchaser he does not have the protection of s. 3(2). Further, under s. 3(1), 'appropriation' includes, where D has come by the property (innocently or not) 'without stealing it, any later assumption of a right to it by keeping or dealing with it as owner'. As the other ingredients of theft appear to be satisfied, it is therefore submitted that Steve will be guilty of theft.

Q Question 5

Alf is a general dealer who specialises in buying and selling secondhand watches. He does not have a house but eats, sleeps and lives in his dormobile while moving around the country. Bert is a rogue, who has obtained a gold watch worth £500 by giving Victor a stolen cheque which he knew would bounce.

Bert met Alf in a pub and sold him the watch for £25, no questions asked. Later, when Bert discovered the true value of the watch, he broke into Alf's dormobile and recovered it. When the police were investigating the incident they discovered safe-breaking equipment in the dormobile.

Discuss the criminal liability of Alf and Bert.

Commentary

This question tests general knowledge of several Theft Act offences. It does not require you to cover all aspects of the relevant offences in depth, but it does require an ability to deal thoroughly with specific principles.

You must cover s. 15 of the Theft Act 1968 (obtaining property by deception) and consider whether Alf could be committing the offence by deliberately paying Bert a sum which is much lower than the true value of the watch. Certainly Alf's expertise raises the possibility of handling stolen goods under s. 22 of the 1968 Act.

The precise status of Alf's dormobile must also be considered in relation to the offices of burglary (s. 9) and going equipped (s. 25). In this context the important case of *R* v *Bundy* [1977] 2 All ER 382 must be discussed.

- **Deception — s. 15 Theft Act 1968**

- **Handling — s. 22 Theft Act 1968**

    - *Bloxham* [1982]

- *Silverman* [1987]

• **Burglary — s. 9 Theft Act 1968**

  - building — *B and S v Leathley* [1979]

• **Going equipped — s. 25 Theft Act 1968**

:Q̇: Suggested answer

When Bert obtained the watch from Victor by giving him a cheque which he knew would bounce, he was committing the offence of obtaining property by deception. Under s. 15 of the Theft Act 1968: 'A person who by any deception dishonestly obtains property belonging to another, with the intention of permanently depriving the other of it, shall on conviction on indictment be liable to imprisonment . . .'. Since *R* v *Hazelton* (1874) LR 2 CCR 134, it has been recognised that by giving a cheque the accused represents that it will be met on presentation. As this did not happen there is a clear deception, and it also appears that Bert has acted dishonestly. This is a question of fact for the jury (*R* v *Feely* [1973] 1 All ER 341), but there is nothing to suggest that the prosecution would not be able to satisfy the test laid down by the Court of Appeal in *R* v *Ghosh* [1982] 2 All ER 689:

(a) Was what was done dishonest according to the ordinary standards of honest and reasonable people? If not, D is not guilty.

(b) If it was, did D realise that reasonable and honest people regard what he did as dishonest? If so, he is guilty; if not, he is not guilty.

Further, since the House of Lords' decision in *DPP* v *Gomez* [1993] 1 All ER 1, stating that D can appropriate property even when the owner has consented to D taking it, Bert would also be guilty of theft under s. 1 of the Theft Act 1968.

When Bert sold the watch to Alf, he may again have committed the offence under s. 15 of the 1968 Act. This is because a seller of goods impliedly represents that he has the right to sell the goods and can pass on a good title to the buyer (Sale of Goods Act 1979). As the watch is stolen, Bert cannot give a good title to Alf and there is therefore a deception. The only argument that Bert may have is that, Alf being a general dealer, he would have known from the low price that the goods were in fact stolen and therefore he was not deceived. However, even if this argument were to succeed, Bert could still be found guilty of an attempt to obtain property by deception under s. 1 of the Criminal Attempts Act 1981 as he has clearly done more than a merely preparatory act with the intention of committing the deception offence.

The fact that the watch is stolen property also raises the possibility of both parties committing offences under s. 22 of the 1968 Act:

A person handles stolen goods if (otherwise than in the course of the stealing) knowing or believing them to be stolen goods he dishonestly receives the goods, or dishonestly undertakes or assists in their retention, removal, disposal or realisation by or for the benefit of another person, or if he arranges to do so.

Thus when Bert sold the watch, he was acting otherwise than in the course of the stealing (as this had already taken place when he obtained it from Victor), and it could be argued that he was assisting in its disposal for the benefit of another (Alf) when he sold it to Alf. This was the point of law for consideration in *R v Bloxham* [1982] 1 All ER 582, where the House of Lords decided that the seller of a stolen car, sold at an undervalue, was not acting for the benefit of another (the buyer) and could not therefore be guilty of handling. Therefore Bert will not be guilty as Alf, the purchaser, is not deemed to be 'another person' within s. 22 of the Act.

However, Alf may be guilty of handling under s. 22 if the prosecution can prove that he has the necessary *mens rea*. They must establish that he knew or believed the goods to be stolen; suspicion is not enough (*R v Grange* [1974] 1 All ER 928). This is a subjective test, but according to *R v Hall* (1985) 81 Cr App R 260:

> a man may be said to know that goods are stolen when he is told by someone with first-hand knowledge (someone such as the thief or burglar) that such is the case. Belief of course, is something short of knowledge. It may be the state of mind of a person who says to himself 'I cannot say I know for certain that these goods are stolen, but there can be no other reasonable conclusion in the light of all the circumstances, in the light of all that I have heard and seen'.

As Alf is a general dealer with specialist knowledge of the value of secondhand watches, the jury may well conclude that in view of the low price agreed for the watch, he did know or believe the watch to be stolen, and that he dishonestly received it. In which case he would be guilty under s. 22. His expert knowledge could also mean that he was charged under s. 15 of the 1968 Act. It is difficult to envisage both parties being charged with deception arising out of the same transaction, but in *R v Silverman* (1987) 86 Cr App R 213, it was held that there was a deception by a builder who, knowing that he was being relied on to quote a fair price, deliberately obtained an extortionate sum from the victim. The prosecution could argue that as an 'expert' in this field, Alf knew that Bert was relying on him to offer him a fair price. However, it is submitted that in view of the nature of this business — buying and selling secondhand goods — it is unlikely that such an implied representation could be established.

When Bert breaks into Alf's dormobile and takes the watch, in addition to committing theft under s. 1 (dishonestly appropriating property belonging to another with the intention of permanently depriving the other of it) he may be committing burglary under s. 9. The prosecution will argue that he has entered a building or part of a building as a trespasser and has stolen something therein (in contravention of s. 9(1)(b) of the 1968 Act). It is submitted that Bert could not argue that he honestly believed that he had a claim of right in law to the watch and is therefore not dishonest (because of s. 2(1)(a)), and his only defence to burglary would be that the dormobile cannot be regarded as a building. There is no definition of 'building' under the Theft Act 1968, but it is generally taken to mean a structure of some substance and permanence. This could certainly include a dormobile, as in *B and S* v *Leathley* [1979] Crim LR 314 it was held that a freezer container detached from its chassis resting on railway sleepers and used to store frozen foods was a building. However, in practice the prosecution will not need to rely on this provision as s. 9(4) of the Theft Act 1968 states that 'building' shall also apply to an inhabited vehicle or vessel, and also at times when the person having a habitation in it is not there as well as at times when he is. Thus Alf's dormobile is a building and Bert will be guilty of burglary.

Lastly, Alf may also face a charge of going equipped under s. 25(1) of the Theft Act 1968: 'A person shall be guilty of an offence if, when not at his place of abode, he has with him any article for use in the course of or in connection with any burglary, theft or cheat.' However, Alf would be able to argue that his dormobile constitutes his place of abode. This was unsuccessfully argued in *R* v *Bundy* [1977] 2 All ER 382, where the accused was actually driving around in his car (which he claimed to be his place of abode) when arrested for the offence. Nevertheless, the Court of Appeal did recognise that a car could be a place of abode if it was on a permanent site, used as a place to live and D was not using another residence. It is submitted that as Alf's dormobile satisfies these conditions he would not be guilty of the offence under s. 25.

Q Question 6

Malcolm is the managing director and owner of 99% of the shares of Arriba Ltd. His wife Orchid is the owner of the remaining shares and the only other director. Orchid takes little interest in the running of the company, and effectively Malcolm is in sole control.

Both Malcolm and Arriba Ltd are in desperate need of money. Malcolm has recently deceived the Midtown Bank to make loans to both himself and the company using property they do not own as security. The bank does not realise this and have sent one cheque to Malcolm for £25,000 and transferred the sum of £20,000 via the CHAPS system to Arriba Ltd's bank account. Malcolm has also written a cheque from the company in his favour for £20,000 and paid this into his own account. No record of this was made in the company records but when questioned by the police Malcolm said this was payment for services rendered to the company.

On his way home after using the London Underground Malcolm sold the ticket he had purchased to Harry who then used the tube without further payment. One month after these events Arriba Ltd went into liquidation owing creditors over £100,000.

Discuss the criminal responsibility of the parties.

Commentary

A question to be tackled only by criminal law students who enjoy analysing the intricacies of offences in relation to cheques and choses in action. Needless to say there are very few such students, or lecturers for that matter! However, there is much academic interest in this area (see, for example, Professor J. C. Smith, 'Obtaining Cheques by Deception or Theft' [1997] Crim LR 396) and therefore much discussion about *R v Preddy* [1996] 3 All ER 481 and the effects of the Theft (Amendment) Act 1996.

In addition to discussing these issues and the offences of theft and deception under s. 15A of the Theft Act 1968 you must also consider the s. 1 offence under the Theft Act 1978 of obtaining services by deception and the recent decision in *R v Marshall* (1998) 2 Cr App R 282. When you consider that reference to corporate liability, innocent agency and s. 22 of the Theft Act 1968 is also required, you can understand why many students would quickly rule this out as an exam question choice.

- **s. 15 Theft Act 1968**

    - *Preddy* [1996]

    - *Graham* [1997]

    - *Williams* [2001]

- **s. 1 Theft Act 1978**

- **s. 15A Theft Act 1968**

- **Corporate liability**

    - *Tesco Supermarkets* v *Nattrass* [1972]

- **Dishonesty**

    - *Ghosh* [1982]

- **s. 1 Theft Act 1968**

    - *Marshall* [1998]

:Q: **Suggested answer**

Malcolm and his company, Arriba Ltd, may face charges of theft and deception under s. 15A of the Theft Act 1968 and s. 1 of the Theft Act 1978 and possibly handling stolen goods under s. 22 of the Theft Act 1968. Orchid and Harry may also face charges under these offences but it is unlikely they will be convicted in view of the difficulties the prosecution appear to have in establishing *mens rea*.

When cheques have been dishonestly obtained or appropriated it has always been difficult for the prosecution to choose the most appropriate offence. Sometimes stealing or obtaining a valuable security under s. 20 of the Theft Act 1968 was used, but in recent years the charge was often framed under s. 15 of the 1968 Act — obtaining property by deception. Many convictions under s. 15 came from the numerous mortgage fraud cases from the mid-1980s onwards. However, the legal deficiencies of this approach were exposed by the House of Lords' decision in *Preddy*. Here the House decided that when a building society sent their mortgage funds either by cheque or telegraphic transfer (CHAPS) to the accused's agent, the only property belonging to the building society (V) was the thing in action represented by the extent of the credit balance in its bank account. No part of this property, V's right to demand from V's bank an amount of money equal to the credit balance or any portion of it, was ever obtained by A. Instead property possessed by A came into existence as soon as A's bank credited his account with the amount of the loan. This property, the thing in action constituted by A's right to demand from A's bank an amount of money equal to the credit resulting from the loan had never belonged to anyone other than A and was not the same as the thing in action originally possessed by V.

A would therefore not be guilty of an offence under s. 15 and in *R v Graham* [1997] Crim LR 340 the Court of Appeal held that if in any case the reasoning in *Preddy* was fatal to a conviction of s. 15 it was likely to be fatal to a conviction of theft also, unless in the case of a chose in action it can be shown that the chose in action appropriated was at the time of the appropriation the property of another. That will not ordinarily be so where the result of A's dishonesty is the creation of a new chose in action. However, in *R v Williams* [2001] Crim LR 253, the Court of Appeal upheld the conviction of an accused for theft who had deceived house-owners who as a result gave him cheques which he paid into his account. The court held that he was thereby appropriating an existing chose in action which belonged to the victim, namely his credit balance, or right to overdraw at his bank.

Another possible alternative in these circumstances was s. 1 of the Theft Act 1978 — obtaining services by deception. However in *R v Halai* [1983] Crim LR 624 the Court of Appeal surprisingly held that a mortgage advance was not a service because such an advance was a lending of money for property. Although *Halai* was distinguished in *R v Widdowson* (1985) 82 Cr App R 314 where the Court of Appeal held that obtaining goods on hire-purchase was an obtaining of services, it was not overruled in *Preddy*. However, s. 4(1) of the Theft (Amendment) Act 1996 adds a new subsection (3) to s. 1 of the Theft Act 1978 and this provides that it is an obtaining of services where the other person is induced to make a loan, or to cause or permit a loan to be made on the understanding that any payment (whether by way of interest or otherwise) will be or has been made in respect of the loan. Further *R v Cooke* [1997] Crim LR 436 in effect overruled *Halai* in respect of transactions entered into before 18 December 1996 (the date when the 1996 Act took effect), so it is clear that now Malcolm would be guilty of an offence under s. 1 of the Theft Act 1978.

As the Midtown Bank have been deceived into transferring funds to Malcolm and Arriba Ltd the key issue in resolving the appropriate charge is to ascertain what the recipients have received. This is where the difficulties concerning cheques, choses in action, property belonging to another and s. 5(1) of the Theft Act 1968 surfaced in *Preddy*. However, these arguments are rendered largely academic as the prosecution can now use the new s. 15A(1) which provides that a person is guilty of an offence if, by any deception, he dishonestly obtains a money transfer for himself or another. Further by s. 15A(2) a money transfer occurs when:

(a) a debit is made to one account;

(b) a credit is made to another; and

(c) a credit results from the debit or the debit results from the credit.

On similar facts to the present case — *R* v *Arnold* [1997] 4 All ER 1 where A had fraudulently used V's bills of exchange — the Court of Appeal upheld A's conviction for theft. This was on the basis that the bill of exchange was property belonging to another (utilising s. 5(3) of the Theft Act 1968) and V had been permanently deprived of it, as the paper that was returned to V was not a valuable security: it had completely changed character. However, this solution is not available when the credit is transferred from bank account to bank account by CHAPS or by telegraphic transfer. Thus a charge of theft could only succeed in respect of the cheque.

As the money has been received by Arriba Ltd it is possible that it could be charged with these offences. This would be on the basis of the identification principle as expounded in *Tesco Supermarkets* v *Nattrass* [1972] AC 153 where the House of Lords confirmed that those who constitute the directing mind and will of the company can be identified with it so as to make the company criminally responsible. However, although Malcolm is clearly the mind and will of Arriba Ltd it is submitted that it would be unfair to prosecute the company which is really one of the victims of Malcolm's criminal activities. This would be a suitable case for utilising the innocent agency principle, thereby treating Malcolm as the principal offender.

Malcolm would also face charges regarding the drawing of £20,000 from the company's account for his personal use. Again there is a choice of offences which could be utilised. As Malcolm has taken a cheque s. 15A might be considered although the prosecution would find difficulties in establishing that there was a deception. Additionally theft under s. 1 of the Theft Act 1968 might be considered as the cheque is clearly the company's property and Malcolm has the intention of permanently depriving the company of it. However, the prosecution must also establish that Malcolm dishonestly appropriated the property. Proving appropriation where the owner consented to the taking of the property had caused difficulties, but now the House of Lords' decision in *DPP* v *Gomez* [1993] 1 All ER 1 demonstrates that the owner's consent is irrelevant; there will still be an appropriation. Further, *R* v *Phillipou* (1989) 89

Cr App R 290 demonstrates that even though a company is controlled by two share-holders who agree to company property being taken, this can still amount to an appropriation of property belonging to another. Especially if the decision has not been made bona fide for the benefit of the company as a whole.

The only outstanding ingredient is dishonesty and as the company has gone into liquidation there is the inference that Malcolm would have known that Arriba Ltd was short of funds when he took the £20,000. The prosecution do not have to prove that Malcolm was dishonest *vis-à-vis* the company, dishonesty in respect of the creditors will suffice. This is a question of fact for the jury, and following the Court of Appeal's decision in *R v Ghosh* [1982] 2 All ER 689 the jury must ask themselves:

(i) Was what was done dishonest according to the ordinary standards of reasonable and honest people? If no, A is not guilty. If yes:

(ii) Did A realise that reasonable and honest people regard what he did as dishonest? If yes he is guilty, if no he is not.

The final issue to consider is the selling of the London Underground ticket to Harry. This situation was recently considered by the Court of Appeal in *R v Marshall* (1998) 2 Cr App R 282 where the accused's conviction for theft was upheld. The key argument centred around the issue of whether the ticket sold by the customer was property belonging to another within s. 5(1) of the Theft Act 1968. The court examined the terms of issue of the ticket and found that there was a term on the back of each ticket to the effect that it remained the property of the company. As Professor J. C. Smith points out ([1998] Crim LR 723, *Stealing Tickets*) notice of such a condition must be known by the accused before he entered the contract otherwise he is not bound by it. Similarly if Malcolm thought that he had the right to sell the ticket he would not be acting dishonestly.

It is possible that Harry might be charged with handling stolen goods (s. 22 of the Theft Act 1968) or evasion of liability by deception (s. 2 of the Theft Act 1978) when he uses the ticket on the underground. However, in both cases it would be very difficult for the prosecution to establish the necessary *mens rea*.

Q Question 7

Dave stopped his car at a petrol filling station and instructed the attendant to put ten gallons of petrol in his tank. When the attendant had put in six gallons Dave realised that he had no money on him, but said nothing. After the attendant had completed the task Dave told the cashier that he was Tim Henman, the well-known tennis player, and that if the garage would send the bill to the Lawn Tennis Association's office at Wimbledon, they would pay the bill. This was untrue, but after asking for his autograph, the cashier allowed Dave to leave without paying.

Discuss the criminal liability of Dave.

Commentary

Yet another everyday situation, which demonstrates the difficulties of applying our complex criminal law. One might assume that such a situation would neatly fall within a specific offence, leaving little room for discussion. However, experienced students of the criminal law know that this is very rarely the case. This has been aptly demonstrated by the case of *R* v *Coady* [1996] Crim LR 518, where the Court of Appeal quashed A's conviction under s. 15 of the Theft Act 1968. In their commentary, the Criminal Law Review pointed out that the prosecution could have presented an alternative argument concerning deception which might lead to a s. 15 conviction being upheld. Alternatively, in the light of the developments extending the concept of appropriation, theft under s. 1 of the Theft Act 1968 may offer the prosecution a greater chance of success. In addition, A might have committed any one of the three offences under the Theft Act 1978.

A good answer must therefore consider the possibility of all five offences, with a detailed analysis of the relevant cases and argument which would apply. In short, this is a testing question, which should only be attempted by a competent, knowledgeable student.

- **Obtaining property by deception — s. 15 Theft Act 1968**

  - *Coady* [1996]

  - *Ray* [1974]

- **Theft — s. 1 Theft Act 1968**

  - *Edwards* v *Ddin* [1976]

  - *Hinks* [2000]

  - *Gomez* [1993]

- **Obtaining services by deception — s. 1 Theft Act 1978**

- **Making off without payment — s. 3 Theft Act 1978**

  - *Hammond* [1982]

- **Evasion of liability by deception — s. 2 Theft Act 1978**

  - *Jackson* [1983]

☼ Suggested answer

Dave might be guilty of any (or all) of the following offences: obtaining property by deception (s. 15 Theft Act 1968), theft (s. 1 Theft Act 1968), obtaining services by deception (s. 1 Theft Act 1978), evasion of liability by deception (s. 2 Theft Act 1978), and making off without payment (s. 3 Theft Act 1978). However, the prosecution would face difficulties in establishing the ingredients of virtually all of these offences.

At first glance, the most obvious offence appears to be obtaining property by deception under s. 15 of the Theft Act 1968, as Dave has obtained the petrol (which constitutes property) and he has deceived the cashier. However, the Court of Appeal decision in *R* v *Coady* [1996] Crim LR 518, makes it clear that for the offence to be made out, the representation relied on by the prosecution must have been made prior to the obtaining of the petrol from the cashier, and must have operated on his mind. To overcome this argument, the prosecution could submit that Dave has made another representation that induced the garage to allow him to take the petrol. This is on the basis that the motorist in driving up to the pump, thereby causing the attendant to operate the switch enabling the motorist to take the petrol, has made a representation that he will pay for the petrol. This argument was rejected by the Court of Appeal in *R* v *Collis-Smith* [1974] Crim LR 716, but in the controversial House of Lords decision in *DPP* v *Ray* [1974] AC 370, the House decided by a 3–2 majority that a diner who orders a meal in a restaurant thereby represents that he will pay for it, so that if he runs out without paying he has deceived the waiter and could be guilty under s. 15. Nevertheless, in view of the court's decision in *Coady*, the prosecution might prosecute Dave for theft.

Under s. 1 of the Theft Act 1968, Dave will be guilty of theft if he dishonestly appropriates property belonging to another with the intention of permanently depriving the other of it. Although the question of dishonesty is one of fact for the jury, it is submitted that following the questions stated in *R* v *Ghosh* [1982] 2 All ER 689, the jury would conclude that Dave was dishonest, as the trial judge would ask the jury:

(a) Was what was done dishonest according to the ordinary standards of reasonable and honest people?

(b) If it was, did D realise that reasonable and honest people regard what he did as dishonest?

However, difficulties arise when considering *actus reus*, as in *Edwards* v *Ddin* [1976] 3 All ER 705, where the Court of Appeal held that ownership of the petrol passes to the motorist as soon as he puts the petrol into his tank, in accordance with the rules of passing of property under the Sale of Goods Act 1979. Therefore, when he appropriates the property by driving off, it is not then property belonging to another.

This decision was clearly based on application of the civil law to determine ownership of the petrol and it is submitted that this is the correct approach. However, two House of Lords decisions have greatly changed the position. Thus in *R* v *Hinks* [2000] 3 WLR 1590, the House held that the acquisition of an indefeasible title to property from a person who no longer retained any proprietary interest in the property was capable of amounting to appropriation of that property. Earlier in *DPP* v *Gomez* [1993] 1 All ER 1, the House decided that there is still an appropriation of property when the owner consents to the thief taking it. Applying these principles, a court could now decide that as soon as Dave starts to put the petrol into his tank he is appropriating it and the fact that he would become the owner, under the civil law principles, of the petrol has no effect on the position in criminal law. Although this is far from satisfactory, the House in *Hinks* justified their conclusion on the basis that the mental element which was required to be proved in a conviction for theft was an adequate safeguard against injustice. Thus, Dave could be guilty of theft.

There is also the possibility that Dave has committed offences under the Theft Act 1978, but again, in respect of two offences, the position is not free from doubt. On a charge of s. 1 of the Theft Act 1978, the prosecution would again face the argument that the deception came after the services were obtained (as in *Coady*). In addition, the defence would also argue that as s. 1(2) of the Theft Act 1978 states the deception must involve a service that must be paid for, s. 1 does not apply. If the garage is self-service, Dave can argue that he is not paying for any service, in as much as all money paid is for the petrol. The prosecution could submit that the very fact of providing a garage with petrol and other facilities is a service which is paid for indirectly by customers, but it is unlikely that Dave would be guilty of s. 1.

Section 3 of the Theft Act 1978 — dishonestly making off without payment when you know payment on the spot is required — was introduced to cover the situations of driving away from garages without paying for petrol, or running out of restaurants, and would seem to be the most apt to cover Dave. However, in *R* v *Brooks and Brooks* (1983) 76 Cr App R 66, the Court of Appeal stated that 'making off' must be given its ordinary everyday meaning by the jury. Further, in the Crown Court case of *R* v *Hammond* [1982] Crim LR 611, where a motorist who gave a worthless cheque to a garage proprietor as payment for repairs to his car, the accused was held to have not 'made off' within the meaning of s. 3, as he had the consent of the proprietor to take away his car. Although, if the proprietor had known that he was receiving a worthless cheque in payment, he would not have allowed the motorist to take his car, the trial judge decided that a departure with the proprietor's blessing could not constitute making off.

However, whilst there may be some doubt as to the most appropriate subsection to use, it is clear that Dave will be guilty of evasion of liability by deception, under s. 2 of the Theft Act 1978. Section 2(1)(a) creates an offence where A dishonestly secures the remission of the whole or part of any existing liability to make a payment, whether his own liability or another's. This subsection was used in *R* v *Jackson* [1983] Crim LR 617, where D obtained petrol from P by tendering a stolen credit card. Because P would then look to the authority issuing the card for payment, this meant that D had secured remission of a liability. It could also be argued that subsections

(1)(b) — with intent to make permanent default, dishonestly induces a creditor to forgo payment; or (1)(c) — dishonestly obtains any exemption from, or abatement of liability to make a payment; are applicable. However, this is a largely academic exercise as the Court of Appeal recognised in *R* v *Holt and Lee* [1981] 2 All ER 854, that although the subsections do overlap, they were not interested in detailed arguments from counsel as to the most appropriate subsection to use in specific cases. As long as Dave is within one of the three subsections, and it is submitted that he clearly is, he will be guilty.

Further reading

Ormerod, D., 'A Bit of a Con?' [1999] Crim LR 789.

Smith, J.C., 'Obtaining Cheques by Deception or Theft' [1997] Crim LR 382.

Mixed questions

Introduction

A typical criminal law exam paper will usually contain one or possibly two mixed questions. A mixed question is one that requires knowledge of a wide variety of topics from different parts of the syllabus. Quite often these topics are unrelated, so you could have to deal with criminal damage, manslaughter, theft, conspiracy and duress in the same answer. Mixed questions will generally be of two types: (1) where you have to cover a vast number of issues briefly; (2) where you need to cover some issues briefly, but others in some depth. Type two questions are obviously the more difficult, as you have to decide which are the points requiring detailed discussion. However, this should be fairly obvious for the well-prepared student.

Because a mixed question may cover so many diverse points, it will often yield comparatively high marks. This is sometimes because a student who does not cover one particular point will not lose so many marks, as the student may do when tackling a question with only three or four major points to cover. So don't be intimidated!

In this chapter there are four typical mixed questions which have generally been answered well by exam students.

Q Question 1

Andy is a member of the Twerton Terrors, a notorious gang of soccer hooligans. Their purpose is to cause annoyance to rival groups of football supporters, although they are not particularly violent and never intend to cause serious personal injury. On one particular Saturday Andy does not wish to travel with the 'Terrors', but Brian, another member, threatens to injure Andy's younger brother severely and damage Andy's new sports car. Andy therefore submits. During the afternoon he sprays 'Up the Rovers' with an aerosol can on a wall adjoining the football ground, pushes Sid's car 100 yards around a corner so that Sid cannot find it, and produces Ken's membership card so he can watch the game without paying.

During the game Andy is so incensed by a bad refereeing decision that he throws an empty beer bottle at the referee. Unfortunately the bottle hits Vernon, an elderly spectator, on the head. Vernon later dies from the head wound.

Discuss the criminal liability of Andy.

Commentary

There are so many points to mention in this answer that you cannot possibly consider them all in depth. The key to a good mark is to recognise the issues on which there is little or no doubt and mention them briefly, while concentrating on the controversial matters.

As well as property offences to consider under the Criminal Damage Act 1971 and the Theft Acts 1968 and 1978, there is also the possibility of the offence of manslaughter in respect of Vernon's death. Reference to the doctrine of transferred malice is also required.

Lastly, your answer must consider the defence of duress. This would certainly be raised by Andy, as if it succeeded it would be a defence to all charges. However, analysis of the principles of duress should lead you to the conclusion that it will not apply on the facts.

- s. 3 Criminal Damage Act 1971 — possession with intent

- s. 12 Theft Act 1968 — taking a conveyance

- Offences under Theft Act 1978

- Murder and involuntary manslaughter

- Transferred malice

- Duress

:ϙ́: Suggested answer

Andy could be guilty of a wide variety of offences arising from these incidents. First, he would be committing an offence under s. 3 of the Criminal Damage Act 1971, of being in possession of an article (the aerosol) intending to damage another's property. Further, when he uses the spray to put graffiti on the wall he will be committing the substantive offence under s. 1(1) of the 1971 Act, of intentionally damaging property belonging to another. In *R* v *Fancy* [1980] Crim LR 171, the Court of Appeal accepted that an accused who was whitewashing over National Front slogans would not be damaging property but merely restoring it to its original state. However, in *Hardman* v *Chief Constable of Avon and Somerset Constabulary* [1986] Crim LR 330, it was held that the defendant was guilty of this offence when he marked the pavement with water-soluble paint, even though it was recognised that the silhouette drawings would have been washed away by heavy rain.

When Andy moves the car, he might be committing an offence under s. 12 of the Theft Act 1968 (taking a conveyance without the owner's consent or other lawful authority). In *R v Bow* (1976) 64 Cr App R 54, the Court of Appeal upheld the conviction of a poacher who moved a gamekeeper's car, which was blocking the poacher's exit, some 200 yards by releasing its handbrake and allowing the car to coast. However, the court suggested that for the offence to be committed the accused must take the conveyance for use as a conveyance, and in *R v Stokes* [1983] RTR 59, the Court of Appeal quashed the conviction of an accused who had pushed the owner's car around the corner as a practical joke so that he thought it was stolen. Thus a charge against Andy under s. 12 might not succeed. He certainly could not be found guilty of theft under s. 1 of the Theft Act 1968 as the prosecution would not be able to prove that he intended permanently to deprive the owner of his property.

The three offences contained in the Theft Act 1978 must be considered in relation to Andy's entrance to the football stadium. As he has used Ken's membership card to gain entry, there is the possibility that he has obtained services by deception and is therefore guilty of the offence under s. 1 of the Theft Act 1978. Certainly the right to see the game would be deemed a service, as s. 1(2) states that it is the obtaining of services where one is induced to confer a benefit by doing some act or causing or permitting some act to be done, on the understanding that the benefit has been or will be paid for. However, whether the offence has been committed will depend on the terms of issue of the season ticket. If the club is prepared to admit the holder of the ticket which has been paid for, it is submitted that the offence is not made out. However, the usual terms of issue allow only the actual member to be admitted, and if this is the case there will clearly have been an operative deception and Andy will be guilty.

The same reasoning would also apply to a charge under s. 2 of the 1978 Act, of evading liability by deception. Under s. 2(1)(a), Andy is guilty if by deception he dishonestly secures the remission of the whole or part of any existing liability to make a payment. As a spectator, Andy would usually have to pay the entrance fee, and as he has avoided this (by representing that he is a club member, Ken) the offence appears to have been made out. Certainly Andy would find it difficult to claim that he was not acting dishonestly (see *R v Ghosh* [1982] 2 All ER 689).

It is submitted that Andy would not be guilty under s. 3 of the Theft Act 1978 of making off without payment, knowing that payment on the spot for services done was required. This is because in *R v Brooks and Brooks* (1982) 76 Cr App R 66, the Court of Appeal stated that the words 'makes off' are to be given their ordinary meaning by the jury. In *R v Hammond* [1982] Crim LR 611, the only reported case on this point, Judge Morrison ruled that a motorist who paid for car repairs with a cheque he knew was going to bounce, had not made off as he had the consent of the garage owner at the time he left the garage. Certainly s. 2 of the 1978 Act appears the more appropriate charge in these circumstances.

As Andy has caused Vernon's death, he may be charged with murder, i.e., the unlawful killing of a human being within the Queen's peace with malice aforethought. However, as the *mens rea* of murder requires an intention to kill or cause grievous bodily harm (*R v Moloney* [1985] 1 All ER 1025), it is submitted that Andy would be better charged with manslaughter, i.e., unlawful homicide without malice aforethought. There are two bases of involuntary manslaughter, killing by gross negligence or recklessness, and constructive manslaughter, where the prosecution must prove that the accused intended to do an act which was unlawful and dangerous. It is this latter category that would be used to convict Andy, as his act of throwing the bottle at someone is unlawful (common assault) and dangerous (as all sober and reasonable people would recognise the risk of harm, albeit minor harm) (*R v Church* [1965] 2 All ER 72). Andy could argue that he did not intend to harm Vernon, but the court would apply the doctrine of transferred malice, and the fact that the actual victim differs from the intended victim makes no difference as Andy had the necessary *mens rea* (*R v Mitchell* [1983] 2 All ER 427).

Andy could claim that as threats were made he has the defence of duress, which is available if he committed the offences because of 'threats of immediate death or serious personal violence so great as to overbear the ordinary powers of human resistance' (*Attorney-General v Whelan* [1934] IR 518). Threats to injure a third party can be taken into account but not threats to damage property or of financial loss (*R v Graham* [1982] 1 All ER 801).

Although the prosecution have the burden of disproving duress once the defence has been raised, there are many difficulties for the defendant. First, voluntary membership of a gang of criminals can rule out the defence (*R v Sharp* [1987] 3 All ER 103), although the prosecution must prove that the accused knew the association to be a paramilitary or gangster organisation for the defence to fail on this ground (*R v Lewis* (1992) 96 Cr App R 412). As the Twerton Terrors are not a violent organisation the defence would still be available (*R v Shepherd* (1987) 86 Cr App R 47).

Secondly, the prosecution could argue that as Andy had the opportunity to nullify the threats and failed to take it, the defence must fail (*R v Hudson and Taylor* [1971] 2 All ER 244). Similarly, although duress is a defence to manslaughter (*R v Evans and Gardiner* [1976] VR 517) there is no evidence that the threats caused Andy to throw the bottle, and therefore the defence of duress cannot possibly succeed on the manslaughter charge against Andy.

Q Question 2

Andy, Barry and Colin went mountain climbing. They were all attached to each other by a rope, with Andy at the head of the group and Colin at the rear. Colin slipped on the greasy rock face and was left dangling in mid-air supported only by the rope attached to Andy and Barry. After three minutes Andy said to Barry 'I cannot hold on any longer cut the rope'. This Barry did, causing Colin to fall. Colin suffered severe injuries and was unconscious. He was hanging precariously on a ledge when a freakishly strong and sudden gust of wind blew him off the ledge to his death.

Discuss the criminal liability (if any) of Andy and Barry.

Commentary

This could be classified as a mixed question, typical of criminal law questions where there are lots of topics to cover. However, the issues to concentrate on are unlawful homicide, causation, and the defences of necessity and duress of circumstances. This particular question has been chosen because the uncertain outcome demands a full, considered conclusion.

The constraints of time dictate that comprehensive coverage of all aspects of causation and necessity is not possible in this answer.

- Murder

- Intention

  - *Moloney* [1985]

  - *Woollin* [1998]

- Involuntary manslaughter

- Accomplice responsibility

  - *Powell and English* [1997]

- Causation

- Aggravated assault

- Necessity/duress of circumstances

:Q: Suggested answer

The most serious offences Andy and Barry can be charged with are murder and manslaughter. Murder is the unlawful killing of a human being within the Queen's peace with malice aforethought. Before the Law Reform (Year and a Day Rule) Act 1996, death had to follow within a year and a day, but this is no longer a requirement, although the consent of the Attorney-General has to be obtained to bring proceedings if three years or longer has elapsed between the unlawful act or omission and the victim's death.

On the assumption that the incident has occurred in England and Wales, the key issue is whether the prosecution can prove that Andy and Barry had malice aforethought. The House of Lords decisions in *R v Moloney* [1985] 1 All ER 1025 and *R v Hancock and Shankland* [1986] 1 All ER 641 confirm that only an intention to kill or to cause grievous bodily harm constitutes malice aforethought. The two cases also state clearly that intention is a question of fact for the jury, and the trial judge should not generally give a detailed explanation of intention as this is a word in common use easily understood by the public. However, if the case is so complex that the judge feels a direction should be given, there is no precise formula that must be used, although the House of Lords in *R v Woollin* [1998] 4 All ER 103 stated that if the simple direction was not enough, the jury should be further directed that they were not entitled to find the necessary intention unless they felt sure that death or serious bodily harm was a virtually certain result of D's actions (barring some unforeseen intervention) and that D appreciated that fact.

The jury must therefore decide if Barry (the principal offender) and Andy (if he is charged as co-principal, which usually happens in practice) had malice aforethought. If the jury conclude that they lacked malice aforethought, they could be charged with involuntary manslaughter, which can be defined as unlawful killing without malice aforethought. Again, this is an area of criminal law in a state of flux, with the Law Commission's most recent recommendations (Law Com. No. 237) being to scrap the existing basis of the offence, despite there being a recent House of Lords decision in *R v Adomako* [1994] 3 All ER 79.

There are three bases of this offence, which are not mutually exclusive. The most commonly and easily established basis is constructive manslaughter. The prosecution must establish that the accused intended to do an act which was unlawful and dangerous. It is irrelevant that the accused did not know the act was unlawful, as this is a question of law. However, it must be established that the accused had the necessary *mens rea* for the unlawful act (*R v Lamb* [1967] 2 All ER 1282). It is submitted that the act of cutting the rope would be unlawful on the basis of criminal damage (under s. 1(1) or s. 1(2) of the Criminal Damage Act 1971, depending upon who was the owner of the rope) or assault (under s. 39 of the Criminal Justice Act 1988) as Barry would have realised that Colin would have been put in fear of impending force.

The act must also be dangerous, but again it is not necessary to establish that the accused recognised the danger (*R v Newbury and Jones* [1976] AC 500). The test is whether 'the unlawful act must be such as all sober and reasonable people would inevitably recognise must subject the other person to, at least, the risk of some harm resulting therefrom, albeit not serious harm' (*per* Edmund Davies J in *R v Church* [1965] 2 All ER 72). In these circumstances it is submitted that cutting the rope is clearly a dangerous act.

The other traditional bases of involuntary manslaughter are gross negligence and recklessness. These terms have sometimes been used indiscriminately, and after the House of Lords in *R v Seymour* [1983] 2 All ER 1058 had applied the *Caldwell* recklessness test, it was believed by many that gross negligence had been subsumed by recklessness. However, in *R* v *Adomako* the House of Lords overruled *Seymour* and confirmed that if a duty of care existed between the parties then gross negligence was the test to be applied. It is submitted that a duty of care would be owed by one mountaineer to another and that, as there was a clear risk of death, there is evidence upon which the accused could be found guilty on this basis if the jury conclude that they had acted in breach of their duty towards Colin.

When Andy told Barry to cut the rope, he would be committing the *actus reus* of incitement, encouraging or persuading another to break the criminal law. However, as Andy was present when the offence was committed, he could be charged with aiding and abetting murder. If this is the case, the prosecution do not have to prove that Andy had malice aforethought. It was held by the Privy Council in *Chan Wing Siu* v *R* [1985] 3 All ER 877, that if the accomplice contemplated death or grievous bodily harm as a possible consequence then the necessary *mens rea* for accomplice to murder was satisfied. This principle has been recently applied by the House of Lords in *R* v *Powell and English* [1997] 4 All ER 545, where the House stated that the accomplice would be guilty if he realised that the principal offender might kill with intent to do so, or with intent to cause grievous bodily harm. However, under the Accessories and Abettors Act 1861, an accomplice can be liable to be tried, indicted and punished as a principal offender.

Both Andy and Barry may argue that they cannot be guilty of murder or manslaughter as they did not cause Colin's death. However, the prosecution need only establish that their act contributed significantly to the victim's death (*R* v *Cheshire* [1991] 3 All ER 670). The court very rarely accepts the accused's submission that a *novus actus interveniens* has broken the chain of causation thereby exonerating the accused, and it is submitted that as Andy and Barry had caused Colin to be on the cliff ledge in a vulnerable condition and that strong wind on a mountain is not unusual, the jury would be unlikely to conclude that they had not caused Colin's death.

If the court did accept this argument, the accused could still be found guilty under s. 18 of the Offences Against the Person Act 1861 of wounding or causing grievous bodily harm, if it can be established that they intended to cause grievous bodily harm (*R* v *Belfon* [1976] 3 All ER 46); or under s. 20 of the Act of malicious wounding or inflicting grievous bodily harm, if the accused intended or foresaw the risk of some physical harm (*R* v *Savage and Parmenter* [1991] 4 All ER 698).

Andy and Barry could also argue that they have the defence of necessity. Despite the Court of Appeal's recognition of the availability of the defence of necessity on a murder charge in *Re A (Children) (Conjoined Twins: Surgical Separation)* [2000] 4 All ER 961, a civil case in relation to the separation of conjoined twins, the long established decision in *R* v *Dudley and Stephens* [1881–5] All ER 61, holding that necessity is no defence to murder, is still good law. However, in recent years, the related defence of duress of circumstances has been developed in a number of cases involving road traffic offences (*R* v *Willer* (1987) 83 Cr App R 225, *R* v *Conway* [1988] 3 All ER 1025);

and in *R v Pommell* (1995) 2 Cr App R 607, a case concerning unlawful possession of a firearm, the Court of Appeal accepted Professor Sir John Smith's contention that 'the defence, being closely related to the defence of duress by threats, appears to be general, applying to all crimes except murder, attempted murder and some forms of treason'. If this defence is raised the prosecution have the burden of disproving the defence's availability on the facts.

In conclusion, it is very difficult to predict the likely outcome of the trial of Andy and Barry. If charged with murder, they could be found guilty only if the jury concluded that they intended to kill or cause grievous bodily harm. If this was the case, it would seem that despite the extension of the defence of necessity/duress of circumstances in *R v Pommell* and *Re A*, following *R v Dudley and Stephens* the defence would fail. However, they may succeed with their argument that the chain of causation has been broken, in which case they could not be convicted of murder or manslaughter. If the jury concluded that they did intend to kill, they could be found guilty of attempted murder (*R v Whybrow* (1951) 35 Cr App R 141). If not, then s. 18 or s. 20 of the Offences Against the Person Act 1861 may apply.

On the other hand, if the jury conclude that Andy and Barry lacked malice aforethought, they could be convicted of manslaughter on the constructive basis. However, as necessity/duress of circumstances is a defence to this and lesser offences, it is possible that the jury will accept that the conditions of this defence have been fulfilled, in which case Andy and Barry would be acquitted.

Q Question 3

Gerry is a member of the Animal Freedom Society, an organisation which believes in total freedom for animals. He visits a local zoo and is so appalled by the conditions in the lions' cage that he saws through the iron bars thereby enabling a lion to escape. The marauding lion attacks and badly injures Sally, a passer-by. A police marksman, Bill, is summoned, but in trying to shoot the lion he negligently shoots Karen, a lion tamer, causing her to break her leg.
    Discuss the criminal liability of Gerry and Bill.

Commentary

After quickly covering the relevant offences of theft and criminal damage, your answer must analyse in detail the possible offences against the person. The most obvious offences to consider are s. 18 and s. 20 of the Offences Against the Person Act 1861, but there is also s. 1(2) of the Criminal Damage Act to analyse. This is an odd offence, but one that the prosecution can more easily establish than s. 18 or s. 20, because of the applicable objective definition of recklessness.

The other major topic to consider is causation, as no doubt Gerry would argue that he is not responsible for any of the consequences of his actions. However, R v *Pagett* (1983) 76 Cr App R 279, if applied, could mean that he is deemed responsible for all of them. Bill, on the other hand, could not be guilty of any non-fatal offences against the person if he has only been negligent.

- **Criminal damage — s. 1(1) Criminal Damage Act 1971**

- **Theft — s. 1 Theft Act 1968**

  - dishonesty — *Ghosh* [1982]

- **Aggravated assault**

  - *Savage and Parmenter* [1991]

- **Causation**

  - *Pagett* [1983]

- **Aggravated criminal damage — s. 1(2) Criminal Damage Act 1971**

  - *Caldwell* [1981]

  - *Steer* [1987]

⦂Ȯ⦂ Suggested answer

Gerry's initial action in allowing the lion to escape could give rise to offences under the Criminal Damage Act 1971 and the Theft Act 1968. His possession of a saw could constitute an offence under s. 3 of the 1971 Act, i.e., being in possession of an article with intent to cause criminal damage, and when he cuts through the bars of the cage this would constitute criminal damage under s. 1(1) of the 1971 Act.

Because the lion has escaped, Gerry could be charged with theft under s. 1 of the Theft Act 1968, i.e., dishonestly appropriating property belonging to another with the intention of permanently depriving the other of it. He has committed an appropriation by assuming the rights of an owner (s. 3) and, although the lion is a wild creature, it is ordinarily kept in captivity and would be regarded as property belonging to another under s. 4(4) and s. 5(1). Gerry could argue that he was not dishonest as he believed it was wrong to keep lions in captivity. This would be a difficult issue for the jury to resolve, and on application of R v *Ghosh* [1982] 2 All ER 689 they would consider the following questions:

(a) Was what was done dishonest according to the ordinary standards of reasonable and honest people? If not, D is not guilty.

(b) If it was, did the defendant realise that reasonable and honest people regard what he did as dishonest? If so, he is guilty; if not, he is not guilty.

Therefore, it will not be sufficient if Gerry thought he was not acting dishonestly, or that his fellow members of the organisation thought the same; he must believe that reasonable and honest people would so believe. This is certainly Gerry's best hope of avoiding a conviction for theft, as it is submitted that he could not claim he believed he had a right in law to the property (and was therefore not dishonest under s. 2(1)(a)) or that he had no intention permanently to deprive as s. 6 includes treating 'the thing as his own to dispose of regardless of other's rights'.

However, the more serious charges will arise out of the injuries sustained by Sally. As she is badly injured it is probable that Gerry would be charged under s. 18 of the Offences Against the Person Act 1861 with wounding or causing grievous bodily harm with intent. The prosecution must prove that Gerry had the necessary intention, and although this is a question of fact upon which the jury would generally require little or no guidance following *R* v *Moloney* [1985] 1 All ER 1025, it is submitted that on the facts this could present the prosecution with difficulties. They may therefore decide to prosecute under s. 20 of the 1861 Act, i.e., malicious wounding or inflicting grievous bodily harm.

At one time it was thought that the prosecution must prove that an assault took place before there could be a conviction under s. 20 (*R* v *Clarence* (1888) 22 QBD 23). However, recent cases (in particular the House of Lords' decision in *R* v *Wilson* [1983] 3 All ER 448) have demonstrated that this is not necessary, and again the major problem for the prosecution will be establishing *mens rea*. Section 20 uses the word 'maliciously', and after much judicial debate the House of Lords decided in *R* v *Savage and Parmenter* [1991] 4 All ER 698 (following *R* v *Mowatt* [1967] 3 All ER 47) that it is sufficient that the accused intended or foresaw the risk of some physical harm. Although wounding or grievous bodily harm is required for the *actus reus*, only intention or foresight of some physical harm is necessary for the *mens rea* as this is another example of the criminal law's use of constructive crime.

Gerry might argue that he was so concerned about the plight of the lion that he did not even consider the risk of some harm; and although the prosecution could maintain that this was an obvious risk to the reasonable man, this state of mind would not be sufficient as *Caldwell* recklessness does not apply for s. 20. Actual intention or foresight by Gerry must be proved. Even if the charge was only assault occasioning actual bodily harm under s. 47 of the 1861 Act, the prosecution would still have to prove intent or foresight on Gerry's behalf, albeit only for common assault (*R* v *Savage and Parmenter*).

Gerry could also argue that he did not cause Sally's injuries and is therefore not criminally responsible. However, the prosecution need only show that Gerry's action was a significantly contributing cause, not the main cause (*R* v *Cheshire* [1991] 3 All ER 670), and a jury directed to apply the 'but for' test would surely decide that Gerry had in law caused this consequence. On authority of *R* v *Pagett* it is also probable that Gerry would be held to have caused Karen's injuries. In this case the accused kidnapped his pregnant girlfriend and used her as a human shield when shooting at the police. A police marksman returned fire and one of his shots killed the girlfriend. Nevertheless the Court of Appeal upheld Pagett's conviction for manslaughter, holding that the return fire was a foreseeable act of self-defence and therefore could not constitute a *novus actus interveniens* breaking the chain of causation. The court also stated that if a stray shot from the police marksman had killed an innocent passer-by Pagett would also be responsible for that death. By analogy, Bill's actions are involuntary and therefore not sufficient to break the chain of causation. As Bill is only negligent, he cannot be guilty of common assault or aggravated assault as he lacks *mens rea*. It is therefore just for Gerry to be held responsible for Karen's injuries, although whether he would be convicted of any of the above offences again depends on the prosecution being able to establish *mens rea*.

Because of these difficulties the prosecution would probably also charge Gerry under s. 1(2) of the Criminal Damage Act 1971 with intentionally or recklessly causing criminal damage being reckless as to whether life would be thereby endangered. This is a very serious offence, and from the prosecution's standpoint it has the major advantage that it does not matter that Gerry did not foresee the consequences as objective recklessness applies. Thus in *Metropolitan Police Commissioner* v *Caldwell* [1981] 1 All ER 961, Lord Diplock stated that a person is reckless if he does an act which creates an obvious risk of that consequence and 'when he does the act he has not given any thought to the possibility of there being such risk or has recognised that there was some risk involved and has none the less gone on to do it'.

The prosecution would still have one difficulty under this offence, however, and that is the condition that the danger to life resulted from the damage to property. Thus in *R* v *Steer* [1987] 2 All ER 833, the House of Lords upheld the Court of Appeal's decision to quash a conviction under s. 1(2) where the accused had fired a bullet, breaking a window and narrowly missing the victim, on the basis that it was not sufficient that the endangerment to life resulted from the accused's act which caused the damage to property. Although in *R* v *Webster and Warwick* [1995] 2 All ER 168 convictions were upheld under s. 1(2) when Webster damaged a train roof by throwing a coping stone on it, passengers being showered with debris, and Warwick broke a car windscreen with glass shattering over the driver, it is submitted that Gerry's case is covered by *Steer*. The prosecution might therefore fail on a charge under s. 1(2).

In conclusion, Gerry would definitely be guilty of offences under s. 1(1) and s. 3 of the Criminal Damage Act 1971, but there are many difficulties for the prosecution if they seek convictions for the more serious offences.

▣ Question 4

Bill is a local businessman with various business concerns. As a sole trader, he runs 'Do It Now' a home improvement shop. He is also in partnership with Jane, trading as 'Eurospares' and specialising in bicycle parts. Jane and Bill are also the sole directors and shareholders of Gnome Improvements Ltd, a company trading in plastic and ornamental gnomes.

Unfortunately, the businesses are doing very badly and creditors are constantly pressing for payment of debts. Bill therefore decides he will take £2,000 from each of the three separate accounts of Do It Now, Eurospares and Gnome Improvements Ltd. He spends the money on a foreign holiday. On his return he tells Jane what he has done, and (much to his surprise) Jane condones his actions.

In an attempt to generate money, Jane suggests to Bill that they could destroy some of the property of Eurospares, Gnome Improvements Ltd and Do It Now and submit an application to their insurance company, claiming the property was stolen in a burglary. Bill destroys some property of each business, but before they submit the insurance form, Jane tells the police what they have done. Gnome Improvements Ltd go into liquidation and both Jane and Bill are made bankrupt.

Discuss the criminal liability, if any, of Bill and Jane.

Commentary

This is a testing question requiring an ability to apply important but difficult principles concerning theft, criminal damage and the inchoate offences of conspiracy and attempt.

The problem highlights the differences in the application of the principles when one is considering the position of a company to a sole trader. Even though the company may be under the control of only two shareholders and directors, it will still be regarded as a separate legal entity, distinct from its members and controllers, under the well known company law case of *Salomon v Salomon & Co.* [1897] AC 22. This means that the outcome will differ when considering the offences of criminal damage and theft.

- Theft — s. 1 Theft Act 1968

- Dishonesty — *Ghosh* [1982]

- Appropriation — s. 3 Theft Act 1968

    - *Gomez* [1993]

    - *Phillipou* [1989]

- Conspiracy — s. 1 Criminal Law Act 1977

- Criminal damage — s. 1 Criminal Damage Act 1971

- s. 5 Criminal Damage Act 1971

- *Appleyard* [1985]

- *Denton* [1982]

• Attempt — s. 1(1) Criminal Attempts Act 1981

⚙ Suggested answer

Bill and Jane could be charged with the offences of theft, criminal damage and the inchoate offences of incitement, conspiracy and attempt. Bill could face charges of theft with regard to his taking of money from the three businesses Do It Now, Eurospares and the company Gnome Improvements Ltd. Theft is defined under s. 1(1) of the Theft Act 1968 as the dishonest appropriation of property belonging to another with the intention of permanently depriving the other of it. However, he cannot be guilty of theft from Do It Now, as this is his business and is not in law regarded as a separate legal entity. He is therefore simply moving money from one of his accounts to another and is not dealing with property belonging to another.

The position is more complicated regarding the partnership business of Eurospares. Although a partnership firm is not a separate legal entity (the firm's assets being regarded as belonging to the partners), both Bill and Jane, as partners, have an interest in the partnership property within the meaning of s. 5(1) of the Theft Act 1968. Thus the Court of Appeal recognised in *R* v *Bonner* [1970] 2 All ER 97 that if one party dishonestly appropriates partnership property he is guilty of theft from the other partner. Further after the House of Lords' decisions in *DPP* v *Gomez* [1993] 1 All ER 1 even if Jane consented to the property being taken by Bill there would still have been an appropriation of property belonging to another, and the ingredients of the *actus reus* of theft will have been satisfied.

However, Bill cannot be found guilty of theft unless the prosecution can prove that he had the necessary *mens rea*, and there will be difficulties in establishing dishonesty. Section 2 of the Theft Act 1968 states that a person's appropriation of property belonging to another is not to be regarded as dishonest if the accused believed that he had the right in law to deprive the other of it (s. 2(1)(a)) or he believed that he would have the other's consent if the other knew of the appropriation and the circumstances of it (s. 2(1)(b)). Although Bill's argument under s. 2(1)(a) may not be convincing, it is submitted that as Jane did consent (albeit retrospectively) this would be strong grounds for success under s. 2(1)(b). Further, as dishonesty is a word in common use, it must be left to the jury (*R* v *Feely* (1973) All ER 341) and in accordance with *R* v *Ghosh* [1982] 2 All ER 689 the jury must ask themselves:

(i) Was what was done dishonest according to the ordinary standards of reasonable and honest people?

(ii) Did the defendant realise that reasonable and honest people regard what he did as dishonest? If yes he is guilty, if no he is not.

Although the prosecution generally encounter little difficulty in establishing the other ingredient of *mens rea* — an intention to permanently deprive the other of it, it is submitted that in view of Bill's arguments regarding dishonesty it is unlikely that he would be convicted of theft from Eurospares.

The third charge of theft would be regarding the company Gnome Improvements Ltd. Bill could argue that, as he and Jane are the sole shareholders and directors of the company, the property is not property belonging to another. In other words as they own the company they also own the company's property. However, this argument will not succeed as since the well-known case of *Salomon* v *Salomon & Co.* [1897] AC 22, it has been recognised that as the company is a separate legal entity, its assets are owned by the company, and although the members have an interest in the assets legally they do not own them. The £2,000 taken by Bill was therefore property belonging to another.

Bill will also argue that as he and Jane, as controllers of the company, decided on this course of action, there was no appropriation. The Court of Appeal accepted this argument in *R* v *McHugh and Tringham* (1988) 88 Cr App R 385 holding that provided the decision was *intra vires* (within the company's objects) there could be no theft. However, the opposite result was the outcome of a differently constituted Court of Appeal in *R* v *Phillipou* (1989) 89 Cr App R 290, and it is this latter decision which has been approved by the House of Lords in *DPP* v *Gomez* [1993] 1 All ER 1 where Lord Browne-Wilkinson stated 'in my judgment [the approach in *McHugh and Tringham*] was wrong in law. . . . Where a company is accused of a crime the acts and intentions of those who are directing minds and will of the company are to be attributable to the company. That is not the law where the charge is that those who are directing minds and will have themselves committed a crime against the company'.

Bill might further argue that as against the company there is no dishonesty as the members (Bill and Jane) are not being disadvantaged. However, it appears that the court will accept the dishonesty *vis-à-vis* the company creditors whose assets are diminished as sufficient to constitute a dishonest appropriation. It is therefore submitted that as the company went into liquidation, there is evidence for a jury to conclude that Bill's action was taken in order to defeat the creditors' interests and he will therefore be guilty of theft.

When Jane suggests that they damage some of the business' property she may be committing the crime of incitement. This consists of the persuasion or encouragement of another to commit a criminal offence, the accused knowing that the person incited will act with the appropriate *mens rea* of the crime in question (*R* v *Curr* [1968] QB 944). Similarly Jane and Bill could also be charged with conspiracy. This could be either the common law conspiracy to defraud or statutory conspiracy under s. 1 of the Criminal Law Act 1977 which states:

> If a person agrees with any person or persons that a course of conduct shall be pursued which, if the agreement is carried out in accordance with their intentions, either —
>
> (a) will necessarily amount to or involve the commission of any offence or offences by one or more parties to the agreement, or
>
> (b) would do so but for the existence of facts which render the commission of the offence or any offences impossible,
>
> he is guilty of conspiracy to commit the offence or offences in question.

Quite clearly if a claim to the insurance company proved successful, this would amount to the offences of obtaining property by deception under s. 15 of the Theft Act 1968 or s. 15A of that Act. Therefore, if the other ingredients of incitement (for Jane) and conspiracy (for Bill and Jane) could be established they would be guilty.

They could also face similar charges for incitement and conspiracy to cause criminal damage, in respect of the property of Gnome Improvements Ltd as s. 1(1) of the Criminal Damage Act 1971 applies to damaging another's property, and as previously stated Do it Now's property is Bill's property and the partnership property of Eurospares belongs to Jane and Bill.

Nevertheless Bill would face the charge under the full offence of s. 1(1) of the Criminal Damage Act 1971 — a person who without lawful excuse destroys or damages any property belonging to another intending to destroy or damage any such property or being reckless as to whether any such property would be destroyed or damaged shall be guilty of an offence.

Bill would no doubt contend that he is not guilty as he has a lawful excuse within the meaning of s. 5(2)(a) of the Act. This provides that if at the time of the alleged offence he believed that the person(s) whom he believed to be entitled to consent to the destruction or damage and its circumstances had so consented he has a lawful excuse. Bill would argue that he and Jane as the company consented. However, in a similar case *R v Appleyard* (1985) 81 Cr App Rep 319 the Court of Appeal rejected this argument in upholding the conviction for criminal damage of the managing director of a company on the basis that he did not have the company's true consent.

Bill might also face an identical charge in respect of the damage caused to the partnership property. However, he could rely on the Court of Appeal's decision in *R v Denton* [1982] 1 All ER 65, where an employee's conviction was quashed when he was acting with the consent of his employer, although he knew that the consent had only been given for a fraudulent purpose (to deceive an insurance company). Bill would hope that the consent of his partner Jane would be treated in the same way as the consent of an employer, although no doubt the prosecution would argue that the reasoning of *Appleyard* should be applied.

As well as being guilty of this offence Bill might also be charged with an attempt to obtain property by deception, under s. 1 of the Criminal Attempts Act 1981. Section 1(1) provides that 'if, with intent to commit an offence to which this section applies, a person does an act which is more than merely preparatory to the commission of the offence, he is guilty of attempting to commit the offence'.

It is for the trial judge to decide if there is sufficient evidence to leave this question to the jury and if there is the jury must then consider if D has done a more than merely preparatory act. Although they are cases decided prior to the 1981 Act, in both *R* v *Robinson* [1915] 2 KB 342 and *Comer* v *Bloomfield* (1970) 55 Cr App Rep 305 it was held that D who had faked a crime with a view to dishonestly claiming the insurance money was not guilty of attempt as he had not submitted the claims form. Indications are that this is likely to be the outcome where the 1981 Act is applied (*R* v *Widdowson* (1985) 82 Cr App R 314) and it is submitted that Bill would be found not guilty of attempt.

Index